One Morning in March

One Morning in March

Dunblane and the Shooting
That Changed Britain

Stephen McGinty

SWIFT PRESS
First published in Great Britain by Swift Press 2026

1 3 5 7 9 8 6 4 2

Copyright © Stephen McGinty 2026

All rights reserved

The right of Stephen McGinty to be identified as the Author of this Work has been asserted in accordance with the Copyright, Designs and Patents Act 1988

Text design and typesetting by Tetragon, London
Printed and bound in Great Britain by CPI Group (UK) Ltd, Croydon, CR0 4YY

A CIP catalogue record for this book is available from the British Library

We make every effort to make sure our products are safe for the purpose for which they are intended. Our authorised representative in the EU for product safety is Easy Access System Europe, Mustamäe tee 50, 10621 Tallinn, Estonia gpsr.requests@easproject.com

ISBN: 9781800756106
eISBN: 9781800753815

For Gwen & the children

CONTENTS

BEFORE		1
I	The Island	5
II	The Scouts	28
III	The Photographs	57
IV	The Families	80
V	The Guns	89
ONE MORNING IN MARCH		115
AFTER		161
VI	The Cabinet Meeting	163
VII	The Snowdrop Campaign	181
VIII	The Gun Lobby	190
IX	The Thursday Night Group	195
X	The Cullen Inquiry	204
XI	The Princess	221
XII	The Cullen Report	246
XIII	The Prince	278
ONE AFTERNOON IN JULY		289
Note on Sources		299
Acknowledgements		302
Index		304

Before

It was better last year, said one little boy of the summer camp on the island in the loch. No one got hit.

This year there was a lot of hitting. You got hit for not doing your exercises properly, if you fainted or said it was too sore or weren't standing up straight enough. You weren't punched, you were only slapped. He held your neck with one hand and slapped you in the face with the other hand, or sometimes he would beat you on the bottom or on your bare legs with a wooden spoon.

If you wanted to go home and started crying, you might get a couple of slaps. One boy got two slaps in the face and he wasn't doing anything, just toasting bread over the campfire. Another boy got a slap for putting wood on the fire when they were all told not to, but it was only a few twigs and other boys were doing it and they didn't get slapped. You could get a slap for scratching your face at the wrong time or even for yawning.

The most slaps any boy got was the boy who said he wanted to go home and when told he couldn't go home the boy said he would tell his dad. He got taken into the tent and everyone outside could hear the slaps and one boy's brother counted up to sixteen or seventeen. The boy came out crying and ran off to his tent and everyone could see that his back and face was all red.

You did get a slap if you played with the whistle on the life jackets. A boy blew the whistle, just lightly, but Sir came across and asked why he had used the whistle. The boy didn't answer. Sir then made him stand on the grass with his feet apart and his tummy in, his head up and his hands behind his back. Sir then slapped him twice across the face. You also got a slap if you didn't call him 'Sir'. He insisted that everyone call him 'Sir'.

I

THE ISLAND

THE waters of Loch Lomond are cold and grey, even in high summer. The Vikings once sailed down the length of the loch, having carried their longships overland from Loch Long, and pillaged the small island communities, stealing livestock and murdering residents. Dotted throughout the vast expanse of water are dozens of little islands, including one populated by Australian wallabies, the fecund offspring of a single imported pair. On the western shore is Luss, the principal location for the popular television soap opera *Take The High Road*, whose honey-coloured stone cottages make it one of Scotland's prettiest villages.

On the afternoon of 20 July 1988, two officers from Central Scotland Police, the nation's smallest police force, were ferried on the mailboat across from the boatyard at Balmaha on the eastern shore to the uninhabited island of Inchmoan. Balmaha is a pretty little village, with a cluster of wooden holiday chalets and a general store. Wedged in the centre of a horseshoe bay, the village has acted for over a century as a natural marina for amateur sailors to anchor their yachts, cabin cruisers, skiffs or rowing boats.

Technically, this part of the loch and islands fell under the jurisdiction of Strathclyde Police, the country's largest police force, but Strathclyde had struggled to source a boat and so asked the officers from Central to go on their behalf. This made sense. Central Scotland Police had received the bulk of the complaints, beginning in the evening of Sunday, 17 July, when the boys from a local camp had been reunited with their parents, and one of the officers on board, PC George Gunn, had taken witness statements. Now Gunn and his colleague, PC Donna Duncan, had been dispatched by Chief Inspector Hay of Strathclyde Police, the head of CID (the criminal investigation division in Dumbarton), to check on the living conditions and supervision of the camp currently being held among the birch and oak trees, the mossy rocks and icy streams of Inchmoan. The parents of several unhappy campers had called both the Central and Strathclyde police forces with numerous complaints that boys in the party had been physically assaulted and slapped.

Gunn and Duncan, dressed in dark blue uniforms and regulation anoraks, clambered out of their boat and made their way through a thicket of trees to a clearing where a cluster of tents were arranged. There were no adults in sight. Instead, several young boys, aged around eight or nine, were playing, unsupervised, thirty yards from the shoreline, the majority dressed only in swimming trunks despite the chill weather, with only a few benefiting from the additional layer of a T-shirt. The officers could see that each child's bare legs were a tapestry of scratches. The boys explained that 'Mr Hamilton' did not permit trousers while at camp: bare legs dried more easily, he'd said, and so the children's legs had got scratched hiking through the thick nettles, bracken and gorse covering the island.

The officers' first impression was that the camp was a dreary mess. The wooden picnic table was littered with dirty dishes, with only tinned and powdered food available; the chemical toilet appeared well used but seldom cleaned. The sleeping bags in the three tents were all damp to the touch. A poll of all thirteen boys established that only three were enthusiastic and actively enjoying themselves, with the remainder complaining that they were homesick and disappointed that they were not permitted to send postcards to their parents or call home during visits back to Luss. Yet when Gunn offered to take anyone home who wished to leave, no child went with them.

After talking to the children, Gunn and Duncan wandered around the island until they came to a large sandy beach, where a portly man with a balding head and square glasses was tying up a large wooden rowing boat with an outboard engine, the only transport on and off the island. Unlike the children, he was fully dressed, wearing cotton trousers and a filthy work shirt with sweat stains around the armpits. Thomas Hamilton had a large moon face and a false smile. He spoke in a soft manner but his tone towards both police officers was measured and confident, with a necessary touch of deference to their authority. He said he was very surprised to see them but would be happy to answer any questions about his summer camp which, he was at pains to stress, had been running successfully for several years. He explained that he ran a series of popular boys' clubs for children aged between seven and twelve in central Scotland, particularly in the towns of Stirling, Falkirk and Dunblane. The clubs, which ran in the evenings from Monday to Friday, with the occasional Saturday morning, focused on gymnastics, physical exercise and football. The highlight was the summer camp, during which groups of boys came to the island for one week at a time. He showed the officers the 'mess tent', and they noted that the first aid box was lying open, a bottle of methylated spirit easily within a child's reach.

When asked about allegations that he had assaulted boys by slapping them, Hamilton insisted that physical punishment was necessary to maintain discipline among boisterous young boys and that the recipients had been disruptive, cheeky and bullying. This kind of punishment for children still remained common in the 1980s. The use of a heavy leather belt, known as the Lochgelly Tawse and designed to inflict considerable pain without drawing blood, had been widespread in Scotland's schools until an August 1987 ban on corporal punishment in schools across the UK.

After completing their enquiries, Gunn and Duncan returned to their boat. Gunn did not consider the children to be in any particular danger, though he was left with an uneasy, ill-defined concern about Mr Hamilton, who waved them off from the shoreline surrounded by a cluster of half-naked children.

While on the island, the officers had noted the names, addresses and phone numbers of each of the thirteen children there. It was decided they would contact the boys' parents to explain about the complaints from other parents, inform them of their visit to the island and offer them the opportunity to withdraw their child if they desired.

The next day, Hamilton and the children were tracked down to a cinema in Alexandria and brought to the police station in Dumbarton, where parents had gathered. Hamilton answered their questions and offered reassurance. Most of the children were then taken home, but five boys, whose parents were the most vocally supportive of Hamilton's clubs, returned to the island. Among those boys returned home, though his mother could not be contacted, was Andrew Hagger.

Doreen Hagger was used to the police at the door. The dark-haired, slim-faced, thirty-something mother of two children – Victoria, aged seven, and Andrew, who was ten – Doreen lived in a grey, pebble-dashed council house with a small front garden in Linlithgow, an ancient town twenty miles west of Edinburgh with a greater past than present. In the Middle Ages, Linlithgow Palace had been the residence of Scottish kings and the birthplace of Mary, Queen of Scots. The town also had the macabre distinction of being the scene of the first murder by firearm in Scotland. On 23 January 1570, James Stewart, the first Earl of Moray, was processing through the town in a royal caravan of coaches when he was hit by a fatal shot from a carbine rifle. The rifle was fired by a man named James Hamilton, crouched in an elevated window of the house of the Archbishop of St Andrews, who happened to be his uncle.

In Linlithgow, Doreen Hagger was 'well known' to the police, who regularly attended disputes. She and her friend Janet Reilly, who lived a few doors down and was a frequent visitor, would often call the police to complain about Janet's upstairs neighbour. The neighbour, in turn, would call the police about the noise Janet and Doreen made.

In May 1988, Doreen's son Andrew came home from school with a leaflet advertising a boys' club starting up in the gym hall of Linlithgow Academy. Andrew was anxious to join. The boys' participation in the club, Doreen later recalled, was conditional on them also agreeing to attend an adventure camp at Loch Lomond over the summer holidays. Although money was tight, Doreen scraped together the £110 fee for the camp. She thought her son 'soft' for his age and hoped the camp would help 'toughen' him a bit. Over the course of May and June, Andrew regularly attended the boys' club, which took place on Thursday evenings. Doreen would come to the school to collect Andrew at 9 p.m. She met Mr Hamilton, briefly, four times before the summer camp began, and he 'always seemed very pleasant'. He assured her that the camp would be properly run, with plenty of adult supervision; the island he had picked, he added, had chalets, indoor toilets, covered cooking facilities, hot showers and excellent radio communications in case of emergencies. Andrew was to attend in July.

The rendezvous point for parents to drop off their sons was Balmaha. Doreen watched as Andrew nervously clambered into a large wooden boat fitted with both oars and an outboard motor and sat down beside a couple of other boys as Mr Hamilton untied the rope anchoring them to the jetty and prepared to cast off. She turned around and walked back to her car.

Four days later, Doreen returned home from an evening with friends to find Andrew back early from camp. He had been dropped off by another mother and left with her uncle, who was staying in the house with them. The first thing she noticed was that her son wasn't wearing his own clothes and didn't have his own bag or personal belongings. The second thing she noticed was how upset he seemed. She phoned the police at Alexandria, the closest station to Loch Lomond and, according to her, was told that they had visited the island and discovered a lack of adequate food and shelter and that it was unsuitable for children. The police had received complaints but did not specify the source. The boys had been in a cinema at Alexandria. All Andrew said was that the camp had been 'horrible'.

That night, Andrew would not settle in bed and 'didn't sleep much'. When she spoke to her son in the morning, he painted a picture of the camp that surprised Doreen. When they first arrived on the island, 'Mr Hamilton', as Andrew respectfully referred to him, had ordered all the boys to strip naked and put their clothes in a neat pile by their bags. They then had to race past Mr Hamilton to grab a pair of swimming trunks. Over the course of the week, Mr Hamilton hit Andrew on his bare legs with a wooden spoon for not eating Smash, the powdered potatoes which were a staple of their island diet. Yet the most traumatic experience for Andrew, who could not swim and was scared of water, was when he and a small group of other boys were taken out on a boat into the loch. The boys were told to take off their swimming trunks so they didn't get wet and given a life jacket to put on. Each boy then had to jump naked into the water. When Andrew's turn arrived he baulked, gripped by a primal fear which Mr Hamilton ignored. Laughing, he kicked Andrew off the boat and into the cold water. The boys were then hauled back into the boat and given a single hand towel to share and dry themselves off before putting their trunks back on. Andrew 'stopped talking about it at that', as Doreen recalled. 'I didn't know if he was maybe exaggerating. He seemed very upset though.' Initially, Doreen thought Andrew's upset was partly caused by being away from home for the first time. 'I hadn't got the impression Mr Hamilton would have been like that, but I also didn't think [Andrew] would lie.'

Two days after Andrew's early arrival home, Doreen received a call from Mr Hamilton, who said that if she wanted her son's bag and clothes, she could collect them from the boatyard at Balmaha. He also said he would appreciate the opportunity to explain himself, as some people were now conducting a 'smear campaign' out of jealousy at how successful his boys' clubs had become. Doreen challenged him about his treatment of her son while out on the boat and Hamilton said it had been essential lifeboat practice, and that he had merely given Andrew a 'tip with his foot' to make him go in the loch, not realising he was genuinely scared of the water. 'He said in hindsight it was a stupid thing to do,' Doreen said.

The following Sunday, Doreen returned to Balmaha with her boyfriend, Sam Davie, and daughter Victoria. Her son stayed home: 'Andrew flatly refused to go with us.' They were met at the boatyard by Mr Hamilton, who had neither Andrew's clothes nor his bag, which he said were still on the island. 'If you come out, we can have a cup of tea and I will explain in detail what has been going on,' he told her. Doreen agreed, and the four puttered out in his motorboat, passing a cluster of other small islands, including the birch-fronted outcrops of Inchfad and Inchcruin, before landing on the western side of Inchmoan.

'The first thing I noticed at the camp was the rubbish everywhere, cans and bottles and things. It was filthy. There were no showers or toilet facilities. There were two tents, a big one and a small one, and that was it.' There was a wood fire, a railway sleeper and a couple of boxes. It was filthy with rubbish where the boat landed.

Over a cup of tea by the campfire, Mr Hamilton explained that they had been supposed to camp on another island, but at the last minute someone had caused the plan to fall through. He also told them that he had been badly let down by fellow club members, but that he was making the best of things for the children's sake. Currently, his only helper was a seventeen-year-old boy, Steven Williams. He was worried that if he didn't get other adults on board, the police would return. 'He was really uptight about that – he kept going on about it. He needed some adult help in case the police came back.'

Hamilton said he had a new batch of boys coming, and he asked Doreen if she would help. She could treat it as a free holiday and keep an eye on the boys, and do some light cooking as well. Doreen may have arrived with plans to remonstrate with Mr Hamilton, but she found herself warming to his quiet manner, and there were the other children to think of. After sipping her tea and pondering the offer, Doreen eventually said she would do it, on the condition that she could bring her friend Janet and her children. Hamilton was pleased and said he'd make sure they had their own tent.

When Doreen arrived home, she called Janet, laid out the offer and was pleased when her friend agreed to go, but was disappointed when Janet said she wouldn't take her own son. Part of the rationale for joining the camp was that they wanted to see for themselves what was going on and step in if Mr Hamilton was acting out of line. 'Otherwise it was only a wee boy's word,' said Doreen. Andrew, after some persuasion, agreed to go back to the camp.

Doreen, Janet, Sam Davie and the two children, Andrew and his younger sister Victoria, returned to Inchmoan two or three days later. Their stay did not go well. The group arrived in the pouring rain and found the remaining boys, about five of them, sitting in their black trunks on the sodden ground eating a cold sandwich lunch. Hamilton didn't want the tents messed up, so Doreen made a shelter out of old tarpaulin and cut up cardboard boxes on which the boys could kneel. There were three tents: a white one used by Hamilton and a couple of the boys, a green tent for the exclusive use of Doreen and her group, and a second green tent for the remaining boys.

On inspecting the larder, Doreen was disappointed by the lack of fresh fruit and vegetables and a preponderance of powdered soup and powdered mashed potatoes, alongside a few tins of corned beef, cold ham, a packet of cornflakes and a solitary pack of digestive biscuits. She told Hamilton that this was unacceptable and wrote out a lengthy shopping list, which he agreed to buy the following day at a cost of £60. During Doreen's stay, the boys eventually received a cooked breakfast, a proper lunch and a hot meal in the evening.

The next area for inspection was the first aid kit, which consisted of a few plasters and a half-empty bottle of iodine. Because there was no fresh water on the island, Hamilton and the boys drank from a bucket drawn from the loch, but he hadn't bothered to boil the water first to kill bacteria. The dry chemical toilet was rarely cleaned, and while Doreen did her best to improve living conditions while there, she was privately shocked at the gulf between what Hamilton had advertised to parents and the privations their sons were enduring.

Hamilton continued to bully the children and insist it was a necessary form of discipline. Cuts and bruises were dismissed as trivial, and when he took the boys on an eight-mile walk from Luss to Helensburgh, he forbade socks, and their feet were badly blistered when they returned.

While the other boys were required to wear only swimming trunks, Doreen insisted Andrew wear both trousers and a T-shirt, which annoyed Hamilton. On occasion, when a boy seemed particularly cold, Doreen made him put on a sweater she kept to hand. On more than one occasion Doreen threatened to leave, only to be persuaded by Hamilton to stay. She did so more out of concern for the boys she would have left behind, but over ten days the situation became intolerable. Hamilton was now being assisted by a couple of teenage boys who were drinking heavily at night; her boyfriend found it hard to resist the temptation to join them for a drink. When their collective rowdiness kept everyone awake, Doreen intervened only to be verbally abused, something which frightened both her and the children. The next night, one of the drunks couldn't find his sleeping bag and tried to drag Janet's one off her, then attempted to slap her face. When Doreen tried to stop him, she was kicked in the shin. Finally, when one of the drunks threatened to attack them with an axe and burn down their tent using one of the cans of petrol used to fuel the boat, Doreen and Janet decided to leave at dawn. The other children were upset and some of them wanted to go with her, but she knew she couldn't take them. Instead, she promised to go to the police.

Steven Williams, Hamilton's original assistant, said he would sit up all night by the campfire to keep watch in case either drunk attempted to make good on their threats. Then, at roughly 4 a.m., Williams quietly pushed the boat into the loch's icy waters to paddle Doreen, Janet, Andrew and Victoria back to the boatyard at Balmaha. The women loaded the children into their car and drove straight to the police station in Alexandria, a thirteen-mile journey over the hills on the loch's southern shore. At the station Janet believed they spoke to a uniformed officer, while Doreen thinks she spoke to a Detective Superintendent McBain, who 'told me it was being looked into'. Over the next few weeks, she phoned Alexandria Police Station several times, seeking an update. 'I began to feel a nuisance.'

The matter of Thomas Hamilton's summer camp for boys was, indeed, under investigation. Constable George Gunn had compiled an initial report based on further interviews with the parents of several boys who had attended the camp, as well as the boys themselves. Gunn learned that the first boy to arrive on Inchmoan had done so alone. The child's mother was a single parent, and although she couldn't afford the fee, Hamilton had said the child could attend for free. On arrival on the island, Hamilton said the child would be stiff from the boat trip and would need to loosen up with exercises, so he had set out two plastic basins a few feet apart and had the boy run between the basins, taking out plates from one and putting them into the other. They did more exercises together in the tent, and every time the boy made a mistake he got hit on the bottom with a wooden spoon. Almost every child spoke of being slapped. They also spoke of the lack of life jackets and how Hamilton overloaded his boat. Once, when they arrived in Balloch, a man had shouted out that the boat was overloaded, that it should only have twelve boys on board and they had almost twenty, but Mr Hamilton told the boys not to mind the man as he was drunk. He told the boys he had a special licence that meant he could decide the boat's capacity.

The final report into Hamilton's behaviour was compiled by Detective Superintendent Ian McBain and submitted to the procurator fiscal on 30 August, six weeks after the police first visited

Inchmoan. (In Scotland, though the police conduct investigations, the decision on whether to press charges remains with the office of the procurator fiscal, who works in tandem with the police to secure evidence.)

This report landed on the desk of James Cardle, who, to clarify exactly what had happened, asked that certain witnesses be spoken to again or 'precognosced', a more formal interview process. Cardle was keen to narrow down the alleged assaults to a number that would hold up in court. While almost every child had testified either to Hamilton striking themselves or another camper, these assaults were either not corroborated by another witness, as was usually required under Scots law, or there were discrepancies between the accounts. One child would state that his friend had been struck, but when questioned the friend would have no recollection of this. In the end, Cardle drilled down and discovered one or two cases for which there was corroboration, but he concluded that the incidents were so minor as not to merit criminal prosecution. Cardle could reasonably have prosecuted Hamilton for assaults on two boys under a breach of Section 12 of the Children and Young Persons (Scotland) Act 1937. What stayed his hand was that the children had not been left with permanent damage, and Hamilton's argument that he was acting with the support of at least some of the parents.

Yet the children's statements raised concerns with Cardle. He informed the police that while there would be no criminal prosecution, he believed they should raise Hamilton's behaviour with the local social work department, the Reporter to the Children's Panel (the Children's Panel is a system unique to Scotland that prioritises child welfare), and the authorities responsible for letting school premises for Hamilton's boys' clubs. Cardle said he was told by police that all the relevant authorities were aware of Hamilton's behaviour.

Thomas Hamilton was also preparing his own retaliation against those he believed had borne false witness. One of his first targets was Doreen Hagger. One August afternoon, the bell rang at Doreen's council house. When she opened the door, she was surprised to see Hamilton standing on the doorstep wearing a three-quarter-length grey anorak with his right hand pushed deep into the pocket. He had heard that she'd been 'telling tales to the police at Alexandria'. He then began to tell Doreen that he owned four guns, that he was an excellent shot, that he considered his guns to be his 'friends', and that his 'friends' didn't like people talking about him. She kept Hamilton on the front doorstep and told her daughter to run and get Janet, and that Mummy was being threatened. 'He was moving his hand in the pocket to make as if he was pointing something at me,' Doreen said.

Janet was sitting at home when there was a knock on the door. Victoria shouted that her mum wanted her to come quickly, as Mr Hamilton was threatening her with a gun. Janet didn't believe her at first, but then the little girl began to cry. So Janet followed her to Doreen's house, where Hamilton was standing on the doorstep. She could see his hand in the right pocket of his anorak, where it remained, unmoving and pointing straight down, 'as if he was holding on to something'. She pushed past him and went into the house, making it clear there was now an adult witness. After a few more minutes Doreen slammed the door in Hamilton's face. As Janet recalled: 'She told me he had threatened her with a gun because she had told the police and some of the other mothers what he was like.'

Doreen said she had definitely seen a gun, but she didn't know or remember what kind. As Janet remembers, she then called Livingston police station (Doreen was aware that Linlithgow police station didn't always answer the phone). Two officers arrived within forty-five minutes; she recognised them from previous visits. The women told the police what had happened; the officers recorded it in their notebooks and said they would visit Mr Hamilton.

The two women next saw Thomas Hamilton about a month later. Janet had been at the shops with Doreen's daughter. It was a school afternoon; a Wednesday, she thinks. When she got back to Doreen's house, she saw a Transit van parked at the gate and Hamilton at the wheel with the window down. Doreen shouted that if he didn't move, she would call the police. The passenger window was next to the pavement and, as Hamilton pulled out, she could see a bulky object under a sheet on the passenger seat. Later, Doreen said Hamilton had wanted to talk to her again about what she had told the police. Again, the women said they had called the police, and again, they said two officers had come out to the house – a different two officers this time, but ones Janet recognised. Again, the officers said they would look into it.

The police investigation prompted Hamilton to strike back at what he believed was unfair treatment, triggered by a cabal of police officers and senior officials from the Scouts with whom he had an obsession stretching back almost fifteen years. The target of his immediate ire was PC George Gunn, and the first salvo in his assault was a series of letters accusing the officer both of incompetence and of repeatedly lying in his report about the initial visit to the summer camp. The letters were copied to Gunn's superior officer, Inspector Michael Mill, who Hamilton knew and was friendly with; other officers at Central Scotland Police; and to Stirling council and Hamilton's local MP, the Conservative Michael Forsyth. Even before the police report had been sent to the procurator fiscal, Hamilton turned up at Balfron's police station demanding to discuss the matter with Gunn, who at first refused to speak to him and finally threatened arrest if he did not leave the premises. On another occasion, Hamilton sat outside the station for three hours, hoping to speak to Gunn.

The letters became more obsessive and granular in their detail. Inspector Mill was sent a lengthy report on the food purchased for the camp and the corresponding till receipts. Hamilton's accusations against Gunn (whom he incorrectly accused of being a Scout leader intent on destroying a competing boys' club) were investigated and dismissed. A letter informing Hamilton of the decision was sent on 19 October 1988. At first, he appeared to accept the decision, before almost immediately changing his mind. He wrote again to the chief constable, stating that Gunn's investigation had been triggered because of 'a long resentment shown to our group by many adult members of the Dunblane Scouts'. He believed a 'brotherhood' between senior police officers and the Scouts in Dunblane was behind his continual harassment.

In October, the *Falkirk Herald* published an article about the summer camp, and Hamilton was vigorous in his defence. He said the matter had all been a misunderstanding and that the police had apologised to him for their overreaction, which was a lie: 'A group of children – all friends – from the Falkirk area came to the camp with the wrong attitude. They didn't like the food or anything about the camp. We spent £1,600 on food but the boys claimed they were starved. Other aspects brought to the attention of the police were that the boys had bare legs and it was alleged that this was cruel in cold and wet weather. The police took this very seriously. However, I must point out that problems of drying wet clothes made us ask the boys to wear shorts. I don't think this means they are treated cruelly.'

By November, Hamilton had made an official complaint against Gunn, forcing Central Scotland Police to follow protocol and appoint an investigator to study the allegations. Douglas McMurdo, the deputy chief constable, asked Inspector James Keenan to re-examine Hamilton's allegations. As part of the internal investigation into Gunn's professional conduct, Inspector Keenan interviewed Thomas Hamilton for almost three hours. He interviewed boys who had attended the camp and also their parents, who praised Hamilton's organisational skills and firm leadership. In addition, Keenan met with Gunn, who argued that Hamilton's evidence was 'untrustworthy, vindictive, wholly unreasonable, malicious and obsessive'. The officer had seriously considered suing Hamilton for slander, but he decided it would be a waste of time.

Inspector Keenan also re-interviewed each of the boys who had attended the summer camp on Inchmoan Island, a time-consuming task which turned up evidence of disturbing and inappropriate behaviour. When, almost nine months after the camp, Keenan visited the home of Doreen Hagger in the late spring of 1989, her son Andrew told the police inspector something he had not revealed to his mother: that Hamilton had insisted the boys rub suntan lotion into his naked torso. He, in turn, would rub lotion into the boys' torsos and legs. It was also said that, on occasion, Hamilton had not been wearing any underwear.

In May, Doreen made a complaint about Hamilton's clubs to her local councillor, but she was also intent on taking the matter into her own hands. She was concerned that Hamilton was still running his boys' club at Linlithgow Academy. She decided that if neither the police nor the local authorities were prepared to put a stop to them, then she would do so herself. In a frustrated phone call with Inspector Keenan, she said, 'If he likes suntan cream that much, I will show him exactly what I think about him and his suntan cream.' Keenan advised Doreen that she would only get into trouble if she assaulted Hamilton, 'but she seemed to believe that if that was the only way she could bring Mr Hamilton to the attention of the court, she was prepared to do so'.

Keenan was left in no doubt that Doreen planned to attack Hamilton in some manner and alerted a duty inspector at Livingston police station, explained the background to the dispute and suggested sending a couple of officers to Hamilton's next boys' club meeting. The duty inspector agreed to put a note in the logbook, but no officers were dispatched.

Doreen hatched a plot with Janet to attack Hamilton in public, with a view to being arrested and charged. The mothers believed that during any trial for assault they would be able to bring their knowledge of Hamilton's behaviour to the public's attention and thus ruin his reputation and force the closure of his boys' clubs. To ensure the maximum amount of publicity, Doreen contacted the *Lothian Courier*, a local newspaper. Chief reporter Karen Butterwick took the phone call. The initial conversation was garbled and confused, but the reporter was intrigued enough to arrange a meeting in person at Doreen's home, where it was claimed Hamilton had 'sexually abused' her son. Doreen briefed Butterwick on her previous involvement with Hamilton and his behaviour at the summer camp. 'As far as I can ascertain,' the reporter said, 'her allegations of sexual abuse amounted to Hamilton keeping the boys wearing only shorts and rubbing suntan lotion on them.' Butterwick pushed for further details that might strengthen the story; Doreen 'was unable to expand any further but was obviously convinced there was more to it ... [she] was unhappy with a number of aspects of the running of the camp.' Butterwick listened as Doreen said that she and Janet had prepared two buckets of slops, which they planned to hurl over Hamilton outside the school.

The next day, in the office of the *Lothian Courier*, Butterwick called the press office at Strathclyde Police and then Central Scotland Police, both of which confirmed they were aware of Thomas Hamilton and that an investigation into his boys' camp at Loch Lomond had taken place. Butterwick was unable to substantiate Doreen's allegations of sexual abuse, and certainly not from the police, who said no charges had been brought against Hamilton. Besides, Butterwick was 'not particularly happy' with Doreen as a reliable witness: 'I felt she was embellishing and making the most of it.' Yet her threat of public humiliation was certainly enough for a 'story'. So Butterwick decided she would go along to Linlithgow Academy on Tuesday evening, with a photographer, to see what kicked off.

With the photographer at the ready, Doreen and Janet were primed to pounce. As soon as Hamilton got out of his car and walked towards the school entrance, the pair tipped over his head two buckets containing a fetid mixture of suntan oil, liquid manure, flour, fish manure, vinegar and wallpaper paste. Doreen shouted that she was sorry she didn't have a 'little boy to rub it in for him'. Hamilton refused to take the bait.

Butterwick followed Hamilton into the school to get his side of the story. They spoke in the janitor's office while he dried himself off. Butterwick's first impression was that Hamilton was 'very calm considering the circumstances, and very soft-spoken'. He could not understand why Doreen Hagger had attacked him in such a manner, and while he admitted to having been questioned by the police, Hamilton said that nothing had come of it. He then began to explain that he was simply 'interested in the healthy development of the boys in his clubs' and described the camps as 'an extension of his clubs'. He was insistent that he would not be stopped from taking boys out in the summer months and that he had plans to take another seventy boys back to Loch Lomond.

The janitor called the police, who despite Keenan's warning were not in attendance. But when they arrived, much to Doreen's anger, Hamilton refused to make a complaint. Instead of flaring into a fury, he remained calm and polite. The newspaper report, which appeared three days later, was matter-of-fact. Butterwick was limited to what she could legally – and ethically – print, but she did quote Doreen saying that 'the boys were standing about blue with the cold, others were sobbing and crying, wanting to go home.' Her hope was that the story might bring out other parents who had complaints against Hamilton, though she did not receive any. About a week and a half later she did receive a letter from Hamilton, in which he once again dismissed Doreen's accusations and claimed, according to the journalist, that people 'misunderstood his motives and had no reason to be concerned'. (When Butterwick later heard that Hamilton's boys' club had been dropped by the school, she considered writing a follow-up, but as Doreen remained her sole contact, she decided it would be 'unfair on Mr Hamilton in the circumstances'.) Hamilton also made a complaint to the council ombudsman, who declined to pursue the matter.

Two days after her assault on Hamilton, Doreen learned that he had taken two handguns and a semi-automatic rifle to the home of two boys who attended Linlithgow Boys' Club. She called the police to say she had been informed by the boys' mother of this visit. The police log recorded that Doreen said Hamilton might become violent and use the weapons against her for telling the police about his behaviour. A report was passed on to Lothian and Border Police, and Sergeant McGrane, based in Bathgate, went out to interview the family that evening. He was told that Hamilton's visit was not in any way distressing; in fact, they reported having posed for pictures with the weapons. (McGrane later said that the family had been uneasy at having the guns in the house, but that he did not put this in his final report.) McGrane took the family's pictures as evidence. A memo on the incident stated: 'It may be quite a harmless display of weapons, but nevertheless an action which leaves a lot to be desired.'

One of the two children Hamilton visited said he had enjoyed the summer camp and insisted he had no memories of anything wrong happening 'other than one occasion when Mr Hamilton punched me in the face ... I had been told to jump into the water whilst wearing a life jacket. This was part of some form of training exercise ... I had refused to jump into the water, so Hamilton punched me in the face.'

At the time of the summer camp, his mother had given the police a full statement, which was largely supportive, and her two sons continued to attend the Linlithgow club. One evening, Hamilton had walked them home after the session and, grateful for Hamilton's concern for the boys' safety, their mother then drove him to the train station. She found him 'very polite and well mannered'. She knew her son had an interest in guns and had discussed them with Hamilton. However, shortly before Christmas, her attitude to the instructor drastically changed. Her son told her Hamilton had struck him after he had been cheeky to one of the camp volunteers. Doreen Hagger was also regularly calling to complain to her about Hamilton. When she asked Doreen what had happened to her son, she said that Andrew had done nothing wrong and 'was just being a typical wee boy'. Privately, she resolved to speak to Hamilton about the slap or punch at the next boys' club meeting, but then, one December evening, he arrived unannounced on their doorstep with a holdall containing a semi-automatic rifle and three handguns: a Magnum, a Browning and a Beretta. Although startled, she and her husband invited him in; Hamilton explained that he thought the boys would like to see his guns, which were wrapped in cloth. Concerned that he had been walking the streets with a small armoury, she asked if this was legal and he assured her it was, as long as they were in bags and had no ammunition. The boys were tremendously excited, and her husband retrieved the family camera to take pictures as they posed with the guns in the sitting room. 'We didn't think there was any harm in it,' she said. 'I remember [Hamilton] kept telling them they had to be very careful and always point them down and never at people.' The impromptu show lasted for an hour and a half. As Hamilton wrapped up the guns, put them back in his bag and prepared to leave, she offered to give him a lift again to the station in Linlithgow.

On the short drive she asked Hamilton why he had slapped her son: 'He said I wasn't supposed to know about that and [her son] was being cheeky … I told him it wasn't good enough and he shouldn't have done it.' Hamilton then continued to defend his actions, before eventually relenting and apologising. Yet her mind was made up; the boys would not return to the club.

Hamilton did not take the family's rejection lightly. When he realised her sons would not be returning, he began to send them abusive letters. At the time of the Inchmoan camp, she had taken a couple of boys who did not want to stay back to her home, as their parents could not be immediately contacted. This was done with the full permission and knowledge of the police. In his letters, Hamilton claimed this was 'tantamount to kidnapping'.

'He sent me a number of letters on that theme,' she said, 'along with various other copies of letters he had received from various authorities which he claimed exonerated him from any blame or wrongdoing.' Yet rather than confront Hamilton yet again, she ignored the letters and threw them in the bin.

11

THE SCOUTS

Thomas Hamilton was born on 10 May 1952 into an unhappy home, a tenement house in Lily Street in Glasgow's Parkhead. His mother, Agnes Graham Hamilton, had married Thomas Watt less than two years before, aged twenty-one. The arrival of young Thomas Watt, as he was named on his birth certificate, served only to break apart an already fractured relationship. A few weeks later, Agnes discovered that her husband was having an affair. Thomas Watt senior abandoned both wife and child soon afterwards.

Agnes moved back in with her parents, who lived around the corner in Bellrock Street, Cranhill. Agnes went back out to work, while Catherine, her mother, looked after the infant Thomas. Catherine suggested they adopt the boy, and this was formalised on 26 March 1956, when he was four years old.

Thomas Hamilton spent the first eight years of his life in Glasgow, where he attended primary school. In the summer of 1963, the family, including his 'sister' Agnes, moved out to Stirling, where his 'father' had purchased a house: 11 Upper Bridge Street, which the family ran as a bed and breakfast. Agnes worked at a hotel in Callander but returned home on her days off. When the family first moved to Stirling, Hamilton attended the Territorial School on Cowane Street, before moving on to Riverside Secondary. Fellow pupils remember him as quiet but intelligent; he was good at maths and an excellent competitive chess player. He went on to Falkirk Technical College, where he completed his O levels in 1968. As his biological grandfather later recalled, they never had any behavioural or truancy problems with him.

Hamilton first showed an interest in handguns and firearms as a teenager, joining a community rifle club in a wooden hut in Irvine Place when he was sixteen. Although his adoptive father would later deny it, there is strong evidence that he helped him buy his first gun, an air rifle purchased at D. Crockart & Sons, a popular ironmonger on King Street in Stirling.

As a young adult, Hamilton also had other interests. He was good with his hands. One of the classes he enjoyed most in secondary school was woodwork. He left school at fifteen and secured an apprenticeship at Stirling County Council, where he trained as a draughtsman in the architect's office. He stayed there for three years, each day walking the short distance to the office from the new family home at 24 Queen Street, again run as a B & B, where he continued to live with his parents and Agnes, whose true identity had not yet been revealed to him.

However, Hamilton was stubborn and knew what he wanted. In 1970, when he was still only eighteen, he decided to leave the safety and financial security of the council, a workplace once so prized for its solidity and security that jobs were quietly passed down from father to son. He wanted to set out on his own, open his own business, be his own boss. He had no wish to have anyone else tell him what he could or could not do. With savings from his council salary and a small loan from his father, he purchased premises in Cowane Street and opened Woodcraft, a DIY store. The store was made up of a small vestibule leading to a counter behind which Hamilton sat, but it was well stocked with ironmongery, a choice of domestic timbers, joists and brackets, an array of saws, chisels, nails, screws and washers: everything the enterprising man about the house would need to build a bookcase or fit a kitchen. When Hamilton arrived in the morning, he would put on a brown overcoat, its breast pocket lined with pens, and always kept a sharpened pencil behind his ear, as the older architects in the office would do.

Hamilton was also fond of young boys, and he liked it when the truants came to hang out in his shop. He would give them money for chocolate and cigarettes and let them stay as long as they wanted, so long as they didn't fool around with the stock or mishandle the saws and chisels.

As a schoolboy Hamilton had briefly been a member of the Boys' Brigade, the uniformed youth club founded in 1883 by Sir William Alexander Smith in his native Glasgow as a means of encouraging city-dwelling children whose parents were toiling through the Industrial Revolution to enjoy camping in the outdoors and experience the spiritual and moral benefits of volunteering. In his late teens, Hamilton was drawn to the Scouts, the Boys' Brigade's younger rival established in 1907 by Robert Baden-Powell, a retired British army lieutenant general. Sir William Alexander Smith may have been first to recognise the benefits of uniformed youth groups, bound by physical exercise and a common charitable purpose, but Baden-Powell was first into print with his book *Scouting for Boys*, published in 1908. The text quickly became an international bestseller. What started with twenty boys and a rural camp on Brownsea Island in Dorset had, sixty years later, become a mass youth movement with troops in dozens of countries around the world.

Thomas Hamilton joined the 4th/6th Stirling Scout troop in 1970 as a Venture Scout. He was invited to join by Robert Deuchars, a regular customer at Woodcraft who in 1973 would be appointed district commissioner for the Scouts in Stirling. He described Thomas as 'young and very enthusiastic'. Three years later, a Catholic priest wished to reactivate the former 24th Stirlingshire troop and asked Hamilton if he wished to step up to assistant Scout leader. Brian Fairgrieve, a surgeon with a senior role in the Scouts, offered him a six-month secondment to organise the new troop. Though 'keen and willing', Hamilton's enthusiasm exceeded his organisational abilities, and what had initially been regarded as leadership potential was later viewed as a cloak to disguise more sinister intent.

Hamilton was initially reprimanded by Robert Deuchars for having extended 'playtimes' with the boys at the expense of the Scout course curriculum. An improvement was noted, but problems increased when he volunteered to take a few boys from the troop out on his boat on Loch Lomond as part of their sailing proficiency badge. (He had acquired a twenty-seven-foot cabin cruiser, which he moored in Balmaha.) When it was discovered that he lacked the correct number of life jackets and oars, or a distress flare in case of emergency, and that his knowledge of the waters was not as comprehensive as required, the planned trip was cancelled.

Among the Scouts in his charge, Hamilton had his favourites. In the winter of 1974, he invited a few boys for a weekend in the wilds of the Cairngorms, an almost three-hour drive north in his Transit van. On arrival, the boys were told their hotel accommodation had been double-booked: they would have to sleep in the van, cuddling up for warmth through shared body heat, as Lord Baden-Powell had recommended. The weather was so cold the van's engine froze. The next morning it had to be towed to Aviemore and defrosted. Hamilton did not join them in huddling for warmth, according to the boys: 'It was all right for Mr Hamilton. He went on the front bench seat of the van with his sleeping bag and blankets and we had to sleep on the cold steel floor.'

The boys complained to their parents, who complained to Brian Fairgrieve, who warned Hamilton that his planning needed to improve. Hamilton insisted that the hotel had been unavailable. He hadn't wished to disappoint the boys, so he had let them sleep in the van, something he'd thought they might enjoy.

Three weeks later, Hamilton set off to Aviemore with another group of boys. Once again, they arrived home with sodden sleeping bags, saying they had slept in the van. This time it was Fairgrieve who made a point of visiting the parents to apologise. When he called the number of the hostel Hamilton had supposedly booked, he was informed that no reservation had been made. Fairgrieve now suspected that the young Scout leader had deliberately sought to spend the night alone with the boys. He contacted Bob Deuchars, and it was agreed that Hamilton should be asked to resign and hand back his warrant book, the card verifying his position as a uniformed leader.

In a letter written to the Scottish Scout headquarters, dated 29 June 1974, Fairgrieve stated his belief that Hamilton was unsuitable to be a member of the Scout movement and should not be readmitted by a troop elsewhere in the country. Fairgrieve would admit that there was no hard evidence against the young leader. No boy had yet made any allegations of inappropriate touching. Instead, his 'suspicions' were what had forced his hand. Fairgrieve organised a meeting with Hamilton, at which he was told he lacked the necessary qualities to be a Scout leader. Hamilton's services were no longer required, and his warrant was withdrawn. Fairgrieve explained that while there was no concrete evidence against Hamilton, 'too many "incidents" relate to him such that I am far from happy about his having any associations with Scouts', and that 'as a doctor, and with my clinical acumen only, I am suspicious of his moral intentions towards boys.'

As district commissioner, Deuchars informed headquarters that Hamilton was an unsuitable candidate on the grounds of immaturity and irresponsibility. The combined consequence of both men's disapproval was to fix the name 'Thomas Hamilton' firmly on the organisation's informal blacklist, ensuring that the organisation would reject any application by him.

Yet Hamilton was both clever and devious. To devise his own narrative, in which he had not been asked but had chosen to resign on a point of principle, he wrote a letter of resignation predated to 28 April 1974 which criticised Deuchars for his own conduct, including being 'appalled at the conditions of safety, hygiene and equipment' and 'the way it is common practice for all the leaders to disappear to the pubs at night and leave the boys unsupervised'.

Hamilton would make multiple attempts to return to the Scouts in a leadership role. First, he requested the organisation hold a Committee of Inquiry into his complaint that he had been victimised, a request the organisation rejected. Over the next three years he bombarded the organisation with letters of complaint. Then, in April 1977, he wrote to the organisation with the announcement that he had abandoned his attempts to secure the return of his warrant card: 'I do not want my good name to be part of this so-called organisation.' He approached the district commissioner for the Trossachs and offered his services as a Scout leader, but when his name was routinely checked with the organisation's headquarters in Glasgow, he received a letter informing him that the Scouts were unable to make use of his services.

In 1974, two events took place whose emotional impact we cannot fully know without Hamilton's testimony. He lost his beloved role within the Scouts, and he discovered that his family had been living a lie all his life. At twenty-two, he was told the truth: that his parents were his grandparents and that his sister, Agnes, was, in fact, his mother. The exact date of this personal revelation is not known, but it was after the family had moved from 24 Queen Street into a new house at 39 Forth Crescent, Riverside. According to his grandfather, Hamilton continued to treat Agnes as his sister despite knowing she was his mother. 'He took it well,' Agnes said of Thomas.

Also in 1974, Hamilton took on a young apprentice, Francis Baird Cullen, whom he first met through a neighbour. Cullen spent the next two years working at Woodcraft every weekend and on Thursday and Friday afternoons after school. 'He was a generous man to work with and a kind man,' Cullen recalled. 'He was definitely a strange man in the way that he spoke and the way that he cut his hair and the way that he walked, his approach to people, and more importantly his nervousness among adult people.' Cullen also said Hamilton was particularly nervous around women.

Woodcraft was a great place for a teenage boy to work. There was an extension at the back of the shop set up with wooden targets at which Hamilton and Cullen would fire air rifles and crossbows. Without the discipline and mental distraction of Scouting, Hamilton was looking for an alternative pursuit. He rediscovered his schoolboy interest in guns.

Until 1903, anyone in Britain could own any type of handgun, revolver, rifle or shotgun, even a military-grade machine gun if one could be sourced – as well as the corresponding bullets and ammunition – without breaking the law. In the United Kingdom there was no 'right to bear arms' as codified in America's Constitution; instead, there was a long-standing tradition that an Englishman should be armed without government interference. The Whig historian Thomas Macaulay long asserted that the ability to arm oneself was 'the security without which every other is insufficient'.

It was not until 1920 that Parliament passed a comprehensive range of laws that finally eliminated the right to be armed. Following the introduction of the Firearms Act 1920, a right was reduced to a 'privilege', one earned through good character and responsible citizenship. The chief constable of each of Britain's constabularies was now tasked with judging whether an applicant could own a firearm without compromising public safety. Over the next five decades gun laws were subject to adjustment, refinement and consolidation.

The British National Rifle Association (NRA) was exempt from some of the restrictions of the new Firearms Act. The organisation had been launched in 1859 to encourage marksmanship among men who could be called upon by their nation to form a reserve military force. The Secretary of War informed Queen Victoria that the NRA was 'to make the rifle what the bow was in the days of the Plantagenets'. In time, the association's martial purpose fell away and became mainly social, with rifle ranges set up in towns and larger villages across England, Scotland and Wales. The Rifle Association promoted target shooting as a sport, saying that 'Target practice ought to form part of the early training of every Englishman.'

In 1920, Winston Churchill, then serving simultaneously as Secretary of State for War and Secretary of State for Air, praised the military value of the NRA and encouraged donations. Five years later, the Prince of Wales added his own ringing endorsement: 'Let us tell the world about ourselves fearlessly. We like rifle shooting. It really is our hobby. But it is something more. Each and every one of us knows that war has not ceased, that the continent of Europe is a seething pot of jealousy and distrust and envy and hatred, and that we may be fighting for our honour, our very existence as a nation.'

Thomas Hamilton, in his mind, would enjoy such illustrious martial company. At the age of twenty-four, he was granted his first firearms certificate, on 14 February 1977. It was the beginning of a 'love affair' with weapons he would eventually describe as 'my darlings'. The licence authorised him to purchase or acquire a .22 target pistol and to hold a total of a thousand rounds of .22 ammunition.

Until this point he had been using an air rifle, firing it off on waste ground at the back of his shop on Cowane Street, but he now felt the need for something more powerful. He began with a small rifle, firing .22-calibre rounds. A week later, on 20 February 1977, he bought a .22 Vostok semi-automatic handgun and on 17 March, a .22 Smith & Wesson revolver. He also purchased a .22 Anschütz rifle and a .22 Browning handgun.

Within less than two years, Hamilton had upgraded his firearms certificate to permit ownership of full-bore firearms. In early December 1979, he purchased a Christmas present to himself: a .357 Smith & Wesson revolver (with 190 rounds) and a .270 bolt-action Sako rifle (with 220 rounds).

Hamilton joined the Dunblane Rifle and Pistol Club in 1977 and would remain a member for almost a decade, until it disbanded. His favourite gun was a .357 Magnum revolver cast from cold black metal, a slightly smaller but only marginally less powerful handgun than the .44 Magnum used by Clint Eastwood in *Dirty Harry* (1971). Hamilton now had his guns, but what he lacked was his boys.

———

Hamilton soon realised he no longer needed the Scouts to get close to the young boys whose company he so enjoyed. He would start his own club, and the boys would come to him. The exact date and location of his first boys' club has never been established, but what is known is that by the late 1970s Hamilton was the sole coach and organiser of both the Dunblane Rovers, which operated out of Duckburn Community Centre, and a second club in Bannockburn, ten miles down the M9 motorway, which operated out of a variety of school premises. (These two clubs are the earliest for which there are records. Between November 1981 and March 1996, Hamilton ran fifteen separate boys' clubs, an average of one new club per year.)

He would draw up a leaflet, photocopy hundreds at a shop near his store and personally distribute them to neighbouring schools and church halls. He claimed he had a Grade 5 certificate from the British Amateur Gymnastics Association which allowed him to coach gymnastics if supervised by someone with a higher qualification. Occasionally he said he was a former Scoutmaster who now wished to branch out on his own. The clubs were advertised for seven- to eleven-year-old boys.

Hamilton explained in conversation that he had a desire to help 'keep children off the streets' and out of mischief, and that the sense of discipline inculcated by gymnastics would stand each boy in good stead for later life. He would sometimes allude to his detestation of overweight boys, whose size he blamed on parents and junk food. In the late 1970s, the cost per boy per class was 20p or 30p. The club's regular attendance would reach seventy boys in the early years, accruing an income of more than £20, from which all expenses would be deducted. In the early days, though, Hamilton was not so interested in turning a profit. He had his DIY store, and derived a personal pleasure from running classes.

In 1980, Hamilton started a youth club, the Stirling Rovers, which was held in an old building on Perth Road. The first club had an army-style uniform, similar to the Scouts: a green jumper with elbow patches, black trousers, black brogues and a khaki belt. As many as twenty-four boys played football, darts and pool, and at the end of the night, Hamilton would allow them to try his .77

and .22 air rifles, holding the boys' arms to show them how to line up the sights of the guns with the target. Some of the boys considered him odd; one described him as 'very effeminate in his speech and actions, but that was as strange as he got'.

One evening, the club was interrupted by two men, who remonstrated with Hamilton for stating on his leaflets that he was a qualified Scout leader. When the men had left, he gathered the boys together and explained why he had quit the Scouts, claiming that the real reason was that he had complained about other Scout leaders getting drunk on overnight trips. 'We were only nine and ten years old, and we obviously believed him,' one attendee said. 'Rumours that Hamilton was "a poof" were circulating, and some boys even called him one to his face. Instead of getting angry, he told them not to be so rude.'

In the late 1970s, Hamilton bought a large cabin cruiser, the *Tropical Linda*, for £3,000 from an executive at Whyte & Mackay, the whisky distiller. He used the boat to take the boys for weekend trips on Loch Lomond, where he taught them how to handle axes and chop firewood. During one trip, a boy scalded his ankle with boiling water from a kettle and Hamilton took him to Vale of Leven Hospital to have the burn treated and bandaged. Instead of then calling the child's parents to come and collect him, he brought the boy back to the camp to collect the remaining boys and drove them all home in the hired minibus. He carried the injured boy up the driveway to his front door, only to be berated by the child's furious parents, who insisted their son quit the club.

Suspiciously, the *Tropical Linda* went up in flames in 1983 due to an exploded gas cylinder. Hamilton, on board at the time, was forced to swim to shore, where a £36,000 insurance payment awaited him courtesy of an insurance broker who also happened to be a friend. As the boat sank in shallow waters, the harbour master at Balmaha asked that it be towed into deeper waters. Chief Inspector Michael Mill, a member of the Central Scotland Police underwater team and a regular Woodcraft customer, assisted in shifting the sunken vessel. (From time to time Hamilton would 'plead his case' about police harassment to Mill, whom he considered a friendly ear.)

On the sprung wooden floor of a school gym hall, 'Mr Hamilton', as he was now known by his young charges, was a stern and forbidding figure. The boys' clubs were modelled on the military, with orders barked out and a focus on regimented uniform. The exercises themselves were described as 'over-strenuous' for the boys' age.

Hamilton liked to look at boys in black swimming trunks. He purchased a bulk order of identical trunks and insisted every boy who attended his club wear them while performing their gymnastic exercises.

The boys were told to change into the trunks not in the privacy of the changing rooms but in the gym hall. If a parent questioned these rules, he explained that some boys arrived unsuitably dressed and so a 'uniform' was required. The colour choice was simply a preference, which he compared to the regional council respraying vehicles in a more desirable hue.

———

The first concerns about Thomas Hamilton's potentially unhealthy interest in boys emerged in the late 1970s, when three sets of parents contacted the police. Their sons were regular attendees of the Forth Valley Rover Scouts, which Hamilton operated out of Stirling High School. The parents had noticed a discernible change in the boys' behaviour. They were pulling away from their parents, becoming more distant and troublesome. A couple of the boys began to skip primary school and hang out at Woodcraft, where Hamilton indulged them with sweets and comic books. The parents had no firm evidence of anything untoward, but they were concerned about 'subversion of parental authority'. The case was passed to Detective James Kindness, an experienced member of Stirling CID. None of the three boys reported any physical or sexual abuse, but Kindness insisted on interviewing Hamilton, who was invited down to the police station in Dunblane. In an interview room, Hamilton was asked directly if he was homosexual. (Homosexual acts in Scotland remained illegal until 1981.) He said no. He was then asked if he was sexually attracted to young boys. Again, he said no. As there was no evidence of any offence, no report was passed on to the procurator fiscal's office, but rumours spread and the club collapsed.

At this point, a police file was opened in Hamilton's name. It contained a flyer for one of his clubs and the following comment: 'Hamilton is a suspected homosexual and operates the above-mentioned youth club. Boys playing truant from school and being members of this group are found in Hamilton's shop. He would appear to encourage these boys and is prone to influencing them against their parents.'

In the early 1980s Hamilton made a friend who went on to assist him with the boys' clubs for a few years. Ewan Anderson was a fire protection consultant, a keen shooter, and a fellow member of the Dunblane Rifle Club. Hamilton asked him about using the old cadet training building on Stirling Road in Dunblane to teach the boys target shooting with air rifles. Anderson agreed to help and went down each Friday night to help supervise. At the time, in early 1982, Hamilton would regularly take boys from his Dunblane Rovers Club to the rifle club and teach them to shoot.

Anderson was impressed by what he saw: 'The discipline was excellent. They all called him "Sir" and there were no hijinks or anything wayward at all.' The pair fell into conversation, and soon Hamilton was visiting Anderson and his wife at home at least two nights each week, a pattern that continued for the next few years.

On two occasions Hamilton brought over his handguns for Anderson to hold and admire. The first time, he brought a 9 mm pistol and his beloved .357 Magnum revolver, which arrived carefully wrapped in a yellow duster, snug inside a leather carrying case. The second occasion, Hamilton arrived to show off his 5.56 mm assault rifle. The pair went shooting on three occasions using a combination of the rifle, revolver and 9 mm pistol. Anderson sensed that Hamilton was 'a very shy, lonely person' and had nowhere else to go. In time, Hamilton asked Anderson if he would help run his new venture, the Dunblane Boys' Club. Anderson agreed to become treasurer, while his wife acted as club secretary. He collected the 50p pieces off each boy and deposited the money in the club account at the TSB on Dunblane High Street. The club operated out of Dunblane High School and the boys exercised topless, in gym shorts and plimsolls, which Anderson felt was not unusual: 'That was the gym kit when I was at the high school in Stirling.'

Anderson was aware of the rumours that clung to Hamilton and that he divided people. Some parents were uncomfortable with his manner, while others were staunch supporters. 'Somebody would always say, "He did this,"' said Anderson, 'and you would say, "When and where?" And they would say, "Oh, I don't know." "Well, how do you know?" "I heard it." They were saying that Hamilton was queer, basically.'

At one point Anderson raised the rumours with Hamilton: '"Tom, I don't know why you bother. Why don't you stop the clubs and just sit back and live your life?" His reaction was that if he stopped, people would immediately consider the rumours to be true.'

Anderson and his wife stopped assisting with the boys' clubs in the mid 1980s. His wife left her role as secretary as she had other work commitments, while Anderson grew tired of Hamilton taking him for granted: 'I didn't like the way I would suddenly be presented with a carrier bag full of receipts, some of which were just little till receipts with no details. I had no boys in the club and lots of other things to do.' Hamilton continued to visit a couple of times a week, but in 1988, he abruptly stopped coming round. The couple were surprised, but privately relieved. It was not until a decade later that they learned Hamilton had visited their house when they were out one evening. Their daughter's boyfriend had answered the door and had told Hamilton he was now 'a nuisance' and that he should not come back.

The first school to give Thomas Hamilton recorded permission to use its property was Borestone Primary in Stirling, then under the control of Central Regional Council. In October 1981, Hamilton wanted to begin operating from the larger gymnasium at Dunblane High School, six miles away. He described himself at the time as the principal leader of the Dunblane Rovers troop, and as the council's policy was to encourage the use of school property by members of the local community, his application was approved. However, a complaint was made by the Scouts, who objected to the use of the word 'Rovers' in the club's name.

In the same month as the lease was approved by the clerk of the school council, the director of education received a memo, written by Mr T. Mack, the Scouts' district commissioner, which made it clear Hamilton had no connection to the Scouts: 'Mr Hamilton appears to be the subject of a confidential report at national level which shows him to be totally undesirable in relation to working for the Scout movement. The report is based on his homosexual tendencies, and he was for obvious reasons discreetly removed from the Scout movement.' The director of education investigated the allegations, but saw no reason to withdraw the lease.

However, it was not long before more influential figures raised concerns about his management style and behaviour towards children. Hamilton had intense relationships with certain boys who attended his clubs, and would regularly overstep what was considered appropriate social behaviour.

A regular at the club, Malcolm Robertson was the son of George Robertson, then the Labour MP for the constituency of Hamilton, an industrial town in Lanarkshire about thirty miles from the family home in Dunblane. Malcolm had received a copy of the club's leaflet and brought it home for his father to sign: 'It was some kind of indemnity where the parent agreed to the child being in the care of the club.' George Robertson assumed the club was 'above board', given that it was operating from the high school, and thought little more about it.

As a young and ambitious politician in the Labour Party, Robertson was intent on protecting his constituents from the excesses of Margaret Thatcher's Conservative government, and he spent most of each week in London at the House of Commons. When Malcolm was unable to attend the club one Thursday evening, Hamilton sent a letter to the family home insisting he meet with Malcolm and his parents to address their son's absence. Robertson, who usually returned home from London late on a Thursday, arranged an earlier train to pay a personal visit to the Dunblane Rovers Club: 'About 7.30 p.m. I went to the gymnasium at the school and looked through the glass doors. I did not enter the gym. I saw that there were about fifty boys, all aged ten or eleven. All stripped to the waist and wearing shorts. I saw Thomas Hamilton and at least two other adult helpers ... there was some form of disciplined marching going on. I had the gut instinct of suspicion and worry as I watched. I felt the discipline and authoritarianism exercised over children was odd.' Robertson watched for ten minutes and, although they did not speak, Hamilton spotted the MP and chose to ignore him. Robertson decided his son would not be returning to the Dunblane Rovers Club.

The following week, after Hamilton had noted Malcolm's absence from class, he phoned and spoke to the boy's mother, Sandra, asking if he could come to the house to discuss the matter. A date was arranged when both parents would be home. When Hamilton arrived, he was clearly annoyed. 'He asked why I had removed Malcolm from the club, and I told him that I was unhappy with the set-up,' Robertson said. 'He was at first belligerent and asked me what I was implying. I responded that

I was the parent and did not require to expand on my reasons.' Hamilton asked what Malcolm thought about his father's decision. 'I am his father and I will decide what is best for him,' Robertson replied. Hamilton's tone then softened, and he seemed to accept this position. He left shortly afterwards.

Robertson was concerned enough to take the matter further. As a Member of Parliament his opinion had considerable sway. He spoke to several other parents whose children were attending the club. Robertson has said he 'may have taken this up with the council' and was most likely to have done so in April 1983. Over the summer, possibly as a result of Robertson's intervention, the Further Education and General Purposes Sub-Committee of the education committee met on 15 August to re-investigate the complaint received from the Scouts two years previously. After some discussion, with only one voice speaking up in Hamilton's favour, the decision was made to cancel his lets. Six weeks later, on 7 October, Thomas Hamilton was at Woodcraft when the morning post brought an unpleasant surprise: a letter from Central Regional Council prohibiting the Dunblane Rovers from using Dunblane High School.

Hamilton refused to accept the decision. He was also not without allies, who leaked a copy of the council's agenda, allowing him to launch a robust defence. In a letter dated 14 October, Hamilton quoted verbatim from the agenda of the August meeting. Pointing out the correct page and paragraph number to demonstrate his access to restricted information, he quoted the following paragraph: 'There is a Youth Organisation operating within the Region which is not formally recognised by the Authority. There have been a number of complaints from various parties concerning the activities of this organisation and it is recommended that their let be terminated.' Hamilton went on to point out that he had not been consulted about any complaints and said he wished to know their nature and the identities of the complainants.

On 18 October Hamilton sent a second letter to the council, insisting that they reconsider at the next meeting on 31 October: 'As very serious allegations have been made, I intend to be available in person on that date. May I assure you of my good character and integrity and I declare that I have no criminal record whatsoever.' In an attempt to refute criticism from the Scouts, he enclosed a 'copy' of the letter he claimed to have sent them back in April 1974, stating the reasons for his 'resignation'.

Prior to a further meeting of the education committee in November, a petition signed by seventy parents, along with thirty almost identical individual letters, arrived at the council's headquarters in defence of the Dunblane Rovers. The signed petition ended: 'We are all proud to have Mr Hamilton in charge of our boys; he has a most activated, excellent quality of leadership and integrity and is absolutely devoted to his lads; above all, he cares.'

Visible support from a considerable number of parents was not enough to change the committee's mind, however. When the subcommittee met again on 7 November, the decision was upheld by a majority. The director of education did agree to meet with Hamilton on 23 November, and at this meeting, Hamilton began by apologising for any inconvenience he may have unwittingly caused. In order to have their let reinstated, he said, his committee for the Dunblane Rovers would be happy to meet any conditions set by the education department. The director was coy and non-committal, stating only that the deliberations of the education committee were confidential.

With polite diplomacy proving ineffective, Hamilton opted to visit the offices of McLean & Stewart, a small solicitor's based on High Street, Dunblane, which then wrote on his behalf to the director of education. The story of Hamilton's battle with the council had made the Scottish national press, and the letter referred to a recent article in *The Scotsman* which alluded to certain complaints against their client: 'If this was the case he should have been given the opportunity to reply to those complaints ... it seems that the council have acted contrary to natural justice.' Aware the decision to cancel Hamilton's let was due to be discussed by the regional council on 14 December, his solicitor insisted that the termination be revoked and the let reinstated. The letter also pointed out the reputational damage that their client had suffered: 'Mr Hamilton feels that his good character has been tainted ... and that it may severely affect his business.'

On 3 January 1984, Hamilton sent a letter to the director of education, declaring that he was now prepared to go to court: 'In the past three months I have been patient in the understanding that mistakes can happen and have allowed ample time for these to be corrected. The slanderous accusations made against me have been so damaging that the majority of the Councillors are not willing to take any chances by reinstating our let. These slanderous accusations, although now realised to be untruthful, have been responsible for further speculative indulgences by Councillors.' He continued to explain that he had instructed his solicitors to begin a series of legal actions and that the 'entire matter may be brought to the attention of Central Government'.

Hamilton decided to make a formal complaint to the ombudsman, the Commissioner for Local Administration in Scotland. One month later, the commissioner wrote to Central Regional

Council requesting all the relevant papers, minutes and correspondence. The council initially pushed back, concluding that the matter was resolved. The commissioner wrote back that he would decide what fell within his purview and to insist on his request for the relevant paperwork and correspondence.

In spring 1984, Hamilton tried again to secure a let, making a fresh application to Dunblane High School under a different name, Dunblane Boys' Club. The education subcommittee chose to defer their decision until after the ombudsman had made his final decision on Hamilton's appeal, which arrived six months later. On 15 November, the ombudsman declared that the Regional Council had acted unjustly and that there was no solid evidence to support the complaints. The council was also criticised for not permitting Hamilton the opportunity to rebut the charges, and the council was instructed to reinstate his lets. For the education department and councillors of Central Scotland it was a bitter blow; for Hamilton it was a sweeping victory.

Hamilton sent a copy of the report to Michael Forsyth, the new Conservative MP for Stirling and Dunblane, who had surprisingly won the seat in the June 1983 general election. Forsyth wrote back to congratulate Hamilton on his success, as he would any constituent who had successfully resolved a problem. (Moving forward, Hamilton would routinely copy in Forsyth on all his correspondence with any official organisation with which he was in dispute.)

The Regional Council was angry that Hamilton's access to the school would be reinstated. George Robertson was both upset and disappointed by the decision. The subcommittee of the education department attempted to set up one final hurdle by insisting that Hamilton's Dunblane Boys' Club have a proper constitution and management committee, but this was cleared by Hamilton, who cobbled together the paperwork and gathered signatures from local supporters. One week before Halloween, when the streets of Dunblane would be crowded with children dressed as witches and goblins, ghouls and devils, Thomas Hamilton returned to the polished wooden floor of Dunblane High School and asked his young charges to strip to their black trunks. Hamilton's victory over the regional council would both embolden him in the coming years and encourage others to act more conservatively with complaints about him.

―――

The week Hamilton returned to the gym hall, he cleared out his personal armoury, selling his .270 Sako rifle, .22 Browning LR rifle, .22 Browning handgun and his .22 Smith & Wesson revolver. He held on to his .357 Smith & Wesson revolver. Later, on 7 November and again on 7 December, he went back to purchase a 9 mm Browning handgun and .223 Browning rifle. In January 1986, Hamilton secured rare permission for a second 9 mm automatic Beretta handgun after a chain of Central Scotland police officers signed off on an incorrect statement that he was active in competition shooting, which he was not at the time.

Shooters were usually prohibited from owning a second gun of the same calibre.

―――

Around this time, in the early to mid 1980s, the former wife of a police officer at Central Scotland Police became friends with 'Tommy', as she referred to him. She would pop into his shop for a cup of tea and, on occasion, borrow his maroon Transit. Hamilton began visiting the home she shared with her partner once or twice a month, usually around dinner time and always accepting an offer to stay and dine.

She recalled that Hamilton's boat at Loch Lomond had recently 'blown up'. Though she had little idea what the incident had involved, she joked with Hamilton that it looked 'suspicious'. He spoke with her about his guns, and she accepted his invitation to visit Dunblane Shooting Club to fire a rifle, which she didn't enjoy as much as she had expected. She was accompanied by her five-year-old son. She was also one of the few people to visit Hamilton at his home. She met his 'father' but barely spoke to him, and noticed that Hamilton's guns were kept in a locked cabinet. 'I recognised one of them as a Magnum purely from Clint Eastwood films,' she said. 'I remember him talking about how strict the gun laws were.'

Hamilton felt that a female presence at the club would help his credibility and so asked if she would help out. She agreed but only attended a few times, assisting with supervision. It was more than enough to gain an insight into Hamilton's character. 'During these visits,' she said, 'I confirmed an opinion I had previously formed about Tommy. He was fascinated, possibly even obsessed with power and control. We'd spoken previously of the forces and police, and at one time he said he would have liked to have joined the police. He spoke of authority, and the military style and discipline involved in his boys' camps. He also stated that children should be disciplined when being brought up.' She said that his father had been strict with him, his sister and mother, adding, 'I formed the opinion that Tommy's attitude to authority and discipline had a lot to do with his upbringing.'

In the summer of 1987 Thomas Hamilton was living at 7 Kent Road, a council house in Stirling, with his adoptive father. The previous year, at the age of fifty-six, his mother Agnes had finally moved into her own home, and shortly after this her mother, Thomas's grandmother, had died. By chance, his upstairs neighbour at this time was Robert Deuchars, the Scoutmaster who had ended Hamilton's involvement with the Scouts over a decade before. When Deuchars saw his new neighbour, he said he felt sick with nerves, but Hamilton proved to be polite and considerate, on occasion mowing their lawn and putting out their bins.

In the house, among the weapons kept in a locked box, was a semi-automatic rifle, similar to the Kalashnikov, one of the most popular rifles in the world. The standard magazine held thirty rounds of ammunition, which on a depressed trigger could be fired in under three seconds.

On the afternoon of 19 August, in the market town of Hungerford in the Berkshire countryside, another man who lived with his parents and legally owned a Kalashnikov-style semi-automatic rifle decided to use it. Michael Ryan was a twenty-seven-year-old unemployed labourer and a member of the Dunmore Shooting Centre in Abingdon and the Wiltshire Shooting Centre in Devizes. He loaded his car with a Beretta pistol, an M1 carbine rifle and his Type 56 semi-automatic rifle, a Chinese-made replica of the Kalashnikov AK-47, and drove off shortly after noon. Over the next eight hours Ryan shot dead sixteen people, including his mother and a police officer, and injured fifteen others before killing himself.

Ryan's first victim was Susan Godfrey, who had been picnicking with her two young children. The infants were spared, locked in the back of her car, but Godfrey was walked back into the woods and shot thirteen times with the Beretta. Ryan would go on to murder his mother, Dorothy Ryan, his neighbours Roland and Sheila Mason, Kenneth Clements, PC Roger Brereton, George White, Abdul Khan, Francis Butler, Marcus Barnard, Douglas Wainwright, Eric Vardy, Sandra Hill, Jack and Myrtle Gibbs, and Ian Playle.

The shooter was finally cornered inside John O'Gaunt School, which was closed for the holidays. Communicating with one of the armed response officers, Ryan said: 'It's funny. I killed all those people, but I haven't the guts to blow my own brains out.' Shortly before 7 p.m., he did exactly that.

When Thomas Hamilton heard about the shooting, his first concern was for his guns. In gun-owning communities, there was anxiety that the murder of sixteen people with an arsenal of legally owned weapons would result in a crackdown on gun ownership. In retrospect, Hamilton should have had greater faith in the powerful advocacy of the British Shooting Sports Council (BSSC). On a visit to the scene, the prime minister, Margaret Thatcher, said that 'tightening' gun laws 'to prevent more events like this' would 'be considered'. Consideration would fall short of wide-ranging and resolute restriction, however.

Home Secretary Douglas Hurd commissioned the chief constable of Thames Valley Police, Colin Smith, to prepare an initial report into the Michael Ryan incident. 'The public,' the report concluded, 'will demand that this tragic event is used as a catalyst for changes in both the law and administrative procedures.' Yet both Smith and an earlier coroner report focused not on all firearms but Ryan's legally owned semi-automatic rifle. Smith argued that sports or leisure shooters should not be disadvantaged by the prohibition on semi-automatic firearms. A review would leave all other high-powered firearms undisturbed.

The BSSC waited until 18 November, three months after the massacre, to make their first comments in defence of gun ownership. In a press statement, the council argued on behalf of the one million people who participated in the sport – a figure they elevated to four million if air rifles were taken into account – that 'Shooting is the second most popular participatory sport in the country.'

The Kalashnikov-style, self-loading rifle was to be the BSSC's sacrificial lamb. There was no argument from their management; it had to go: 'We therefore agree with the Home Secretary that self-loading rifles of the type used by Michael Ryan should be banned.' Anyone suspecting that a big 'but' was brewing would not be disappointed. The BSSC argued that an overall ban on semi-automatic rifles would disproportionately affect women, disabled people, international shooting competitions and British gun manufacturers anxious to maintain a civilian home market for their lethal wares: 'Without the possibility of any home market ... there will be little incentive to compete against other world market manufacturers.'

By 15 November 1988, the government had pushed through the Firearms (Amendment) Act 1988, which banned semi-automatic rifles and restricted pump-action shotguns with the capacity to fire more than three cartridges. At the time, the Home Secretary said: 'There is no point in pretending that by making changes in the law we could guarantee the safety of the public against the quiet, withdrawn citizen who answers every question, fills in every form and keeps every law until the moment when he commits an atrocious crime. We cannot give Hungerford an absolute guarantee against Ryan.'

However, powerful semi-automatic handguns, including the Beretta which Ryan had used to kill most of his victims, remained untouched by the new proscriptions. Tony Hill campaigned for the ban to also include the handgun that had killed his daughter Sandra, Ryan's youngest victim, but he was unsuccessful.

The government announced an amnesty period during which owners of guns now rendered illegal by the new act could hand them to the police and receive a small sum in compensation. At the time David Mellor, previously a Home Office minister, had argued vehemently for an extensive ban to include powerful semi-automatic handguns and revolvers such as the .357 Magnum, but his protestations proved unsuccessful. Mellor now moved to the Foreign Office, felt bound by the collective responsibility of Cabinet to remain silent about his disappointment and fear for the future. Yet the majority of Conservative MPs, including Michael Forsyth, were persuaded that the changes to the legislation were adequate. Douglas Hurd, the Home Secretary, said the changes should be 'robust enough to stand the test of time'.

In the months following the Hungerford shooting, Hamilton visited Ewan Anderson and his wife. He had popped in on his way to the Dunblane Shooting Club with his semi-automatic rifle. When he brought it out to show the Andersons, he complained that it had cost him over £1,000, and that he would be lucky to receive £100 from the police under the current gun amnesty. He was pleased to be able to keep his handguns, which he had wrapped in dusters and carried in a plastic shopping bag.

However, the buy-back scheme was more generous than Hamilton had imagined, permitting the gun owner 50 per cent of the weapon's value as of September 1987, a month after Michael Ryan's massacre. Hamilton wrote to Central Scotland Police on 14 January 1989, offering to donate his .223 Browning semi-automatic rifle, but the deputy chief constable wrote back, saying, 'unfortunately I am unable to accept such a gift', advising Hamilton instead to 'surrender' the weapon under the government's scheme. Two months later, on Saturday, 18 March, Hamilton visited the police headquarters in Stirling with a bag containing his automatic rifle, several spare magazine clips and 820 rounds of ammunition. As the firearms department was closed for the weekend, the duty clerk accepted the weapon and ammunition and wrote out a receipt. However, on 20 March, the department pointed out that the ammunition could not be accepted as the government scheme extended only to the rifle. The police now required written consent for the destruction of Hamilton's legal property, and so a junior officer, only a few weeks out of the police academy, was sent to secure his signature. On arrival at the house, the young man asked to speak to a 'Mr Hamilton', but the signature he received was that of Thomas's adoptive father.

This mistake required the deputy chief constable of Central Police to write a letter of apology to Thomas Hamilton for the accidental destruction of 820 bullets: 'Apparently the officer concerned, who is young and fairly inexperienced, failed to ensure that he was speaking to the "correct" Mr Hamilton and, in fact, got your father to sign the form. This unfortunate error resulted in the items being destroyed without your express authority. I offer my sincere apologies for this and trust you have not been duly inconvenienced.'

III

THE PHOTOGRAPHS

SHE first saw the leaflet at Christmas. Copies had been distributed to the local schools in Denny, and she spotted one lying on a table alongside the tinsel and paper chains and green nylon Christmas tree. As her son was active in the Boys' Brigade, she didn't give a second thought to the advert for the new club. Then, in March 1993, she arranged for her son to sleep over with a friend, who had two boys of a similar age that attended the new sports club at Denny High School on a Friday night and Saturday morning. She gave permission for her son to go along to the club with the two boys. When he returned home on Saturday afternoon, he was excited and clutched a video of the sports club's summer camp in Loch Lomond. The family watched the VHS tape, which lasted around fifteen minutes and contained various sequences of boys playing football in a rustic, woodland setting. Her son was keen to attend, but his mother didn't feel he had been going long enough to sign up to a summer camp that involved spending two weeks away from home. Perhaps, she suggested, they should start with a few more classes and see how it went.

The following week, she assumed the sports club would be closed for the Easter holiday. Yet that evening she received a phone call from a man she had never met. Thomas Hamilton, in his soft voice, explained that the club would not be running over the weekend but that he hoped her son would return. He was a 'lovely boy', who he believed would settle in well at the club. She agreed to bring her son along next week and introduce herself. 'He seemed quite happy with that and rang off,' she said.

Mother and son attended the club the following Friday and she met briefly with Hamilton, who seemed relatively pleasant. The next morning, she dropped off her son at the Saturday session. When he returned home, it was with exciting news that 'Mr Hamilton' had invited him to play five-a-side football next Wednesday evening. The match was to be played at Stirling High School, and Hamilton would come and collect him. His mother agreed, and so, the following week, Hamilton arrived at their home in a rented Transit van carrying three other boys in the back. Her son climbed inside, and they drove off.

The blue van returned three hours later to drop off her son, who explained that, unfortunately, their opponents hadn't shown up. The team had done some gymnastics instead. That evening she listened with increasing alarm as her son explained that in preparation for their gymnastics class, each boy was told to change into very small, tight, black swimming trunks. Hamilton had said they might go swimming, but that the wrong janitor was on duty so they couldn't access the pool. She asked where Hamilton had been when the boys had changed into their trunks, and her son said he had been in another room. This was a mild relief. Her son said Hamilton had instructed the boys to jump over the vaulting horse and then to stand with their heels together and crouch down on their haunches, and that Mr Hamilton had taken photographs of them as they performed the exercises. 'This concerned me very much,' she recalled, 'and I thought, in my mind, there was something perverse about the whole thing.'

And yet, perhaps fearing confrontation or believing she was overreacting, she decided to let it go – for the time being. After all, her son was happy and enjoying himself and she didn't want to disappoint him without cause, particularly given that she had recently separated from his father.

Her son was allowed to return to the boys' club on Friday, 30 April and Saturday, 1 May, and when he came home, he was full of chatter about how 'Mr Hamilton' had said what a 'nice woman' his mother was. The boy went back to the club the following weekend, and he returned home with a second invitation to play five-a-side football on 12 May. The same routine unfolded. He was collected, this time from his father's address, and, once again, the opposition failed to turn up and the children were told to change into black swimming trunks, perform gymnastics and be photographed. Afterwards, Hamilton gave the boys £1 and bought them each a bag of chips and a Mars bar.

Despite both parents' concerns, their son was enjoying the boys' club and anxious to go back, so they allowed it. The next Saturday, his mother was at work in Stirling town centre when Mr Hamilton turned up with her son and another boy. He explained that the power had been turned off at Denny High School. He had sent the other boys home and taken the remaining four, whose parents were not at home, into Stirling. He had found the parents of two of the remaining boys in the shopping precinct and now planned to take her son and the other boy for something to eat. She assumed this would be at Wimpy or McDonald's, one of the fast-food restaurants nearby, and asked if he needed some money. Hamilton said he would take care of it. He took the boys to a local butcher's shop, where they bought meat pies, and then back to his house.

When the boy's mother returned home that night to learn that Hamilton had taken her son and his friend to his own house, it was the last straw. But she now had suspicions without proof, and so the following morning she called her friend, whose two boys attended the club, and they decided together that they would follow Hamilton on his next five-a-side trip, scheduled for Wednesday, 19 May.

With her son due to be picked up by Hamilton, she arranged for her husband to stay at her home with their son while she and her friend waited, discreetly, by the garage on Glasgow Road in Denny, along the route Hamilton's blue Transit would take on the way to Stirling. Once the van had passed to collect the boys and then returned, the two women would follow the vehicle from a safe distance.

They had arranged to meet shortly after 5 p.m. Neither woman had been on a 'stakeout' before, and both were deeply worried about what they might discover.

Hamilton was due to be at the boy's home at 5.30 p.m., but by 5.50 there was no sign of the blue van. She phoned home, and the boy's father said Hamilton hadn't been yet. But then the van passed by, en route, the women believed, to pick up the boys. They waited for its return. At 6.10, she called home again and there was no answer. She assumed her son had been collected and her husband had gone home. (In fact, Hamilton had failed to arrive; her husband had taken their son out with him.)

The women decided to set off in search of Hamilton. First, they drove by Denny High School, but there was no sign of the van. Then they drove up the A9 to Stirling High School. As they pulled into the car park, they spotted the Transit close to the school entrance.

They went through the main school entrance, down the linoleum-clad corridors, to the glass-panelled janitor's office, where they asked where the five-a-side class was booked. The janitor looked perplexed and explained that no five-a-side class had been booked for tonight, nor any previous Wednesday night. Yes, Mr Hamilton was in the school, but he was giving an extracurricular gymnastics class. The gym was right down the hall and to the left. Fearing her son was involved, she rushed down the corridor, but when she reached the gym door and tried to pull the handle it would not budge. The door was locked. She rapped on the door. Eventually, she could hear footsteps, then the lock being turned. The door opened, partially. Thomas Hamilton's face appeared in the crack.

When she demanded to see her son, Hamilton said her boy wasn't there. She said he had agreed to collect him from her home at 5.30. Hamilton assured her that there had been a misunderstanding; he had agreed to pick up the boy at a bus stop, but only if he had phoned first, which he never had.

Behind Hamilton, she could see a tripod with a camera fixed on top. Disturbed by what exactly he was photographing with a young boy in a locked room, she forced open the door. 'I pushed past him,' she said, 'and there was only one boy present and dressed in the briefest of black trunks.' The boy was on the parallel bars, about four feet off the ground, legs spreadeagled across the bars, 'moving his torso in an up and down fashion', unaware of how it would look through adult eyes.

When she demanded to know why there was only one boy in the gym, Hamilton told her that the team hadn't turned up. Convinced the child was unsafe, she told him she was going to take him home. Yet Hamilton refused and insisted that if the child had to be taken home, then he would be the one to do so. He was the child's current guardian. 'At that I turned and walked out,' she said. 'I spoke to the janitor about the matter.'

She waited outside by her friend's car and watched as Hamilton, carrying his tripod and camera cases, left the building accompanied by the boy. As the two walked past, she asked if the football would be on again, now knowing that no such fixtures had been arranged, but he clung to his lie and said he didn't know, because it took a long time to set them up.

By then it was shortly after seven. The two women drove home and, having discovered the child's name, she phoned his mother and told her what she had seen and about her own concerns. 'My son told me Mr Hamilton has taken a lot of photos of him because he was a new boy,' the other woman told her. He also said that 'Mr Hamilton promised Mitre footballs and tracksuits to him as prizes for having "A" marks.' According to her, the boy 'has twelve such marks', but other children 'who have been going for over six months know nothing about such grades or marks'.

One week later, on 26 May, the boy's mother sat in her living room and gave a detailed statement to Gordon Taylor, an officer from Central Scotland Police based in the Bannockburn Family Unit. After recording the mother's statement, Taylor began his own enquiries, which confirmed that Hamilton had never booked the separate hall used for five-a-side football, only the room used for gymnastics, and despite his suggestions to the boys, swimming would not have been available at the school. Around this time, he received a second complaint from another mother, whose nine-year-old son attended Hamilton's boys' club at Dunblane High School. Again, Hamilton had photographed her son in black swimming trunks without her knowledge and consent and had him perform an array of gymnastic exercises. Yet what particularly concerned Taylor was the revelation that Hamilton had asked the boy to lie on top of another boy, also clad in small trunks, while he photographed the pair. Taylor had no doubt Hamilton was engineering photographic scenarios for his own personal sexual arousal.

The detective knew that to build a case against Hamilton he needed to get full access to his photographic archive. However, this investigation triggered a great deal of discussion among parents, and Taylor was concerned that Hamilton would find out and destroy any incriminating photographs and 'make a tremendous amount of fuss in order to thwart the investigation'.

Earlier that year, Hamilton had become a regular at a photography shop in Stirling. On an early visit, he explained to the store manager that he ran a boys' club and would be taking numerous photographs. The owner was unprepared for the sheer volume of film Hamilton bought. His visits were every two or three days; each time he dropped off six cartridges of negatives, each containing thirty-six photographs. On one day he brought in thirty spools of film for development. In addition, he began bringing in slides from a professional Hasselblad camera. Each film was sent to ColourCare in Livingston for development and arrived back in a sealed packet, which was then handed over to the customer without the contents being scrutinised. This was standard practice.

Over time, the manager grew suspicious, and one day in May, he looked inside the envelopes. 'I saw pictures of boys jumping over gymnastic equipment and hanging onto wall bars,' he said. 'The boys were all dressed in navy blue or black pants.' He phoned the lab at ColourCare and spoke to the staff responsible for developing the film, all of whom shared his unease. His second phone call was to the police, who transferred him to the Family Unit, where Taylor worked. An officer attended the shop the same day and examined the photographs. Technically, they did not break the law, and so the manager was asked to continue to monitor the situation, with the agreement that he would alert the police if the contents became criminally pornographic. Yet as the manager explained, 'All the photographs that I saw, the boys always had shorts or pants on.' In all the hundreds of rolls of films developed over the summer, not a single frame was of anything other than young boys.

The manager also remembers Hamilton acting strangely around this time. Once, he called into the shop to collect the latest round of photographs, but the delivery hadn't arrived. 'I noticed Hamilton loitering outside the shop for one and a half hours until the delivery arrived,' he said. 'Hamilton appeared to be very agitated by this delay, and shortly after that, or possibly at that time, Hamilton stopped having his film developed at this shop.'

The only way forward, Taylor believed, was to secure a search warrant that allowed him and his team to catch Hamilton by surprise, search his home and document all photographic evidence. To do this, he needed to persuade the local procurator fiscal. In early June, he prepared a memo detailing his findings and concerns, to which he attached a 1991 police report into Hamilton's summer camp at Loch Lomond. He decided to hand-deliver the memo, with a view to impress on the fiscal the depth of his concerns.

Taylor soon discovered that this would be more difficult than he had thought. Once he found the office of William Gallagher, the procurator fiscal depute – a lawyer responsible for the day-to-day handling of criminal cases – in the fiscal's building, he learned that not only was Gallagher familiar with Thomas Hamilton and his photographic proclivities, but that he also remained unconvinced a search warrant was an appropriate course of action. Hamilton's aggressive tactics towards all who questioned his motives had left the procurator fiscal's office both frustrated and jaded. In their view, he had a remarkable ability to stay just within the law.

The reason for Gallagher's reticence was that he and the procurator fiscal's office had seen this behaviour from Thomas Hamilton before. In July 1991 Hamilton had organised another camping trip to Loch Lomond, this time to a campsite on Milarrochy Bay, nearly two miles past Balmaha on the east bank of the loch. The camp would last two weeks. Parents were told there would be as many as six adults supervising, but there was only Hamilton, with support from one other adult during the second week. Again, one of the parents had made a complaint to the police, who had again visited the camp to investigate Hamilton's activities.

On 23 July, Detective Sergeant Paul Hughes, the senior officer in charge of the Family Unit at Bannockburn, assisted by Detective Constable Grant Kirk and accompanied by a social worker, arrived at the camp, where they interviewed Hamilton under caution. The parents had accused Hamilton again of striking the boys, and also of filming them in their swimming trunks. This had taken place on a nearby island, thought to be Inchmoan, where the boys had recreated scenes from *Lord of the Flies*, William Golding's novel about warring tribes of shipwrecked schoolboys. (One boy thought the film was called *The Monsters at the Bottom of the Sea*, and another that it was *The Wild Ones*.) The boys had been ferried across to the island, where they were encouraged to daub themselves with Ambre Solaire tanning cream to give themselves an orange complexion. One boy had had the lotion rubbed on personally by Hamilton. He had then been chased by the other boys, who burst out of the undergrowth while Hamilton filmed the 'action' on a new Sony 8 mm camcorder. One boy had been forced to lie in freezing water despite his obvious distress, and the boys weren't allowed to dress during frequent, heavy rain showers. Slaps had, once again, often been delivered for minor 'infractions', but what had coarsened in the past three years was Hamilton's language and the anger with which he spoke to the boys, who were aged between eight and eleven. He called them 'bastards' and 'fucking cunts' and shouted orders such as 'You need fucking disciplined, ya bastard,' which made the younger boys cry.

The detectives interviewed the boys in turn, and one said Hamilton had taken him to a smaller, individual tent, asked him to put on a pair of red swimming trunks, which he kept easily to hand in his trouser pocket, and photographed him. The boy didn't like doing it; he complained that the red trunks were far too small and rode up in an uncomfortable manner, and that he disliked the poses. Hamilton had told him that his mother wanted a lot of photographs of the camp. 'The one I hated most was where I had to hold two cans of soup, with my legs bent and my head in the air and my body was crouched over and my arms were behind my back,' the boy said. 'The other ones that I didn't like were when I was having to stand straight and show my muscles.'

At night, all the boys would sleep together in one large tent. Despite one boy's desire to sleep beside his big brother, Hamilton would pick him up in his sleeping bag and lie him down next to him instead. Then Hamilton would tell the boys horror stories that made them frightened to go to sleep.

Hamilton admitted striking the boys to maintain discipline, and to filming them, but insisted there was no sinister motive. They were to be warm memories for the boys and their parents to watch over the winter.

Hughes was concerned Hamilton might be grooming the boy in the red trunks for later abuse, but when questioned, Hamilton initially denied such plans or taking photographs of any of the boys. Hamilton handed over his video camera while at the campsite, but it was not until a week later, on 30 July, that he also passed on six boxes of slides and around 150 photographs, claiming he had forgotten he had taken them. But Hughes spoke to the shop in Stirling that Hamilton was using to process his films and found that eight boxes, not six, had been returned to him. Two boxes were missing. The content of the photographs had been enough to disturb the film processor at the lab in Livingston to which the original negatives had been sent. They had then contacted the shop in Stirling to raise concerns. As to the contents of the missing boxes, the police could only speculate. Had they contained photographs of the boy in the red swimming trunks?

The photographs handed over to the police featured various boys in different poses, wearing black swimming trunks, yet they were not deemed to be explicit or indecent. Hughes had little doubt, however, that Hamilton's interest in young boys was unhealthy.

And he was not alone in his doubts. One evening, Grace Ogilvie, Thomas Hamilton's neighbour, was invited into his home to watch a video with him. She had been coming home when she bumped into Hamilton, who extended the invitation. 'I walked in behind him and into his sitting room and he asked me to sit down,' she said. 'Well, I did sit down ... He asked me to look at a video. Small boys. He fast-forwarded it and stopped it and let it go for a bit and then he would fast-forward it again and let it go for a good bit. He did this all the time, and he was very proud. "These are my boys." That is what he said. I sort of had my back to him and I was looking out the window more often than I was looking at the video. The bit he showed me, well, I think it was about forty minutes. Just small boys, walking along or maybe running. I can't remember if they were running over a wooden horse. I can't remember that. But they just seemed to be marching in lines, the boys. They turned their heads to the camera as they walked past, but from the waist down they had very small, shiny bathing pants on.'

Hamilton also took the opportunity to show Mrs Ogilvie an old box with rope handles in which he kept his favourite photographs: 'He opened it and there were a lot of frames in it. Picture frames. He took out one picture of one boy and said he was his favourite or his star pupil or something to that effect, but I just glanced at it because I was uneasy. He was just from here up – bare skin ... I wouldn't say it was indecent, but I just didn't like it. I was just uncomfortable.' As she left that evening, she passed his bedroom. The door was open, and she could see pictures on the walls of small boys in bathing trunks.

Mrs Ogilvie was also witness to the fires Hamilton frequently lit in the back garden. She didn't see what Hamilton was burning but remembers the distinctive smell, like plastic.

Under the police's spotlight, Thomas Hamilton went on the attack. In August 1991, almost immediately after his initial interview with Detective Sergeant Hughes, he made an official complaint to the chief constable and deputy chief constable, and copied in his MP, Michael Forsyth. This proved effective. Hughes continued his investigations and planned to interview Hamilton under caution, but as he was now himself the subject of a complaint, Hughes asked the procurator fiscal in Stirling about the best way to proceed. The procurator fiscal, Keith Valentine, suggested that instead of interviewing Hamilton under caution, Hughes should invite him on a voluntary basis. Hamilton refused the request, stating that he had said everything he wished to about the camp.

Despite this refusal, Hughes put together a list of ten charges: various physical assaults, unnecessary suffering or injury to health, and obstruction of justice. Hughes had concluded that Hamilton was a manipulative man with clear paedophiliac interests and the potential to be deeply dangerous to children. He had also discovered that Hamilton owned a collection of handguns, rifles and thousands of rounds of ammunition. From his conversation with Gallagher and the other procurators fiscal, he was aware that his recommendation of criminal charges was unlikely to proceed. On 11 November 1991, he sat down to write a memo to the detective superintendent at CID, requesting that serious consideration be given to the withdrawal of Hamilton's firearms licence. He wrote that he was 'firmly of the opinion that Hamilton is an unsavoury character and unstable personality' who 'has an extremely unhealthy interest in young boys which to a degree appears to have been controlled to date', and that he 'would contend that Mr Hamilton will be a risk to children whenever he has access to them' and would be 'an unsuitable person to possess a firearm certificate in view of the number of occasions he has come to the adverse attention of the police and his apparent instability'. He concluded his memo with the following: 'I respectfully request that serious consideration is given to withdrawing this man's firearm certificate as a precautionary measure as it is my opinion that he is a scheming, devious and deceitful individual who is not to be trusted.'

The memo was submitted to his superior, Detective Superintendent Millar, who wrote on it the following note to Deputy Chief Constable McMurdo: 'While appreciating DS Hughes' concern, I cannot recommend the action proposed for obvious reasons, ie Hamilton has not been convicted of any crime and it seems the PF is likely to No Pro the recently reported case.'

McMurdo chose not to communicate with Hughes. He wrote 'no action' on the memo on 11 November 1991, the same day he received it. The memo was not widely distributed. It should have been added to Hamilton's firearms file, but it wasn't, nor was it added to the appropriate file for criminal intelligence. It simply drifted, like a snowflake, into a blizzard of paperwork.

Thomas Hamilton's formal complaint against Hughes was investigated and later found to be entirely spurious by Chief Inspector Ferguson, who wrote: 'I have completed thirty years' police service, a long number of these as a CID Officer. Throughout these years I have interviewed many hardened criminals, many aggressive people, many reluctant witnesses, many complainers against the police, but I can honestly say the interviews with Mr Hamilton were the most exasperating of my career.' Hamilton then made a complaint against Ferguson for the way he had dealt with his complaint against Hughes. This led to the chief constable of Central Police seeking advice from the legal services at Central Regional Council about raising a defamation case against Hamilton on his officers' behalf. The idea was dropped on the grounds that it would provide Hamilton with a public platform for his paranoid conspiracy theories about the Scouts, the police and the Regional Council.

Hughes filed his report to the procurator fiscal on 6 September, which included ten charges against Hamilton. While Valentine believed Hughes' 11 November report lacked the evidence to merit court proceedings or secure a conviction, he did ask that the boys be interviewed again, and he was troubled enough by the contents to have other child service agencies informed. A procurator fiscal depute also examined the report and concluded that many of the charges could not be substantiated, with the possible exceptions of those charges of assault and breach of the peace.

On 18 November, William Gallagher, the procurator fiscal depute, marked the papers 'no pro: no crime libelled: not in the public interest'. On the same day, he wrote to Thomas Hamilton informing him that no charges would be brought against him and that he had instructed the police to return his photographs of the boys.

The police investigation into Hamilton's summer camp on Loch Lomond in 1991 did, though, force him to organise a 'camp' closer to home in 1992: the gym hall of Dunblane High School. Once again he attracted the attention of the police when three children, tired and homesick, walked out in their pyjamas and were found on Old Doune Road late at night, trying to make their way home. Hamilton said they had left the building after lights out. The police constable who found them was PC Gunn, one of the officers who had questioned Hamilton in 1988. Upon learning where the boys had been, he expressed no desire to be directly involved. Instead, he brought them back to the station, where their parents were called and Gunn allowed a fellow officer to investigate. The boys had slipped out via the fire escape after having gone to the toilet. Although no charges were ultimately brought, the incident did prompt a prophetic memo from a reporter to the Children's Panel: 'I feel that the events of 29 June 1992 in Dunblane in a sense serve as warning. If the kind of circumstances as described are allowed to continue without some kind of intervention, I consider that other children may be placed at risk. In like situations arising unchecked, I fear that a tragedy to a child or children is almost waiting to happen.'

So in June 1993, it was merely a new detective standing in the office of the procurator fiscal telling William Gallagher a familiar story. The view of his office remained that there was insufficient evidence to support a search warrant. Gallagher admitted that the photographs were disturbing and clearly a cause for concern but concluded that they did not cross the line into criminality. Gordon Taylor argued that the parents' concerns could be construed as a breach of the peace, but Gallagher was unpersuaded. According to Taylor, when he said that there were still enquiries to make, Gallagher replied that if there were other reports in the future of Hamilton photographing boys in swimming trunks and nothing more, 'I should not report them as they would not be proceeded with.'

Not easily dissuaded, Taylor pushed for a charge of breach of the peace. Gallagher asked him if any of the boys had been alarmed or distressed. Taylor said that they had been concerned enough to tell their parents, who had indeed been both alarmed and distressed.

Yet to Gallagher this separation of 'alarm and distress', present in the parents but not demonstrably present in the children, meant that he and his office could not make a case.

Taylor's request for a warrant was denied. As far as Gallagher was concerned, no further action would be taken. He did agree, however, to re-examine the report in three months' time. He also asked to be informed of any further investigations or developments, but only if they provided evidence of criminality. On 10 September 1993, Gallagher reviewed the papers and added a note stating that no proceedings were to be taken. Once again, as he had done in 1991, he recorded: 'no pro: no crime libelled: not in the public interest'.

Now, Taylor had little choice but to return to the parents and explain that no action would be taken by the procurator fiscal. He also told his boss, who was then in charge of the Family Unit, that Gallagher had warned them off further reports. Yet Taylor, without the support of the procurator fiscal, decided to continue his search for any additional evidence. He called the headquarters of the Scout Association, who were 'rather reluctant to let me see their files on Hamilton'. Over the phone, he was told they had 'no evidence on their files of any crimes being committed by Hamilton'.

Despite this, on 20 October Taylor visited the Scout Association headquarters in Dunfermline, where he spoke to staff and was permitted to examine their file on Hamilton: 'We were left to browse through the file,' he said. 'There was nothing specific in the file that assisted my enquiry.' Taylor asked to take the file with him, but 'they were reluctant to hand it over to me'. He then made an appointment to visit the home of Brian Fairgrieve, the retired doctor who had first raised concerns about Hamilton's behaviour and possible paedophiliac tendencies. 'He was unable to substantiate the comments he had made in the file to me due to the obvious lapse in time between when they were made and my present enquiry, this being some nineteen years,' Taylor said. Yet Fairgrieve did say the Scouts had been unhappy with Hamilton's character 'due to an apparent unhealthy interest Hamilton had in young boys'. It was for this reason that his position had been terminated.

Also in October 1993, the deputy chief constable asked DS Joseph Holden and DS James Moffat to interview Hamilton at his home.

Thomas Hamilton now lived alone. His relationship with his adoptive father had become increasingly hostile, an atmosphere not helped by Hamilton senior's heavy drinking and inadvertent destruction of his son's ammunition. The men might have been living in the same small council house, but they had stopped talking. In time, Hamilton senior explained his plight to the council offices and was eventually provided with his own home, one his adopted son would never visit. When they encountered each other on Stirling High Street, they would both avert their eyes.

The interview in October 1993 lasted almost two hours. Hamilton was calm, exceedingly polite and verbally articulate, but also suspiciously evasive. He extolled at length the efficacy of the exercises and the logic behind the boys' state of undress. Moffat felt his verbal fluency was the result of practised repetition, while Holden believed he was lying, especially when quizzed on the 'missing' members of the club committee.

Shortly after the interview, Moffat received yet another complaint from parents whose sons were attending a club of Hamilton's in nearby Balfron. Their complaint concerned Hamilton taking pictures of their children in swimming trunks. Moffat had the frustrating task of explaining that this behaviour was not new, and that both the police and the procurator fiscal were aware of Hamilton's practices. There was nothing they could do.

At this point, Thomas Hamilton was offering his services as a professional photographer and videographer, filming weddings and engagement parties. He also ran an off-the-books business buying and selling camera equipment through small ads in magazines such as *Amateur Photographer*. He boasted to friends that he would deliberately cheat customers; when contacted for a camera he could not source cheap enough to make a profit, he would cash the customer's cheque and send them the wrong product. When the product was returned, Hamilton would refuse to refund the order on the grounds that the camera was 'damaged'.

In spring 1994, Hamilton put a flyer for his photography business through George Robertson's door. Ten years on from his first encounter with Thomas Hamilton, the MP decided he would try again to substantiate his suspicions. Robertson called a contact at the *Sunday Mail* and suggested Hamilton was worth investigating. After a few days of digging, evidence of Hamilton's photographic fetishes, as well as of copious allegations, were unearthed by reporters Marion Scott and Angus Macleod. On 18 March 1994, they confronted Hamilton outside one of his clubs. Dressed in scuffed trainers, denim jeans, a white shirt and a grubby tie under a beige anorak, Hamilton sounded more polished than he appeared. He was remarkably calm. Of course he had heard the rumours, he said, but they were untrue. He had a lengthy explanation for each of Scott and Macleod's questions, and even agreed to pose for the newspaper's photographer – but not, he insisted, with any of his boys. His voice was quiet, reassuring and, as parents walked by, he called out, 'Your lads will be okay with me. They'll enjoy themselves here. You've no worries.'

There were parents for whom Hamilton was a strong, supportive figure, running clubs their sons enjoyed. 'Why take the risk with your child?' Scott asked one parent, who replied, 'I have heard some things being said. But Mr Hamilton is always so polite. I just can't believe the gossip.' 'Mr Hamilton would not be here unless he had the full support of the authorities,' another parent told her. When Scott pushed back and asked if Hamilton was going to behave otherwise in front of a parent, she was greeted with a shrug. As Scott and Macleod couldn't persuade any parents to put their names to their private concerns, the newspaper's lawyers insisted that it was inadvisable to publish the story.

Hamilton's behaviour and sinister photographic practices did not go entirely unpunished, though. When Alexander Robb learned that his girlfriend's son had been photographed by Hamilton without the family's knowledge, he enlisted two friends, William Wardlaw and Fraser Gillies, and on 9 December 1994 they arrived at Hamilton's Kent Road home late at night. They hammered on the door but received no answer.

The next morning, Robb visited the former premises of Woodcraft, which was now a kitchen appliance store, to verify Hamilton's address. The new owner asked if Hamilton was 'up to his old tricks', and said they were not alone in trying to track him down.

Later that afternoon, Robb and Wardlaw returned to Kent Road, and again there was no response. As they were driving off, however, Wardlaw spotted the curtains twitching. Robb slammed on the brakes and both men got out of the car, ran back to the address and started kicking at the front door, screaming obscenities such as 'Beast', a colloquial term for sex offenders. Robb demanded the photographs back. Hamilton refused to let them in and called the police, who arrived within minutes. Robb and Wardlaw were ordered into the back of an unmarked police car, where they said that Hamilton had taken photographs of a child they knew and that they wanted the photographs back. An officer went inside to talk to Hamilton and returned a few minutes later with a colour photograph, eight by five inches, of a young boy in trunks, photographed from his knees up, arms stretched out wide. It was the boy Robb was concerned about. The officer said Hamilton was not prepared to part with the photograph, which technically remained his personal property. The police knew there wasn't much they could do. They explained that they were aware of the rumours about Hamilton, and that he was already under investigation. The two men were released without charge and told to go home.

Later that night Robb called Hamilton, threatened him, and insisted that any photographs of the boy be returned to him. Four days later, an envelope arrived at the home Robb shared with the boy's mother, containing a selection of photographs so warped and dissolved that only the child's face remained identifiable. Yet, as the boy confirmed, there were still photographs missing. Hamilton included a receipt for one bottle of bleach, which they believed he had used to sabotage or cleanse the photographs.

———

Back in 1991, Chris Deerin, a young reporter with the *Stirling Observer*, received a phone call from his aunt, Sandra McInally.

A nurse with the local NHS trust, Sandra had taken her seven-year-old son to one of Thomas Hamilton's boys' clubs at Stirling High School. Afterwards, Hamilton had walked both her and her young son home. She felt uneasy in his presence and disturbed by how effusive he was about her son's performance. He spoke about the need for firm discipline, how he would brook no dissent and favoured contact games such as British Bulldog. So uncomfortable did she feel that she walked past her house rather than let him know exactly where she lived. Then he stopped, opened his briefcase and handed her a video cassette. After putting the children to bed, she popped the tape into the player. The footage was about fifteen minutes long. 'The video showed children aged between five and ten years old,' she said. 'I noticed that the children, all boys, about a dozen, wore football shorts. The camera appeared to pan along the line of children and concentrate on their waists and below. This hall was outside, and I think on a football pitch somewhere. There was also a section where the boys were in a canteen of some sort – it did not look like the university – and sitting perfectly still, as though they were having a snack, but not speaking at all. Throughout there was music in the background – not dubbed – like Marc Bolan T. Rex stuff. I found it quite eerie and unnatural that kids should behave in such a way – not laughing or speaking, but afraid to move or say anything. In the second half of the video, I saw all the boys were wearing black swimming trunks and were doing exercises on these ropes that hung from the ceiling with steel hoops on the end, which I felt were way beyond the physical capabilities of children at that age, and some appeared close to tears.'

Sandra called her sister-in-law, who came round with Chris and his girlfriend. All four rewatched the video; the consensus was that they were 'not happy' and that her son would not be returning. Sandra also decided to contact the police, who visited her at home, took the video away for inspection and returned, saying that there was nothing criminal in the tape but advising her not to send her son back to the club. Yet the matter preyed on her mind, and so she later decided to make an official report. Two officers interviewed her son, who said that Hamilton had not touched him in any improper way but had asked him to take off his top so he could photograph his body. 'I was not happy with my son being photographed in such circumstances without parental permission,' she said, 'and this formed the basis of my complaint.'

Sandra McInally then wrote a letter of complaint to the education department, asking why Hamilton was permitted to lease council property when he had an open police file. A week after she posted the letter to the council, she received a letter to her home address, delivered by hand. It was from Thomas Hamilton. In the letter he offered to release to her all photographic material he possessed of her son – if she agreed to come to his home in person. McInally was deeply concerned. She had deliberately concealed her home address on the evening of their first encounter; clearly someone within the council had passed on her name and address as the complainant. She did not reply or meet with Hamilton, who continued to send her letters for the next four years complaining that his name had been blackened by innuendo. The final letter arrived in 1995. She called the police, and two officers visited her home to collect the letter. She asked the officer why it was that Hamilton's disturbing behaviour had been allowed to persist without prosecution. The police officer told her that Hamilton was 'getting older', and that he 'would make a mistake at some point'.

IV

THE FAMILIES

Dunblane is an ancient settlement. The Roman army marched through its lands, building three camps, a signal station and a small fort. Faint traces of a road are still detectable after two thousand years. Eight miles north of Dunblane today are the earthen defences of what may be the finest preserved Roman fort in Britain. Yet at the heart of the town is the Christian church, and for many years, centuries even, this church was the heart of Dunblane.

At 3 Kilbryde Crescent, Isabel MacBeath did not have her troubles to seek. Born in 1960, the younger of two sisters raised by a gentle mother and an alcoholic and physically abusive father, she lived in a council house in Kilsyth, just outside Glasgow, the family outwardly respectable but privately troubled. A bright student with an agile, questioning mind, education would provide an escape. Isabel completed a religious studies degree at Stirling University, before embarking on a master's in which she wrestled themes of exile and restoration in the Old Testament into an accomplished and compelling dissertation. As she told friends, it was an exploration of why people continue to believe things without evidence. By the age of 21 she was a schoolteacher in religious education.

THE FAMILIES

Curious minds were deeply attractive to Isabel, and they didn't come more curious than Murray MacBeath, an older academic in the Philosophy and Religious Studies department, whom she met on a blind date. The relationship was on again, off again until Isabel returned from her travels in Israel; one evening, she was babysitting at a friend's house when Murray, who she had not seen for six months, arrived on the doorstep with an engagement ring. The couple married twenty-one days later.

On an academic exchange to the University of Zimbabwe, Murray had a stroke which left him with bilateral paralysis and forced the pair back to Scotland. He made enough of a recovery to return to teaching at Stirling University, while Isabel continued to teach, but the consequences of Murray's stroke were considerable. Despite their everyday difficulties, though, Isabel and Murray decided to start a family, and their daughter Mhairi was born in 1991. They lived in a comfortable terrace house in Dunblane, only a few hundred yards from the primary school.

As a baby, Mhairi didn't sleep. She was also an extraordinarily fussy eater, which left Isabel in a permanent state of exhaustion. But as she grew, Mhairi's personality began to emerge, and it became apparent that she would not be following the expected path.

Dr Mick North lived in Willowbank House, in the Bridgend area of the town. But in early March 1995, he was among the red sandstone mesas of Arizona. For the academic and his young daughter, Sophie, it had been a long physical and emotional journey from their family home in Dunblane, which was quieter since the death of his wife and Sophie's mother, Barbara, two years before.

Father and daughter lived in a spacious Victorian cottage with pink-washed stone walls and a slate roof. Close to the train station, the cottage had once been used by the stationmaster and his family, and from the back room you could see the spire of Dunblane Cathedral, while the upstairs study looked out over the gently flowing waters of the Allan.

The couple had met at Stirling University. North, a Londoner, had taken up a lectureship in biochemistry there in 1975. Barbara Lockwood, a research scientist from Yorkshire, had moved in 1983. After the collapse of North's first marriage, they began a relationship in 1988. Despite Barbara being offered a research post in America, they decided to build a life together in Scotland. When Barbara fell pregnant with Sophie, they moved from the neighbouring town of Bridge of Allan to a larger property in Dunblane within walking distance of the primary school. Sadly, it was a walk Barbara would never take with Sophie: she was diagnosed with breast cancer in 1991, the day before the couple's wedding. Despite a mastectomy, malignant cells were found in her lymph nodes, and then in her bones. She would die at home, in the front room, a few days after her daughter's third birthday.

An older father, with a shock of silver hair, Dr North had been forty-two when Sophie was born. He'd spent the past eighteen months adjusting to life as a widower and single father. Luckily the staff at Arnhall Nursery, which Sophie attended while North was at university running a research lab and teaching students, rallied to his and Sophie's side.

In spring 1995, North accepted an invitation to lecture and discuss collaborative research with colleagues in America. He also wanted to take Sophie to see the Grand Canyon, which he described to Sophie as one of the largest holes in the ground

THE FAMILIES

anywhere in the world. He booked a steam train journey to the canyon's rim, and while North was aware the excursion included live entertainment, he had no idea of the specific form it would take. When armed outlaws arrived on horseback to 'hijack' the train, he was caught by surprise. Sophie was terrified by the gunfire and the shouting and buried her face in her father's jumper. When one of the gunmen who came swaggering through the carriage tried to attract her attention, she screamed.

On 13 March 1995, the drama ended when the sheriff arrived and the gunmen were arrested.

Pam and Kenny Ross lived on George Street. Pam had known Kenny since she was fourteen. She liked his easy charm and quick wit, and although the pair didn't begin dating until after they left school, everything happened quickly once they did. A first date was in May 1990, followed by an engagement in August and a December wedding. By the next May they were cradling baby Joanna, the first grandchild, adored by everyone.

Kenny was an electrician, at one point working at Balmoral, the Queen's Highlands estate. Pam worked for the Royal Bank of Scotland, first as a teller in the local branch in Dunblane, then in Stirling, processing paperwork couriered by surrounding branches.

The couple's house on George Street had a garden backing onto a lane in which the local children played. Kenny's parents, Jimmy and Betty, lived on the other side of the lane on Charles Street and looked after Joanna while her parents were at work. Betty would take the toddler to the Dunblane Hotel, where she met her friends for coffee, and the little girl would sometimes wander into the bar. Joanna's striking blonde hair made her instantly recognisable, and her natural curiosity made her friends. Even as a small child, she always wanted to be part of whatever was going on. On holiday in Gran Canaria, she would be lifted through the restaurant hatch by staff to meet the chefs. She didn't sit on a sofa; she did handstands on the cushions, her legs waving in the air. Then there were her imaginary friends. At the table she would have conversations, laughing and nodding at whatever they had to say. When Pam and Kenny asked for their names, Joanna would say they were 'Boy' and 'Sister'. Always 'Boy' and 'Sister'.

Her parents thought she was hilarious, but when Joanna got a little older, she could also be stubborn. When she was five, and shortly after her baby sister Alison was born, Pam was returning from the town centre with Alison in the buggy and Joanna wouldn't take her hand or hold on to the buggy and kept running along the road to where a new Tesco was being built. Pam was frightened something would happen to Joanna, but she couldn't leave the buggy and baby Alison, and the more she shouted after Joanna the more her elder daughter refused to heed her call. When mother and daughters finally got home, Pam and Joanna had an argument. Joanna was furious at being berated and stormed off to her room. By the time Kenny got home, Pam was still upset at how their daughter had behaved. She had felt so frightened that Joanna might come to harm; a thought too much to contemplate.

The fear and the anger passed, and later that evening, lying in bed beside Kenny, listening to the snuffly noises of baby Alison asleep in her cot and with Joanna sleeping in her bedroom next door, Pam reflected on how fortunate she was to have her husband and two beautiful daughters.

THE FAMILIES

When Gwen Mayor wanted to make beef stroganoff or vegetarian curry, onion chowder or her celebrated meat loaf, she would reach for the small red notebook of handwritten recipes. Sometimes she would draw a curvy cloud around the name of the dish, like her lentil chicken. She even had a recipe for play dough, which she coloured with blue or green food dye and brought into the classroom for her pupils.

Above the entrance to Mrs Mayor's class in room thirteen at Dunblane Primary School was a colourfully decorated sign declaring *Welcome to Mrs Mayor's class*, the words enclosed within a cloud. When a colleague complimented her on the sign, she made them one too, dropping it off the next day. Gwen Mayor liked to craft, to work with her hands, and she had her own personal, creative flair. If you were invited to dinner at Gwen and Rod's home in nearby Bridge of Allan, you were in for a treat.

The couple had bought the detached house when it was newly built. The garden had a fish pond, verdant rockeries teeming with flowers and, at the side, strawberries and raspberry bushes. At lunchtime, Gwen would drive home from Dunblane and spend twenty-five minutes sitting outside, resting among the greenery, before heading back for her afternoon lessons. Inside the house, in which she had raised their two daughters, Debbie and Esther, who were at this point teenagers, Gwen had her own sewing room, where she meticulously crafted her own clothes.

Gwen, the daughter of a police constable, was fourteen when she first met Rod, who was twenty-one, at a youth club in Great Harwood in Lancashire. She studied teaching at Nottingham University, graduating in 1971, the same year the couple were married. An engineer by trade, Rod had expected to work in Yorkshire, but an opportunity at a power station in Fife took the couple to Scotland. As Gwen's qualification was from an English university, she was required to do two years' probation, so she secured a position at a primary school in Bothkennar, near Airth, which meant Rod could drop her off in the morning and collect her on his way home. Their first home was a rented flat in Stirling, but later that first year they decided to buy a three-bedroom house on a new estate in Bridge of Allan.

Money was tight. The television was rented, and the only pieces of furniture they owned were a coffee table and a bed. When Gwen's parents visited with a gift of curtains, they tacked them up because curtain rails were too expensive. Yet over the next twenty years, the couple built a good life for their daughters and expanded their home from three rooms to six. Gwen was fluent in French, and the family would spend the first three weeks of the school summer holidays camping in Toulouse or the Dordogne.

By autumn 1995, Gwen was happy with her life. The girls had left home, and though she missed them deeply, she was proud that they were making their own way in the world. Esther was working in Glasgow, while Deborah was in London studying hospitality and catering.

The money worries of their younger years had eased. The couple were now members of the health club and spa at Gleneagles, the luxury hotel and golf course, only a twenty-minute drive away in Gwen's new turquoise sports car. They were beginning to make plans for their twenty-fifth wedding anniversary in the August of the following year. Gwen loved a party. She once broke her wrist dancing. She loved the Beatles, Kate Bush, Phil Collins and the Supremes.

As a primary school teacher, she had a sixth sense for the quiet anxieties tucked inside little lives. On one occasion she announced that the class would be having a pyjama party, then noticed that one little girl was less than excited by the prospect. A discreet conversation revealed the truth: the girl slept in a nightie, which she believed would exclude her from an invitation. Reassured by Gwen, the girl arrived the next day with both nightie and her teddy.

In a small terraced house in the suburbs of Dunblane, a young mother opened a worn fabric bag and emptied out a bundle of soggy tennis balls. She then tied up the bag and placed it inside the tumble dryer, switched the dryer on and listened to the trundling din as the bag rolled around inside the drum. Judy Murray was a part-time tennis coach, a full-time mother to two young, boisterous boys, James and Andrew, and a pragmatist. If there was a problem, there was a solution. Scotland did not have the climate for tennis. What few courts the country had were outdoors. Heavy rain was an accepted part of play; tennis balls absorbed so much rainwater that her young players were lucky to hit them, so low was their bounce.

Judy had been born in Dunblane and raised in the town by two tennis-obsessed parents. Her father, Roy, was the town's optician and her mother, Shirley, had founded the Toy Box, a family toyshop on High Street. Judy was raised in a household where silence was expected during the fortnight Wimbledon was broadcast on the BBC. A promising tennis player, Judy won sixty-four titles in Scotland before embarking on a professional career in 1976. A robbery in Barcelona, combined with persistent homesickness, convinced her to fold up her dreams, pack them into her tennis bag and come home.

After graduating from Edinburgh University with a degree in French and Business Studies, she became a sales rep. She met her husband William, a manager with the newsagent chain RS McColl. After the births of the boys she began coaching tennis in the early 1990s, on the condition that her pupils' mothers took turns pushing Jamie and Andy round the park. Beginning as an unpaid volunteer, Judy slowly began to make money, though rarely enough to cover her costs.

The boys' introduction to tennis was batting a balloon over the family sofa. Soon they graduated to swingball in the garden, and both were given miniature tennis racquets shortly after they could walk. By the time Andy was six and a little taller than a tennis net, he announced to his mum: 'I'm bored playing with you and Gran. I want to play a proper match.' His complaint inspired Judy to ring around other club coaches in Scotland and organise the nation's first under-tens tournament in 1993. Yet Andy and Jamie were both huge football fans and so, for a time, they attended the boys' club at Dunblane High School run by Thomas Hamilton, who, on occasion, would be given a lift to the train station if Judy and the boys were heading that way.

V

THE GUNS

THE firearms licence Thomas Hamilton had possessed for almost twenty years was due for renewal in 1995. This involved a mandatory interview with a police officer and the inspection of the applicant's storage facility for safety and security. The task fell to Detective Constable Anne Anderson, the local community officer for Hamilton's address. Although she had been a probationary officer in firearms, shadowing more experienced officers as they interviewed applicants, her only previous unsupervised renewals had been for four shotguns. The home visit to 7 Kent Road was brief, around fifteen minutes, and disturbing.

Anderson said she experienced a 'strange feeling' when she first entered the property, triggered not only by the way Hamilton looked at her but by the manner in which he referred to his guns. She felt intimidated by the way he held them, as if he was gloating. She checked his gun cabinet, which was of regulation standard and bolted to the wall. His ammunition was stored separately in locked boxes whose keys he always kept on his person.

She had been told not to sign off Hamilton without first examining his criminal intelligence file. But as she was not authorised to use the computer on which it was stored, her colleagues reported that it showed only three lines related to his attempts to set up a boys' club in Bannockburn. Missing was the lengthy memo written four years before by Detective Sergeant Paul Hughes, stating his belief that Hamilton would be a risk to children whenever he had access to them, and that he would be 'unsuitable' to possess a firearm certificate. Also missing was any reference to the two previous investigations, or the charge sheets prepared in connection with his summer camps. As Anderson still felt uncomfortable about signing, she discussed her concerns with a senior officer, who suggested she raise the matter with Inspector John Anderson. The inspector explained that there had been several reports about Hamilton, but that nothing had ever been solid enough to charge him, and he told her that there was nothing they could do. Failing to find any supporting evidence for her concerns, Anderson felt that perhaps she had misinterpreted Hamilton's manner. She made no entry in the criminal intelligence file about her concerns.

The final sign-off on the renewal of Thomas Hamilton's firearms licence was made by Deputy Chief Constable McMurdo, who was only too aware of the complaints Hamilton had been making about his officers and council employees, the concerns of parents about how his clubs were run and the sinister nature of his photography. Yet when required to state whether Thomas Hamilton was a 'fit and proper' person to possess multiple handguns, rifles and as much as 5,000 rounds of high-calibre ammunition, McMurdo said he was.

An argument could have been made. Hamilton had committed physical assaults on multiple young boys, been neglectful and indecent, vindictive and deceitful. By failing to hand over potential evidence, he was also potentially guilty of a breach of the peace.

This point was never raised, though, and Hamilton's licence was renewed.

———

We don't know the exact day or time when Hamilton began to imagine and plan a homicidal mass shooting. We do know that nine months prior to its execution, his life began to decline, alongside his bank balance and the attendance at his clubs.

One date, 22 September 1995, was significant. (By this time, Central Scotland Police's lax firearms certificate system erroneously permitted him to own two weapons of the same calibre without a persuasive 'good reason', as the firearms legislation required.) In recent years Hamilton had rarely fired his arms or attended gun clubs or shooting ranges, preferring to hold and stroke his guns instead. But on 22 September, for the first time in eight years, Thomas Hamilton purchased ammunition. Eleven days before this, he had paid York Guns £304 for a competition model Browning 9 mm and quibbled over the price, having first sent his freshly renewed firearm licence in the post. In return, the shop had couriered the gun to his home address.

Between the September of the year before and 27 February 1996, when Hamilton reloaded his firearms for the final time, his total purchases amounted to 1,700 rounds of 9 mm and 500 rounds of .357 ammunition.

In March 1995, Hamilton's clubs in Menstrie, Alva and Tillicoultry had closed. A new club in Callander failed to get off the ground when only one boy turned up to the first session; the rumours surrounding Hamilton's behaviour had taken hold among local parents. To address the matter, on 18 August he sent out a long, circular letter which claimed that all allegations against him were false and had been started by the Scouts. Consequently, he wrote, 'many young athletes had been lost needlessly over the years and others deterred from attending.' Hamilton pushed photocopies of the letter through doors across Dunblane. Kenny Ross picked one up, read it and then binned it. The father of two daughters had little interest in boys' clubs.

To escape the rumours, Hamilton moved further afield. In autumn 1995, he was able to secure a let for a new club at Thomas Muir High School in Bishopbriggs. To get a discount on the room rent, he obtained recognition as an approved youth organisation, for which he had to provide a character reference. This was supplied by Councillor Robert Ball, who was now convener of the Education Committee of Central Regional Council and had considerable influence. (Ball later admitted he had not paid the request as much attention as he should have.) Hamilton's application claimed the club was supported by a committee of twelve parents, that his mother Agnes was the club's treasurer and that Ian Boal, a sports development undergraduate, was club secretary.

Boal believed he would be running the club himself and so was disappointed when Hamilton turned up every week, distributing leaflets that claimed he was the coach. Eventually, Hamilton went further, writing a letter to Boal criticising his coaching methods. 'I wasn't going to put up with the hassle he was giving me through writing a letter like that to me,' said Boal, who resigned but still agreed to continue to coach until Easter rather than let down the boys. Boal also noticed a change in Hamilton's behaviour and preferred conversational topics. Where previously the older man would talk incessantly about photography, lens sizes, film stock and development solution, now his focus was guns, a theme which dominated his conversations even with those previously unaware of his firearms collection. He would talk about the impressive firepower on display in the *Alien* and *Terminator* films. During one coaching session, Hamilton showed the boys his gun catalogues and told them about the day he had shot a moose. He explained to the group of eight-year-olds the devastating effects of bullets on the human body. When Boal learned about this and suggested it was an inappropriate conversation to have with young children, Hamilton was dismissive, telling him, 'It's okay, kids play soldiers all the time.'

The younger man also remembers Hamilton expounding at length on the differences of various bullets. He said that he favoured dumdum bullets, which disintegrated and 'sprayed', ripping through a target instead of passing through. Around this time, Hamilton was actively experimenting to see which bullets were most efficient and least likely to jam in the barrel of a handgun. He also fired through stacked books so he could judge the 'spray' of a bullet as it passed through a series of thick hardbacks and paperbacks.

In early January 1996, Hamilton's home was visited by two Trading Standards officers who accused him of operating as an unlicensed trader in photography equipment. As a result, he was no longer eligible to advertise in *Amateur Photographer*. This ban torpedoed his sole means of income; in a phone call around this time, Hamilton told Roger Allston, a fellow photographer, that he would fight the ban but that his photography business was doomed.

Over the coming weeks, Hamilton became more active as a shooter. On 23 January he shot at the Whitestone range used by the Stirling Rifle and Pistol Club. When he returned for a meeting in February, G. F. Smith, the club president, noted that his shooting was reasonably good and that he had a surprisingly rapid fire rate. This was always the case with Hamilton, who cared less about accuracy than the explosive jolt in his hand.

In late January, Hamilton visited the photography shop in Stirling, accompanied by his mother. When she attempted to follow him into the shop, he spun around and thrust his palm into her face to physically prevent her from entering. He told her never to follow him in there. 'There was a lot of venom in his voice when he said this, and it was the first time I had heard any aggression from him,' recalled the shop's owner, who had known him for more than fifteen years. Disturbed by Hamilton's behaviour, the owner told him to leave the shop and never to return. Hamilton's response was surprising: 'He was very pleasant to me, never threatened me but thanked me for my assistance over the years and left the shop.' The next day, the shop owner received a handwritten letter from Hamilton in which he remonstrated with him about his decision, which Hamilton felt was unfair given his many years as a loyal customer. The owner crumpled Hamilton's letter into a ball and tossed it into the bin.

On 26 January, Hamilton again set pen to paper to begin a long letter to Councillor Ball. He marked the letter 'private and confidential' but afterwards made copies which he posted to the head teachers of St Francis Xavier Primary in Falkirk, Bannockburn Primary and Dunblane Primary. He also sent copies to the Scout Association. In the letter he complained that Bannockburn Boys' Club had been destroyed because teachers at Bannockburn Primary had told pupils and their parents he was 'a pervert'. As a result, he wrote, all twenty-six members of the club had never returned. He said that the education department had done nothing to correct these false rumours: 'At Dunblane Primary School, where teachers have contaminated all the older boys with this poison, even former cleaners and dinner ladies have been told that I am a pervert. There have been reports at many schools of our boys being rounded up by the staff and even warnings given to entire schools by Head Teachers during assembly.'

These statements had been detrimental not only to his clubs but to his ability to earn a living, he continued, adding that 'I have no criminal record, nor have I ever been accused of sexual child abuse by any child.' This matter, he explained, had started in 1983 when an official in the education department had warned head teachers that he was interfering with boys, had been evicted from the Scouts for such behaviour and that he had a long criminal record. Hamilton said this official had been discredited but the information had never been corrected and had 'over the years reached epidemic proportions'. (Hamilton would make personal visits to both the Bannockburn and Dunblane primaries to complain to their heads that their teaching staff were warning off pupils and potential new club members.)

Two weeks later, on 11 February, Hamilton continued his correspondence, this time writing to MP Michael Forsyth to complain again about the 'malicious gossip' being spread by certain officials in the Scouts. He rehearsed his various conflicts with the local authority and referred to the police visits to his summer camps in 1988 and 1991. Though the police had been satisfied with his behaviour, he claimed that the persistent rumours had 'been a death blow to my already difficult work providing sports and leisure activities to local children as well as my public standing in the community'.

It was true that Hamilton was in increasing financial difficulties. The money he had received from the insurance payout for his boat in 1983 and the sale of his business property in 1985 had long since depleted. For the next eight years he had claimed unemployment benefit, which he had supplemented by buying and selling camera equipment. However, the 1993 investigation by the Department of Social Security had led to the loss of these benefits, and camera sales had slumped. Hamilton had debts accruing on his credit card, an overdraft at Barclays, and a further debt thanks to a bank loan he had used to set up his camera business. His application for a further loan at the beginning of the year had been unsuccessful.

On 24 February, Hamilton approached an official of the Callander Rifle and Pistol Club and enquired about shooting regularly with them. Two days later, after passing a basic marksmanship test, he was allowed to shoot on their range. The club had a small clubhouse with a twenty-five-metre shooting range which was divided into twelve firing positions, eight for small-bore rifles and four for both small-bore and full-bore pistols. The club extended a courtesy to visitors and invited guests: they were invited to shoot once for free, but if they wished to attend a second time they were asked to join as full members, something which required a character reference. Applicants could then attend for a six-month probationary period before the committee would vote on membership.

Hamilton approached John Moffat, secretary of the Callander Rifle and Pistol Club, and enquired about shooting regularly with them. The Dunblane club was now 'too sissy'; he'd moved beyond it and wanted more of a challenge. 'He told me that he had been a member of Callander years ago and I have been going there since 1979, and I didn't remember him, and I said that to him. I said: "It must have been before my time then, Tom, because I don't remember you." He said, "Oh, I used to come with Clive Woods." Now, I remember Clive Woods and so placed him as attending in '81, '82, '83. Around the early eighties. I could easily remember Clive, but Tom was a blank.'

On 26 February, Moffat was surprised to find Hamilton already at the club when he arrived. He led him onto the range, where the other shooters were hanging up targets and patching up bullet holes at the other end.

While Moffat was distracted, Hamilton took out his guns and put them on the upper shooting bench, which irritated the secretary because it was against protocol. Yet Moffat was taken with Hamilton's handguns: both Browning 9 mm self-loading pistols. The first was a standard Browning, but the second was either the Target or the Competition model, with an extended barrel that had a cosmetic muzzle weight at the front. What most surprised him was that both guns were the same calibre, given the reluctance of British police forces to sign off on a licence for duplicate guns. New guests were required to complete a supervised marksmanship test from twenty-five metres. The aim was to keep ten shots within the scoring rings of a standard two-foot-square target known as a P17. With his ear protectors on, Hamilton took aim and, over ten shots, hit the target. Moffat agreed that he was free to use his own weapons.

The next thing to surprise the secretary was Hamilton's insistence on setting up his own targets. He recalls saying to him, 'Tom, there are plenty of targets there, pin one up, shoot and we'll watch to make sure you don't do anything daft.' But Hamilton took the target from Moffat only to put it down again. His idea of a target was two pieces of white A4 stuck together and decorated with 'little fluorescent stickers'. The other man thought this was odd, but he remembered that some shooters who had problems with trigger control would shoot at blank paper so they didn't distract themselves. Moffat assumed Hamilton was trying to save money on club targets, but then he spotted that he was using factory ammo, which was expensive. At the club most members didn't use factory ammunition and instead made their own, but Hamilton was using an expensive 9 mm Parabellum with a 115-grain bullet encased in a full metal jacket. He was reloading from an open carton of bullets. He clearly had the money – or, if he didn't, he wasn't bothered.

That night, Hamilton participated in a shooting challenge known as Police Pistol 1. A target is placed at twenty-five metres, and the rules state that you have twelve shots and two minutes. However, it quickly became clear Hamilton had no intention of following club rules. He immediately let off a 'fusillade of shots', which prompted a warning about his behaviour. The target was then moved to just ten metres. Two shots were required within two seconds. Again, Hamilton broke protocol and fired four shots before he could be stopped. Before he left, Hamilton handed in his probationary membership form, but it lacked a supporting signature.

Hamilton's friend John Gillespie was the first to notice how erratic Hamilton's behaviour had become. Gillespie was used to visiting him at home and chatting over a cup of coffee while he oiled his guns. In early February, Gillespie visited his friend, who made him a coffee; they talked while Hamilton cradled his Browning 9 mm automatic handgun. As it often did, their conversation turned to the 'conspiracy' against him and the declining attendance at his boys' clubs.

The evening took a sinister turn when Hamilton asked Gillespie if he would allow his own children to attend Hamilton's clubs, even though he didn't have any. Gillespie thought for a second and said no. Hamilton then turned the gun, pointed it at Gillespie's head and pulled the trigger. There was an audible click as the hammer fell on an empty chamber.

Gillespie's rising surge of terror was instantly replaced by an endorphin wave of relief which quickly turned to anger. He shouted, 'You stupid bastard!' hurled his cup of coffee at Hamilton and stormed out of the house. He considered reporting Hamilton to the police, but he had no doubt his former friend would deny the incident ever took place.

The two men would never speak again.

Another friend was asked a similar question. The young boy who had burned his leg at Hamilton's camp in the early 1980s had grown into a dependable friend. Now married with two young children, he had his own gardening business and often used his work van to ferry around gym equipment for Hamilton's boys' clubs. But by February 1996, they had become estranged because Hamilton had shouted at his wife after she had advised him against making a fuss about local rumours.

The previous week, Hamilton had called to ask why his friend no longer came to visit, and the day after that, he had spotted Hamilton walking along Burghmuir Road talking to himself.

When he bumped into Hamilton in Stirling town centre on 22 February and saw how troubled the man looked, he offered to buy him a cup of tea. When Hamilton declined, the friend drove him home. When they arrived, the sitting room was strewn with letters and envelopes. Hamilton was writing to everyone. He said he was getting 'hassle' from people; they were 'spitting' on his back. His friend had never seen him so upset and angry. On the coffee table, a few bullets were scattered around an automatic handgun. Concerned that Hamilton was suicidal, he asked what they were doing there. Hamilton said he had just been cleaning the gun, and not put it away. He had then spoken obsessively about how he was being targeted by 'the people of Dunblane', how all he had ever done was help children. He had never been thanked, he said, and now people were saying he was touching kids and that he had never touched kids.

Then Hamilton asked if he would trust him with his own two children. Yes, the friend replied, but told Hamilton that if it turned out that he had touched his kids, he would break his legs.

Over the next couple of weeks, the friend tried calling Hamilton to check on him, but the older man never answered the phone. When he called round in person, Hamilton wouldn't open the door, even though the television was on and it was clear he was home.

On 1 March, Isobel Martin, the head teacher of a primary school in Bishopbriggs, received a complaint from a parent. The mother was concerned about Hamilton's interactions with her son, who was eleven. Hamilton would pick him up on the way to one of his clubs, but he was steadily extending the time the pair were spending alone before he picked up other boys. Hamilton had shown him a gun he kept in his car and offered to take him shooting as well as to lend him his videotape of *Alien*. Martin made a note of the parent's concerns and wrote a letter to the social work department in Bishopbriggs. She received no reply. On 12 March, she decided to call the department. She was told a social worker would be contacting the parent in due course.

Hamilton was given a lift to Largs, a town on the Firth of Clyde around sixty miles from Stirling, on Saturday, 2 March. He had phoned William Campbell, the range conducting officer and competition secretary of the Stirling Rifle and Pistol Club. Campbell had met Hamilton in January at the Whitestone range and thought him exceedingly shy but competent, so when he received a call on the Friday evening asking if Hamilton could get a lift to the competition at the Inverclyde shooting practice scheduled for the next day, he agreed. His friend Alex Woods drove, taking Campbell, his cousin Alexis Fawcett, and Hamilton. Woods arrived in his car at Campbell's house. As they loaded the holdalls into the boot, he asked Fawcett to wait a few minutes for Hamilton, whom Woods hadn't met. When Hamilton arrived, they all got into the car and set off on the journey down to Largs. They arrived at the range at midday and were the first people on site. Hamilton and Woods carried the bags from the car, then helped prepare the range for the session.

There were three people in each of the five booths; Woods and Hamilton shared a booth with a third club member. There were two targets prepared for the day's shoot: a simple circular target and the 'advancing man'. The target was an army-type figure, camouflaged in black and brown. Hamilton tried to put his favoured yellow stickers over the target's head and heart but was told he wasn't allowed.

Each marksman was to enter their booth with a loaded gun and exit only after all their bullets had been fired and the weapon had been checked to ensure it was empty. Woods had brought a Browning .22 and a fancy Browning 9 mm: the Capitan model, top of the range, with a polished walnut handgrip and specialist sight. Hamilton had been admiring it for the first couple of details (a shooter's turn at the target is known as a 'detail'), and then, around 1.30 p.m., asked to try out the Capitan. Hamilton used it for one detail and passed it back, commenting that the gun was 'very nice'.

About an hour later, Hamilton took up his position and fired his entire round of thirteen bullets at the head of the target.

By 3 p.m., Hamilton switched from his Browning automatic to his .357 revolver. So great was the din from each shot that everyone was immediately aware of it. 'There were terrific shock waves and sound coming from the gun when he discharged it,' said Woods. (The booth's third man was so impressed that he asked to try the revolver.)

The afternoon's shooting ended with a short round of Police Pistol 1. All the shooters had been firing at targets from twenty-five yards until Hamilton insisted he move his target closer, to fifteen yards, before proceeding to fire round after round from his 9 mm Browning. At such close range, many of the shooters were struggling to see the point of the competition.

At around 4 p.m. the range closed, and the group drove back to Stirling. Hamilton was in the back seat complaining again about how much he missed his Kalashnikov. But he took comfort in his handguns, which he had repeatedly stroked, much to everyone's discomfort.

It was dark by the time they reached Stirling. Woods got out with Hamilton, opened the boot and handed over his gun cases.

THE GUNS

Hamilton thanked him for the lift and offered to pay for the petrol, but Woods waved him away. As he climbed back into the driver's seat, he heard Fawcett breathe a sigh of relief and exclaim, 'Thank God he's away. What a weirdo.' She said he had been talking about his guns as if they were children.

On the evening of 6 March, Hamilton spoke on the phone with Roger Allston, a freelance photographer based in Gravesend, Kent. The pair had become friends when Allston answered one of Hamilton's adverts in *Amateur Photographer*. He was selling an exposure meter, and Allston was impressed by Hamilton's photographic knowledge and the vast array of equipment he said he had access to. Allston suspected he was secretly dealing.

The men spoke most weeks, and Allston found 'Tom', as he knew him, 'a very jovial man and very talkative'. In recent weeks the calls had dropped off, and when they did speak Tom was 'very subdued and depressed'. Allston, who was unaware of local rumours about his friend, attempted to cheer him up. Hamilton had lost his case against Trading Standards and was seeking solace on the shooting range. It took his mind off his problems. 'I can recall Tom telling me that he was keen on guns and was a member of a shooting club,' Allston said. 'He told me once that he thought the Clint Eastwood films were totally unrealistic because Eastwood continues talking when using his Magnum. Tom said that his Magnum was so loud that if he didn't wear ear defenders he would be temporarily deaf.' The last thing Hamilton said to Allston before cradling the phone was, 'I'm going back to my guns.'

Others who knew Thomas Hamilton noticed he was changing. Geoffrey Wood, a cameraman, had known Hamilton for more than ten years, since their first meeting at the Callander Gun Club around 1981 or 1982. During this time, he'd given Hamilton lifts, visited him at home and had once bought a Beretta handgun from him.

Wood's first thought on seeing Hamilton at the gun club was that he was putting on weight. His second thought was that he had never seen anyone fire so many bullets in so short a time: 'He certainly fired a lot more rounds that evening than I would ever have seen anybody else firing.'

Hamilton was using a sheet of white A3 from a sketchbook, with red or orange rectangular stickers placed in the middle. He liked to group the bullets around the sticker, and was so pleased with one round that he asked Wood to stop shooting so he could show him that he had struck the bull. He would then place the targets back into the sketchbook. He said he hadn't been shooting for some time but wanted to get back into it. Wood asked if he had a competition coming up, but Hamilton said no, he simply needed the 'practice'.

Prior to his call with Roger Allston, on 6 March Hamilton attended the Callander Rifle and Pistol Club, where Nigel Bell, a probationary member, was disturbed by his manner. Hamilton expressed interest when Bell mentioned he was from Dunblane. 'He was very deliberate and very intense,' said Bell. Hamilton insisted he try out his Browning handgun. At the end of the night, Hamilton asked Bell if he could give him a lift to Dunblane railway station. Bell agreed despite not wanting to. 'I couldn't put my finger on anything specific other than I was just very uncomfortable in his presence,' he said, 'but I would never have seen anybody stuck for a lift home.'

When they got to the car, Bell realised he had left the baby seat in the front. He went to move it, but Hamilton insisted he sit in the back. Bell felt a wave of fear and anxiety: 'Panic is pretty close to the case. I, as I have said, was very uneasy in the gentleman's presence ... I was really, really uncomfortable at this stage, with Mr Hamilton being in the back of the car, particularly with firearms and particularly given that nobody in the club, unless they overheard the conversation, knew that I was giving him a lift.' In his mind, he imagined Hamilton taking out his gun and shooting him in the head. Rather than take this risk, Bell insisted it was no trouble, unclipped the car seat and insisted Hamilton ride in the front with him.

Once they set off, Hamilton began to talk. 'The conversation started off really just about his shooting and the fact that he enjoyed shooting,' Bell said. 'He mentioned that he had had a firearms licence for more than twenty years. He got a bit agitated at one point because he explained to me that he had had something like a .243 rifle, a self-loading rifle, and he was quite aggrieved obviously at the police for having taken it off him. I asked why it had been taken off him, and he said it was because of what happened at Hungerford. I was under the impression that he hadn't had his rifle very long and it cost him £1,200. And that, as a result of the law change, the police actually bought the firearms back from the owners. He mentioned that he had only been paid £700 for it, and he was very angry about that.'

The conversation continued in fits and starts. Hamilton said he was a gym teacher at 'the high school'. He said his club was on a Thursday, and when Bell said he played badminton there and had never seen him, Hamilton got annoyed and demanded to know why he was questioning him. Bell backed off and said he wasn't.

Moving onto safer subjects, the two men discussed the various guns Hamilton owned. Bell asked Hamilton how many rounds he had fired that night; the average person might only fire between five and fifteen, and Bell himself had fired only fifteen rounds. Hamilton claimed he had fired several hundred. When Bell arrived home, he said to his wife that he was worried about Hamilton working with kids. She reassured him that the council would be aware of his background and would never allow Hamilton to work with children if there were any doubts about his character.

Also on 6 March, Hamilton called the headquarters of the Scout Association in Scotland and began a rambling conversation with the receptionist in which he rehearsed all the ways in which he had been wronged by the Scouts. He asked for the names of the association's high-ranking officials and, when told these were not to hand, asked for the current patron. He was told this was Her Majesty Queen Elizabeth II. After hanging up, Hamilton began to compose a long letter to the Queen, in which he complained about how he had been treated by the Scouts and how it had caused him 'untold damage', and that he was writing to her 'as a last resort ... appealing for some kind of intervention in the hope that I may be able to gain my self-esteem in society'.

The letter arrived at the mailroom of Buckingham Palace in London over the weekend of 9 and 10 March. (The Queen was not in residence, having left the previous evening for Sandringham.) Copies were also sent to the Secretary of State for Scotland, Bannockburn Primary, Dunblane Primary, DS Moffat of the child protection unit, the police family unit, *The Scotsman* and the *Daily*

Record. The Queen, as befitting her status, warranted a first-class stamp; the other copies were sent second class, arriving at their destinations on 12 and 13 March.

After completing his letter to the Queen on the evening of 7 March, Hamilton made his way to Dunblane High for one of his remaining boys' clubs. As the boys ran around the gym hall playing five-a-side football, Hamilton beckoned over one nine-year-old to sit beside him on the wooden bench. For some time, he had peppered this particular boy with questions about the school, including about the way to the gym and to the hall, what time certain classes went to the gym, and where the fire exits and the main entrance into the school were. He asked the boy the same questions every week for two years.

Around 11.30 a.m. on Friday, 8 March, in the kitchen department of a Debenhams in the Thistle Centre, John Wilson was weighing up cooking utensils. At sixty-two, he had retired from Central Scotland Police and was now spending his time developing his culinary skills. He was browsing an array of spatulas when he heard a familiar voice: 'Hello, John, how are you?'

Wilson knew Hamilton from Woodcraft, where he received a 10 per cent discount (as did other officers). Wilson was also an instructor at the police firearms club, whose weekly sessions took place on Wednesday nights at the police headquarters at Randolphfield.

It had been five years since they had last met, but Hamilton hadn't changed: 'It was his usual wringing of hands,' Wilson said. The pair spoke about Hamilton's camera business, and his recent shooting trip to Callander. He complained that the Linofix, the screen which stops the spatter from bullets, was badly damaged. He reminded Wilson that the same thing had happened at the range at the police headquarters, which had had to close due to excess lead and insufficient ventilation.

Hamilton then turned to the subject of his own shooting: 'My conventional shooting is okay, but I am not very good at ten yards. I could do with some instruction.' Wilson fended off this implied invitation by telling Hamilton that he had developed tinnitus in his left ear, which meant he no longer shot, and that he was now 'anti-blood sports'. Wilson told Hamilton that he was claiming medical compensation from Central Police for the tinnitus, and Hamilton asked how his claim was progressing. The issue of police obstinacy provided him with an excuse to update Wilson on his litany of complaints about the police, local politicians and the wider public: 'He said the authorities were against him, the parents of the children were against him, the police tried to get kids to say he had done things that he hadn't done. He certainly was anti-police.'

During their conversation, Hamilton raised the subject of Michael Ryan's mass shooting in Hungerford eight years before. In Hamilton's opinion, the police had been too scared to go in after him, and this had allowed Ryan to kill so many. Wilson felt responsible for defending the police and the conversation became heated, prompting a frustrated Wilson to say, 'Anyhow, these nutters normally kill themselves anyway, they don't want to be wounded by police firearms officers.' Hamilton said it was better that they did.

Hamilton also directed the conversation to a recent incident closer to home. In Cowie, just outside Stirling, the police had been called to an address following reports of a man firing a shotgun.

On their arrival, their police car had come under fire. A shotgun blast had shattered the back window. Hamilton commented that the firearms team should have been quicker off the mark and taken him out. Did Wilson know if firearms were kept at all police stations? Or just certain ones? Wilson said he didn't know. When he'd been on the force, not every station had had an armed officer. Usually, police stations that were manned round the clock had access to guns. Hamilton thought for a second, then said he believed there should be an armed response unit at *all* police stations, as a precautionary measure.

Robert Togneri, Hamilton's childhood chess teacher, was standing outside RS McColl, the newsagent on Murray Place, on the morning of 11 March. He had just left the post office when he heard a voice behind him call out his name. It was Thomas Hamilton, wearing a grubby anorak and a hat with ear flaps. They exchanged pleasantries and crossed the road together to the old arcade side, then walked along Murray Place and into the shopping precinct on Port Street. He thought Hamilton unusually quiet, although they had only met half a dozen times over the years. Usually with Tom, he remembered, you 'couldn't get a word in'. He seemed to have something on his mind. When Togneri asked about how his boys' clubs were doing, Hamilton replied, 'Not very good'. Then he did something unusual: he invited Togneri to join him for dinner. Togneri thought this strange, as Hamilton hardly knew him, and politely declined. After that, Togneri said, 'We both went on our way.'

On the morning of 12 March, Ron Taylor, the head teacher at Dunblane Primary, was in his office, a small room decorated with artwork made by his pupils. He opened his mail and was surprised to see a photocopy of a letter addressed to 'Her Majesty the Queen'. He glanced through it and saw it had been written by Thomas Hamilton. He'd met Hamilton a couple of times and considered him a troublesome crank. He showed the letter briefly to his deputy, then continued with his day.

That same morning, Hamilton was on the phone to his old friend William Macdonald. The pair had bumped into each other up at the Thistle Centre the previous month, and when Macdonald mentioned his plans for a new fitted kitchen, Hamilton offered to help. There had been a flurry of phone calls. This morning, he was calling up to give advice on the size of specific units, but his usual focus and attention to detail was absent. 'I felt it was a little bit odd,' Macdonald said, 'because he did mention … he was very concise and I felt very up on kitchens et cetera, but he did suggest a 1,000 unit then a 600 unit to me, which would knock the whole context of the kitchen out, and I thought that was a bit unusual for him. He is quite a deep thinker.'

At around 3 p.m. that day, Hamilton made his way to a car hire centre in Stirling. He told the receptionist he wished to hire a van for a single day and that he was happy to pay the full charge in advance. He was told to leave a deposit of £50 and settle the bill upon his return the following day. Yet his manner was memorable. 'He unnerved me quite a bit … the way he spoke mainly. He spoke very slowly, very clearly, precisely, but with no emotion or expression. There was just nothing, nothing in there. You couldn't have held a conversation with him.'

Hamilton then paid a visit to his mother, where he had a cup of tea and a hot bath. They talked for a couple of hours, then he went home.

THE GUNS

At around 8 p.m., the telephone rang in Kent Road. It was David Macdonald, William's son and his former shop assistant at Woodcraft. For the past five years the pair had talked on the phone a couple of times a week, usually about cameras and Hamilton's market for second-hand Canons, Minoltas and, more recently, the more exclusive Hasselblad brand. (At one time, Hamilton's calls had been so frequent and long that David would avoid picking up.) Hamilton left two messages on David's new answering machine, and that evening, David called him back. The conversation lasted a little less than an hour and largely concerned the kitchen Hamilton was helping David's dad install. However, on that evening the conversation also took a rare personal turn. 'For a while he had said that he was quite a lonely person,' David said, 'and that it wasn't good to be alone for all your life, which I thought was a bit strange.' It was a subject they had touched on before. 'I said to him, I mean that, you know, it is possible for anyone to be lonely at some point in their life, so it's not a big deal.' David then tried to engage him with talk of cameras but sensed a lack of interest. Hamilton was speaking slowly and the conversation started to 'fizzle out ... It just started to go quite flat, so I said it was getting late.' They hung up.

It was a cold night, and ice had formed on the outdoor steps and the slate tiles on the roof of Hamilton's house. In the kitchen there was a pot on the stove and a half-empty packet of Kellogg's Frosties on top of the fridge. A shirt was hanging up to dry above the radiator, next to pots hanging from their handles. In the back bedroom, Hamilton sat at a wooden table. In front of him were three steel strongboxes full of ammunition. He had twenty larger box-type ammunition magazines, which could each store twenty 9 mm bullets. Each of the magazines was layered, with three different types of bullet. Once loaded, each magazine was carefully labelled with two coloured stickers to minimise reload time: orange to indicate the back, yellow the front. We do not know if Hamilton slept soundly, content with his plans, or spent the night staring into the darkness that now had all but consumed him.

―――

Dunblane dawned cold on Wednesday, 13 March 1996. There was frost on car windscreens and in the corners of windows. Frost on the grass and on the pavements. Frost at the base of the snowdrops, the first flowers of spring, which were beginning to push up through the icy earth.

Amy Louise Hutchison, a five-year-old pupil at Dunblane Primary, started the day battling with her mother over her choice of footwear. Her uncle had sent her a new pair of Kickers boots. but as the early spring morning was frosty, damp and cold, her mother wanted Amy to wear her wellington boots. Amy was adamant that she was going to wear the Kickers boots. Amy won.

For Isabel MacBeath it was a day wreathed in sadness. The previous autumn, her husband, Murray MacBeath, had suffered a further catastrophic stroke and died a week later. Their daughter, Mhairi, was five, and Isabel was six months pregnant. In December she had given birth to a second daughter, Catherine. Mhairi missed her daddy deeply. 'Mhairi was very sad,' Isabel said. 'That is the only way I can describe her in the last three or four months, that she was very sad.' She also doted on her new baby sister, whose portrait she drew in crayon, complete with a giant fresh nappy. On 13 March, a memorial service had been planned for Murray at Stirling University. Isabel would drop Mhairi off at school and return home to Kilbryde Crescent, where her mother had agreed to babysit Catherine during the service.

In the family's terraced house Judy Murray rushed to round up Jamie and Andy for school. Over the past three years she had become the first woman to pass the Lawn Tennis Association's performance coach award and had been appointed national coach for the Scottish Lawn Tennis Association; she was now responsible for building a national team for home international matches and nurturing the nation's contribution to Great Britain's hopes in the Olympics and the Davis Cup. She had a busy day lined up – a meeting in her office at Craiglockhart on the outskirts of Edinburgh, then a coaching session at the indoor courts on the campus at Stirling University – but first she had to get to her mum's toyshop to help with stocktaking.

At 8.15 a.m., Hamilton left his house dressed in a dark jacket and black corduroy trousers and began scraping ice from the windscreen of the white hired van. He stopped to have a brief conversation with his neighbour Robert Deuchars. Deuchars was surprised to see Hamilton up so early, knowing he liked to sleep late, and asked Hamilton to put his newspaper through his letterbox as he was going out. Hamilton said he would, and he returned to finish cleaning the windscreen. He needed a clear view.

Hamilton then went back inside to prepare himself. The telephone directory was on a glass-topped coffee table; it was open at the page containing the telephone number and address of Dunblane Primary.

Each ammunition magazine was fully loaded. The magazines were positioned for ease of access and to reduce the risk of jamming. They were then loaded into two canvas camera bags, into which he had fitted cardboard inserts to keep them propped open. He loaded 501 rounds of 9 mm ammunition and 242 rounds of .357 ammunition.

He pulled on four leather holsters and secured his four guns: two 9 mm Browning semi-automatic pistols, one with an extra-long barrel, and two .357 Smith & Wesson Magnum revolvers, including his oldest and favourite.

Hamilton slung a canvas bag over each of his shoulders and loaded the twenty 9 mm magazines into them. The bags were left open to allow swift access. He put on his woolly hat. After all, it was cold outside.

The drive from his home address in Stirling to Dunblane Primary took around twenty minutes. The traffic had begun to ease after the morning rush, but he was too late for assembly.

He got out of the van, walked to a wooden telephone pole and cut the wires at its foot.

Then he walked up the driveway towards the school.

One Morning in March

D UNBLANE Primary was one of the largest primaries in Scotland, twice the average size, with 640 pupils on its roll. It sits on a hill off Doune Road, which runs through the centre of the town. Built in the 1960s, the school had since expanded to cope with increased numbers by the addition of six wood-framed 'huts', separate from the main building and used as classrooms for older pupils in Primary 6 and 7. The main building was T-shaped, with the trunk consisting of the main entrance, offices, dining area and assembly hall with a wooden stage. A corridor led to a large, modern gymnasium with a polished sprung wooden floor and expansive windows looking out onto the school's grass playing fields.

On the morning of 13 March, the minister closed morning assembly with a prayer. As Reverend George Cringles, the minister at St Blane's, stood on the stage of the assembly hall, he could see the first row of children were dressed for PE in blue shorts and white T-shirts, wriggling excitedly.

Ron Taylor, the head, was agitated. A few classes had arrived late, and they hadn't begun until 9.15. Once under way, he rattled through the principal points of discussion before introducing the minister, one of three local chaplains who served in the school.

Meanwhile, Mary Blake had a small errand to run. The learning support assistant visited the machine room for ten minutes to cut some covers for the schoolbooks used by her class of Primary 1s. Afterwards she popped back to Gwen Mayor's classroom, where she had left her handbag. There, she bumped into Claire McLeod and reminded her that her class should be at the assembly. Then Blake returned to the machine room, finished the covers and looked out of the room at 9.30 as assembly was finishing. The corridors were crowded with the chatter and din of children corralled by teachers, all readying themselves for the first lessons of the day.

PE teacher Eileen Harrild wasn't required at morning assembly. She arrived at the gym at nine to prepare for her class, having first dropped off her own two children, also pupils at the school. A dedicated teacher, she loved to encourage even the shyest child to get involved. In the past she had taught in the local secondary, and both Kenny and Pam Ross were former pupils, as their daughter Joanna liked to remind her. That morning, she had laid out the long wooden beam used for balance work and had moved a second, curved beam into position. To allow the children space to run around, the centre of the hall was left empty.

Outside, Thomas Hamilton had parked his van, cut the telephone lines and fixed his ear defenders over his woollen hat. He had planned to arrive at the school during assembly, but he was three minutes late.

Gwen Mayor was a loving but firm teacher, and, after assembly, her young class stood in a neat line outside the gym. When three pupils pushed their way into the hall early, they were ordered out again.

When it was time to go inside, Mayor followed her pupils into the gym and told Harrild she wouldn't be staying long, as she had a meeting. Instead, Mary Blake, who had arrived earlier, would take over the class. Mayor was holding a diary, which Harrild put on the bench next to the door. Harrild then took one of the children's glasses from them for safekeeping and placed them down carefully on top of the diary.

Harrild asked the children to find a space in the gym on their own. She liked the children to spend a minute or two standing alone to help develop their own spatial awareness, reminding them that they were their own person, their own unique personality.

Meanwhile, Thomas Hamilton was walking the school corridors. He had not entered through the main door, where he was likely to have been seen, but by an unlocked side entrance. He then fired two shots into the side of the wooden stage in the now-empty assembly hall, followed by others into the girls' toilets outside the gym hall.

Inside the gym, the noise startled the teachers, who instinctively looked towards the door. Harrild saw Hamilton walk through the door with a gun in his hand.

'He walked towards me. He did not pause or speak, he just continued walking straight towards me, looking at me. He pointed his gun at me and shot me. The first shot hit me on my right forearm. I put my hand up to defend myself. There was a succession of shots. I knew I was hit on my right forearm and my right hand, and also my left forearm and left breast. There was a terrible noise of continual firing. He started to spray shots everywhere. The children started to scream.'

Badly wounded, Harrild began to stagger towards the gym store cupboard.

Hamilton then turned and shot Gwen Mayor in the face. The bullet pierced her right eye, killing her instantly. She had been standing near and perhaps shielding her pupil Emma Crozier, who was also shot dead.

The room now filled with gunfire. Harrild stumbled towards the storeroom, clutching her bloody arms across her chest. She had lost her glasses. A small group of children joined her. They had also been shot but, incredibly, were still able to move.

Bullets were coming fast. Mary Blake recalled seeing a dark figure with some sort of headgear, and then feeling the impact of the first bullet. There was a terrible pain in her head as another round grazed her scalp. The bullets knocked her to the floor. Somehow, with wounds to both legs, she struggled to her feet and began to shepherd the children in front of her to the storeroom. Elsewhere, other children were running hysterically, while some classmates were already lying on the gym floor. Blood was everywhere.

The noise of the gunshots and screams was deafening, so loud it seemed to be inside her head. She could see Harrild a few feet away, limping badly, clutching her arm and struggling to reach the storeroom with a group of children.

Amy Hutchison, who only two hours earlier had been arguing with her mother over what boots to wear, remembers skipping in her plimsolls when her legs turned to jelly and she fell to the floor, having been shot multiple times. She then managed to drag herself to the gym cupboard.

Coll Austin was shot in the foot but still managed to follow Mrs Harrild and Mrs Blake. Limping and struggling towards the storeroom door, he was shot again, this time in the back, then fell face first onto the gym floor. Blood pooled around him.

By the time Blake turned the corner and made it to the storeroom, Harrild and three children were already inside. Harrild was lying on her back; Blake then sat to the right of her. Four children were at their feet.

In front of the entrance to the storeroom lay a couple of children, badly wounded.

Inside the storeroom, which was full of PE mats, Harrild hunkered down with the children. She wanted to pull the mats around them as an added layer of protection, but with her arms badly wounded, she struggled to move them. The children were lying across her legs, and she could see the bullet wounds in their own pale thin legs.

At the far end of the storeroom was a large rolled-up mattress. Harrild thought about trying to hide one of the children inside, but she feared they would make noise reaching the mattress and attract the gunman's attention.

Blake could see one little boy holding up his arm, a bullet wound in it. Another was wounded above the knee. Amy managed to crawl into the storeroom and began to cry for her mum.

At one point, Harrild and Blake tried to hush the children by putting their fingers over their lips. One little boy kept repeating, 'What a bad man … what a bad man … what a bad man.' Then they fell quiet. Outside, they heard the creak of footsteps. There was a period of deadly silence, followed by the punch of rapid gunshots.

Blake could feel blood running down her neck and an agonising pain in her legs. She tried to pull one of the heavy gym mats onto her and the children closest to her. She gripped it, pulled as much as she could manage, but the mat would only move a couple of inches. Instead, she covered the children with her own body. Through a gap in the door, she could see children outside in the gym hall, 'screaming and wailing'.

This went on for approximately three minutes, but to Harrild, Blake and the children in the cupboard it felt like a lifetime. Lots of little lifetimes. 'The next few minutes, I don't know how long, seemed to last like an absolute eternity,' Harrild later recalled. 'It seemed to last for ever. We just lay there on the floor helpless, just waiting for him to come round the corner and finish us off … I wasn't feeling any pain. It was as if I was anaesthetised. All things were going through my mind. I remember thinking, "What can we do to save ourselves here? What can I do to save the children?"'

Although both women were aware of how much blood they were losing, there was nothing they could do but wait. Harrild began to pray. All the old prayers of her childhood returned to her mind.

Hamilton had begun by firing twenty-nine shots around the gym, killing and wounding on his way. He then walked along the east side of the gym, firing six more bullets. At one point, midway across the gym, he fired eight bullets at the opposite side of the room.

He then walked to where a group of seven children lay wounded. He walked in a semicircle, standing over each child, and fired at point-blank range. He fired a total of sixteen bullets.

At one point, Hamilton was briefly distracted. A boy from a Primary 7 class had been sent on an errand by his teacher and was outside in the playground, walking along the west side of the gym. When he heard the shots, he looked in and saw Hamilton shooting. Hamilton caught his eye and turned and fired at the boy, who was missed by the bullet but struck by the shattered glass of the gym window.

This prompted Hamilton to move back down to the south end of the gym, where he fired a further twenty-four bullets in various directions. He shot through the window next to the fire escape, probably at an adult walking across the playground.

Across the playground, a boy sitting at the back of his Primary 6 class looked outside. From his seat, he could see through the floor-to-ceiling windows of the gym hall. He could see an overweight man in dark clothes, wearing glasses and what he thought were earmuffs. The man was standing a few feet in front of the basketball net with his arms outstretched. The boy thought he was firing a gun as he kept putting one hand on top of something as if to reload. The boy watched as the man walked around, firing in all directions. The pupil then saw a boy, who was halfway down the gym, drop to the ground.

His teacher, who had heard the bangs but assumed they were harmless, noticed her pupil wasn't paying attention. 'My teacher told me to face the front of the class, which I did,' he said. 'I didn't see anything else after that.'

Inside the gym, the air was thick with smoke and the acrid smell of cordite. Bullet casings littered the floor. There were splintered bullet holes in the wooden floor and white flecks of plaster breaking off the walls.

Hamilton pushed open the fire doors and fired four shots from within the gym. He briefly stepped outside, into the chilly open air, and fired four more shots at the library cloakroom towards the back of the main building. One of the bullets grazed the head of teacher Grace Tweddle, who was near the cloakroom.

Turning around to face Hut 7, used by Primary 7 pupils, Hamilton opened fire. As nine bullets shattered the windows, teacher Catherine Gordon screamed for all the pupils to get down on the floor. One pupil hurled himself onto the linoleum, where he could see two girls, his classmates, crawling towards him in tears of shock. When he turned round again and looked up, he saw a bullet hole in the plastic back of the chair on which he had been sitting seconds before. The other eight bullets had embedded themselves in schoolbooks, the wall and other pieces of school equipment.

Across the playground, Hamilton stepped back inside the gym. He then walked back across the varnished floor to where Coll Austin was lying in a pool of blood. The boy could see the gunman's boots as he approached. Aware Coll was still alive, Hamilton shot him once more in the back.

A few seconds later, Hamilton made the decision to kill himself. He had used the 9 mm Browning automatic for the last four minutes, reloading six times and firing 105 rounds. He preferred a weapon with more personal meaning for his own death. He threw down the Browning and pulled out his .357 Smith & Wesson Magnum, a weapon he had owned for almost twenty years, from its leather holster. He put the black barrel in his mouth and pulled the trigger. His head jolted backwards, his knees folded, and he landed on his back on the gym hall floor where he began to twitch in a pool of his own brain and blood. The bullet passed through his skull, bounced off the stone wall behind and fell tinkling to the wooden floor.

'Then there was silence. There was no shooting or screaming,' said Harrild. 'I don't recall a lot of screaming towards the end. It seemed to go quiet. There was an uncanny silence.'

Blake asked Harrild how she was doing. 'He got me in the chest,' she replied. But Blake could see Harrild had also been wounded in the arm, which she was holding across her chest. Blake had been shot four times. One bullet had skimmed her scalp, giving her a dreadful headache, and she had also been shot once in her left thigh and twice in her right.

Agnes Awlson, the assistant head, heard the shots as she lined up her Primary 7 class in preparation for an art lesson. Her teaching assistant had been sent on ahead to prepare the classroom, one of the temporary Portakabins. Seconds before, she had led her pupils out into the playground. She was explaining to one of her pupils where the scissors were when she heard eight to ten loud bangs, followed by the screams of children.

Awlson ran towards the sound, heading through the door closest to the library. At the staff offices she met another teacher and together they headed for the gym, but as they reached its doors, they saw several metal objects on the floor that she recognised as bullet casings. The noise changed direction and Awlson and her fellow teacher became convinced the gunman was now coming after them, so they turned and ran.

Ron Taylor was standing outside his office; the corridor was busy with pupils making their way to class. He had been in conversation with two teachers before walking back into his office, where his secretary had asked him to return a call he had missed. He sat down at his desk around 9.35 a.m. and placed the call. The office windows afforded a clear view of the playground and the Portakabins. Taylor was pleased to see the playground was empty of any stragglers.

Taylor was a couple of minutes into his phone conversation when he heard a 'burst of three or four bangs' in the distance, which infuriated him. Clearly it was construction work he had not been informed about. He looked out of the window and into the playground but couldn't see anything. By this time the noise seemed to be getting louder, with short breaks in between. He then stood, with the intention of hanging up and investigating the source, when Awlson pushed open the door. She was crouched down with a look of terror on her face, her eyes wide open. 'Somebody is in the school with a gun. Get down.'

The head immediately hung up and dialled 999. When he was put through, he said there was a man in the school firing a gun, possibly blanks, and to send someone right away. By the time the call to the police was complete, the noise had ended.

Taylor ran out of his office into the main hallway to see Grace Tweddle lying in the foyer being comforted by another teacher, who shouted to him, 'It's the gym.' Taylor ran on into the main assembly hall, which fifteen minutes before had been packed with hundreds of pupils. He headed towards the gym with two kitchen staff as well as David Scott, a student teacher who had been looking through his art class window and seen Hamilton turn the gun on himself. Scott shouted that the gunman was dead. Taylor kept running along the gantry area leading to the double doors, then through the corridor connected to the gymnasium.

As soon as Taylor reached the gym door, he could hear children crying. He burst through the door, stopped and stood still. What he saw was almost impossible to comprehend. In his words, 'It was a scene of unimaginable carnage, one's worst nightmare.' At his feet lay the body of Gwen Mayor and beside her, lying partially across her, was Emma Crozier, a little girl he recognised. Both were obviously dead.

Looking across the full length of the gym hall, Taylor saw a group of injured children close to the storeroom entrance. Taylor told Scott to get them out of the gym, then turned and ran back towards his office, where he told another member of staff to 'phone for ambulances'. He then ran back to the gym, calling for more help from the kitchen staff. By the time he got back, Scott had four or five children beside him in the corridor and was attempting to tend to their wounds. Taylor went back into the gym and again struggled to make sense of what he could see.

In the centre, close to the climbing ropes, a silent group of children lay on a gym mat, huddled together, some partially on top of others. There were benches next to them. They all appeared to be dead. In a state of shock, Taylor, unable to take his eyes off the children, was briefly unaware of the arrival of John Currie, the school janitor, who walked towards where Hamilton lay with his right hand still twitching.

Taylor shouted to Currie that the gunman was still alive. He could also see a handgun on the floor and, afraid the killer might reach for it, shouted to Currie to kick the gun away.

Currie also spotted that Hamilton still had the Smith & Wesson Magnum in his left hand, so he reached down and prised it from his grip. He threw it across the gym, where it bounced and landed near the fire exit. As he was throwing the handgun, a voice behind them shouted either 'Put the gun down' or 'Leave the gun.' It was an off-duty police officer who, only minutes before, had dropped off his older child at the school's nursery. He had been standing with his son when a teacher ran past and said there had been a shooting. He had identified himself as a police officer, passed his son to the closest teacher and set off running through the corridors.

In the gym, Currie, startled by the officer's shout, explained that he had only wanted to get the gun away from the shooter.

When Taylor asked him what they should do, the officer told them to put pressure on the gunshot wounds and to find some rags or clothes or anything else to hand. He ran back out to the shower room opposite the assembly hall stage and grabbed as many green paper towels as he could. Upon his return, he noticed that two young girls in the group in the centre of the gym were still breathing. He pushed the paper towels against the bullet wound in one girl's back, but he then saw that she also had serious bullet wounds to her chest. She died in Taylor's arms.

It was at this time that the first uniformed police officers arrived in the gym hall.

Taylor went to the left side of the gym, where three young boys and a girl were lying. One boy's arms were moving, but then Taylor saw the bullet wound to his head. He could see no way to help. All he could do was say sorry and move on.

Next, he went to a young boy who was lying on his back with his hand holding his wounded shoulder, quietly whimpering. Taylor passed him some paper towels and told him to hold them tight against his wounds.

When Taylor next stood up to look around, he noticed the storeroom. It was there he found Mary Blake, Eileen Harrild and the children. He passed them paper towels and assured them that help was on its way.

Agnes Awlson, who had alerted Taylor, was not far behind. When she arrived at the gym she bent down to check on Gwen Mayor, but Mayor's skin was cold to the touch, as was that of the child at her side. Both were clearly dead. When she approached the group of children on the mat at the centre of the gym, the janitor said, 'You can't help them, Mrs Awlson, they're gone, they're all gone.'

She then saw a child crying on the right side of the gym, approached him and asked his name. He was lying on his back, and although she couldn't see any obvious bullet wounds, there was blood on his legs and arms. She spent only a minute or two comforting him before moving on to the next child, a boy, motionless and face down in a pool of blood. She presumed he was dead, so didn't touch him. She heard crying from another boy, who was lying near the corner of the gym hall. She put him and the boy beside him, who was barely conscious and lying on his front with blood around his neck, in the recovery position.

When Awlson looked up, she saw a fellow teacher holding a young girl who was sobbing. She asked if she could help but was told there was nothing she could do.

Meanwhile, the off-duty police officer was now in the head's office, where he asked for an outside line. He called the operator at police headquarters, then asked for the control room. He explained that he was at Dunblane Primary, that there had been a major firearms incident, that there were at least a dozen dead or wounded and that they needed ambulances, lots of ambulances. He was passed onto a sergeant who asked about the whereabouts of the gunman. The officer said he was dead.

It was then that the first two uniformed police from the local station in Dunblane entered the school and ran down the corridors towards the gym.

One of the officers had borrowed a mobile phone from a member of the public. The officer accidentally pressed 9 – a built-in emergency line which automatically directed the call to the owner's home answering machine, which recorded a brief conversation between the officer and his colleague, a senior officer, and then a police controller at headquarters, later transcribed phonetically by the Crown Office. (One of the officers knew Hamilton from when two men attempted to secure the return of photographs he had taken.)

POLICE OFFICER 1: 'There's going to be people hammering down here now … Aye, get the ambulances as close as you can, and eh.'
POLICE OFFICER 2: 'What are we goin tae dae if it's blocked off? We'll pit the ambulances round there tae, cause they can get in.'
POLICE OFFICER 1: 'Well they will get directed up this way, and that might be a problem, that might be a problem, when the thingummy's come.'
POLICE OFFICER 2: 'Who?'
POLICE OFFICER 1: 'The parents come down … that's the … fucked. No, we need tae stop them though, we really need tae stop them. Hello, sir.'
POLICE OFFICER 3: 'How many's dead?'

POLICE OFFICER 1: 'Eh, several, over a dozen – it's Tommy Hamilton. He's a fuckin' nutter.'
POLICE OFFICER 3: 'Where does he live?'
POLICE OFFICER 1: 'Stirling.'
POLICE OFFICER 3: 'What did he use?'
POLICE OFFICER 1: 'Eh – a gun.'
POLICE OFFICER 3: 'Shotgun?'
POLICE OFFICER 2: 'Eh no – a wee gun.'

In Motherwell, the ambulance control room log recorded a 999 call at 9.43 a.m., with ambulances dispatched from Callander at 9.44, Falkirk at 9.45 and two from Forth Valley Ambulance Service, based in Stirling, at 9.46.

The Stirling Royal Infirmary initiated its major incident protocol at 9.50 a.m., cleared space in the emergency room and called in additional off-duty staff. The hospital sent their own medical team at 10.10, while Falkirk Royal Infirmary also sent a surgical team.

The first ambulance arrived at the school at 9.57, followed by two more in the next ten minutes.

A team of doctors and a nurse from the health centre in Dunblane arrived at the school at 10.04 and were joined shortly afterwards by one of the centre's community nurses.

At 10.15, the first of multiple teams from the Stirling Royal Infirmary arrived and took over the process of triage. Each casualty was assessed and prioritised for dispatch based on their injuries.

In the storeroom, Harrild could see a bullet wound through the knuckle of her ring finger. She had been shot multiple times, but it was her chest wound that most worried her. She was terrified that she was going to die. She kept thinking of her family: of Tony, her husband, and their children, Anthony, Andrew, Jennifer and Jack. The first face she remembered seeing was Linda Stewart, the nursery assistant. She told Linda she'd been shot in the chest and wasn't going to make it. She asked Linda to tell her family she loved them.

Linda looked at her and said, 'Tell them yourself.'

Soon, doctors from Harrild's own local surgery began treating her. She was lying on the floor beside the horse apparatus, her head against the wall. 'The doctors tore open the shirt I was wearing and started to tend to my chest wound,' she later said. When they tried to put a saline drip into her arm, she grabbed one of the doctor's ties and tugged, pleading for help. 'It seemed like ages before the ambulance arrived. I remember someone holding my drip and telling me to keep breathing and keep my eyes open.' She couldn't stop shaking and felt close to death, always conscious of the hole in her right arm. When she moved her hand away from it, blood 'poured out like a fountain'.

Mary Blake, in a state of delirium, had to be reassured twice that someone would look after her handbag. She was told repeatedly to hang in there.

The kitchen assistant suggested using the door at the bottom end of the gym's storeroom, which was always locked and blocked off by PE equipment, as the access point for the ambulance crew. She began moving the equipment, but there was a problem: in the way was a little wounded girl being comforted on a chair by one of the nursery teachers. Together they slid the chair backwards towards the gym and cleared the passageway.

When the paramedics first arrived, a female paramedic stayed with Blake and Harrild while her male partner went into the main hall. He quickly returned to say that there were more seriously injured victims in the hall who had to take priority.

John McEwan, the divisional manager of Forth Valley Ambulance Service, took the lead coordinating the ambulance response at the gym. An experienced medic who had worked in Lockerbie in the immediate hours after the bombing of Pan Am Flight 103 in 1988, he was faced with an emotion he had never experienced on the job: a visceral desire for revenge. He wanted to mutilate the body of the gunman and had to force himself not to kick the corpse each time he walked past.

Most immediately shocking about the scene for McEwan were the stricken faces of the wounded children. Shock served, briefly, to cauterise their wounds. They didn't scream or cry but seemed only to stare uncomprehendingly at the bullet holes in their arms and legs.

As the paramedics were now on the scene, the kitchen assistant went out to the corridor between the gym and changing area, where a five-year-old boy with light brown hair was only just managing to stand by himself. He had two bullet wounds between his waist and buttocks. She lifted him up and carried him into the assembly hall, where she laid him down and covered him with a curtain, a jacket and eventually a doll's quilt taken from the school's nursery.

When more paramedics arrived, they treated the wounded teachers. Mary Blake's head wound meant they first had to fit a neck support and manoeuvre a stretcher underneath her, something which proved difficult in such a confined space. Blake was covered with a blanket, loaded into an ambulance and driven at speed to Stirling Royal Infirmary.

Among the many police officers in the gym hall, one of the first was Constable George Gunn, who had first met Hamilton on the island of Inchmoan and spent a few years as the target of his insults and accusations. His two children were pupils and, although he was off duty, he had heard about the incident and rushed to the scene. Gunn only found out his children were safe after first staring in horror at the inside of the gym.

———

The first ambulance left for Stirling Royal Infirmary at 10.15, eighteen minutes after arrival, with a single casualty, Mhairi MacBeath. She was triaged by doctors in casualty and assessed as beyond medical assistance. She died with a stranger by her side, sometime after 10.30 a.m.

At 10.18 a.m., a second ambulance left the school bound for Stirling Royal Infirmary with two patients. A third, also carrying two casualties, departed at 10.31.

At 10.54, one of the Forth Valley ambulance crew informed the control room that there had been twelve fatalities. Two minutes before, the control room had been advised that no further medical resources were required at the scene.

By 11 a.m., all the injured victims, including fourteen children, had been sent, at least initially, to Stirling Royal Infirmary. After examinations, some were then sent to Falkirk and District Royal Infirmary, while others were sent on to the Royal Hospital for Sick Children at Yorkhill in Glasgow for specialist treatment. The bullet in Coll Austin's back had exited into his head, breaking his jaw and fracturing his cheekbone. He had two collapsed lungs and broken ribs, but he was alive.

Harrild's journey to hospital was memorable. The shooting had heightened her senses. The noise in the ambulance was now deafening as the medics radioed updates; the smell of the paramedic's cigarette-stained fingers made her want to vomit. As they rattled along the motorway, he kept lifting off her oxygen mask and slapping her face to keep her conscious.

Too weak to speak, she could only lie on the stretcher thinking, 'Please don't hit me. I've just been shot.' As she began to feel warmer, the shaking subsided and she noticed the ambulance's sirens. 'The sirens are not for me', she thought. 'They can't be for me.'

Harrild was rushed into an emergency room. Her clothes were cut from her body, which was then examined by an A & E doctor. A minute later he came to her side and whispered that her injuries were serious but not life-threatening, and said, 'You are going to live.'

The *Daily Record*, the nation's largest-selling newspaper, prided itself on being first with the news. It received a call from a reader in Falkirk who had a scanner that picked up police and ambulance short-wave radios. He called the news desk to tell them an emotional officer was shouting, 'We've got dead children,' and requesting doctors and ambulances. The picture desk organised a helicopter, but before this could get there, the police announced a shutdown of the airspace in the local vicinity. A dozen photographers and thirteen reporters were dispatched to Dunblane, as well as the paper's features editor, who had children at the school.

At Stirling Sheriff Court, the reporter for Central Scotland News Agency found out something was wrong when the procurator fiscal announced that several court cases had been cancelled. An unspecified 'emergency' had detained all police officers who had been due in court to testify. Tim Bugler returned to the news agency's offices, where he called the Scottish Ambulance Service, who confirmed there had been a shooting at Dunblane Primary School. He put the first news story about the incident on the wires at 10.40 a.m.

Within minutes, dozens of reporters were driving to Dunblane, as were a fleet of TV news vans. British correspondents for the international press, headquartered in London, headed to Heathrow. The BBC sent dozens of reporters, camera crews, lighting technicians and a back-up generator. Kate Adie, the BBC's war correspondent, was told she might soon be required to fly to Scotland.

At the Scottish Office in Edinburgh a short briefing note was prepared: 'Details are still sketchy, but these are the latest: Dunblane Primary School near Stirling. A lone male gunman entered the school gym full of five- to six-year-olds at about 10 a.m. He fired a gun indiscriminately and it is believed thirteen are dead, including a teacher, and eight are injured. The gunman turned the gun on himself, but it is believed he is injured rather than dead. The injured have been taken to Stirling and Falkirk Infirmaries. The Secretary of State for Scotland will be at the scene at 13.30.'

Detective Superintendent Joseph Holden was in his office at Central Police Headquarters in Stirling when he was informed of a shooting at Dunblane Primary. Just twenty minutes later he was on the school premises.

Around the same time, Detective Chief Superintendent John Ogg, a thirty-year veteran of Central Police, had arrived and was appointed senior investigating officer by Chief Constable William Wilson. Ogg met with Holden in the gym hall and asked him to secure a cordon around the perimeter of the outer school grounds, with a second inner cordon enclosing the school buildings.

The chief constable had tactical command and sequestered an office in the school foyer, next to the main entrance, while they waited for a police incident caravan to arrive and be parked in the playground.

Holden was instructed to take personal responsibility for the care and welfare of the parents of any child who was a pupil in Gwen Mayor's Primary 1 class. He was told that Mayor and many of her pupils were dead, but that identification of the dead and wounded had only just begun. His concern was how to best handle briefing all the parents who were already gathering at the school entrance.

On Holden's arrival he had spotted a large, detached stone villa on the east side of the school. Given its location, it fell within the outer cordon, so he approached the owner and asked if they would allow all the parents to gather in their home. They immediately agreed.

Holden walked down to the school gates, where a crowd of several hundred, mostly women, had gathered. Some were in their dressing gowns with a winter coat over them; others were pushing prams or buggies with babies, rosy-cheeked in the cold. All were in a state of confusion and gripped by fear. All had heard rumours of a shooting, of dead children. All were frantic that one of the victims could be their own child.

Among the worried crowd of parents was Isabel MacBeath. She had been at home in Kilbryde Crescent preparing to attend her husband's memorial service at Stirling University. Her mother had agreed to babysit Catherine, who was asleep in her buggy in the front porch, but hadn't yet arrived when the phone rang. It was Barbara, her friend who lived in Dunkeld, asking if everything was okay.

Barbara explained that there were reports of a gunman loose in Dunblane Primary. Isabel thanked her for the call and concern but didn't believe a word of it. When she went to the porch to check on Catherine, however, who was asleep in her buggy, she could see that the street was filled with people running towards the school. When she opened the front door she saw Liz, a member of her babysitting circle, who shouted that there was a gunman in the school. Still Isabel remained calm. Without waiting for her mother to arrive to babysit, she grabbed her jacket, pushed the buggy outside and even locked the front door before joining the throng of mothers surging up the road.

Joanna Ross's mother Pam was at home playing with Alison, who was four months old, when her brother called from Dundee. Had she heard about the shooting at a primary school in Dunblane?

She immediately called the school and then the police. Both were engaged. Pam then called her mother-in-law, who came across to babysit Alison while Jimmy and Pam drove towards the crowded school gates.

The mass of parents was asked to follow a police escort up to the house near the school. In a few minutes every ground floor room was packed with anxious parents, whom the host made diligent efforts to comfort with cups of tea. Dozens more were gathered in the garden. Among the anxious parents inside was Judy Murray, who had been swept along in the crowd. She had been in her mother's toyshop when a co-worker answered the phone and was told by her daughter that the radio was reporting a shooting at Dunblane Primary; that a man with a gun was in the playground.

When Holden arrived, he first spoke to the parents gathered outside, unaware the media were behind the garden's stone wall. Then he went into the house and spoke to the parents crowded onto the stairs, standing by the windows and crammed into the kitchen. He said that there had been a shooting incident, that a man had entered the gymnasium and discharged a firearm, that there had been both fatalities and casualties, and that the only class affected was Class 1/13, taught by Gwen Mayor. For the majority there was a wave of relief; for a small group there was anxiety and anguish.

Among the commotion, one parent asked Holden if it was true that twelve children were dead. He said he couldn't confirm the figure but would return soon with more information; arrangements were being made to transport the parents affected to a second house. He left Detective Sergeant Alan Moffat, who had arrived from the Family Liaison Unit at Bannockburn Police Station and was waiting in the corridor, to look after them.

The parents of Mrs Mayor's class were then escorted by police, in full view of the gathered television cameras, across the road to a second house, in which nurses and members of the clergy were waiting to comfort them.

Shortly before 11 a.m., Mick North left his laboratory in the science block at Stirling University and walked across the snow-covered grounds to the Macrobert Arts Centre. When he got back to his office, an agitated colleague told him he'd received a call from a student and wanted to know if Mick had heard about a shooting at Dunblane Primary. Mick's automatic response was to rationalise: if it was serious, someone would have phoned him. After all, the school had his office number for emergencies. He checked. There was nothing on his answering machine. He then tried calling the police station in Dunblane, but the line was busy.

Mike and Sylvia, who worked in the same department, offered North a lift, as Mike also had a child at the school. As they drove from Bridge of Allan and up the hill towards Dunblane, he thought that it would all be fine, that it would be someone else's child, not Sophie. The school had more than six hundred pupils; the odds were firmly in his favour.

Sylvia turned off the bypass at the top of Doune Road, but her car was immediately obstructed by a police roadblock. Mick and Mike got out of the car, told police that they both had children in the school and were told to go the Westlands Hotel, another liaison point for parents. On arrival at the hotel, they were each given what appeared to be a numbered cloakroom ticket.

In the lobby, Mick spotted a parent, Olwen, whose child had attended nursery with Sophie, and they sat together. Olwen was Sophie's nursery teacher and had helped to look after North's young daughter during his wife's declining health and in the months after Barbara's death. He was thankful to be with her.

Ten minutes later, a police officer came into the hotel and informed the group that the incident involved only one class and that any parent whose child attended Mrs Mayor's Primary 1 class should walk down Doune Road to Cairnbaan, a large, detached villa beside the school, where they would receive further information.

On the walk down, North was in a daze. He was aware of the gathering media, including photographers with telephoto lenses aimed at the school. On arrival at Cairnbaan, he accepted a cup of tea from the owner and looked around, recognising at least three sets of parents with children in Sophie's class. The police were uncommunicative. Everyone seemed to know that twelve children were dead, but no one in authority could – or would – confirm it.

When the families were told they were being moved to the main school building via minibuses, North was annoyed, thinking they could walk in seconds if the police would only clear a path. The first minibuses took social workers; the second the first group of parents. North was on the third bus, whose driver had problems negotiating the tight corner into the school drive and so parked next to the press photographers.

By 12.30 p.m., all the parents had been escorted along the corridors to the staffroom, a quiet beige room with worn armchairs, a couple of sofas and a wooden table. An atheist, North could take no comfort from the black-clad clergy, moving between the parents, 'silently touching us on the shoulder'. (He would later write: 'It was as if the angels of death had arrived.') Once all the parents were inside the staffroom, Holden closed the door and went back to the temporary operations room for an update.

The news was not good. No one had a complete and accurate list of every child in the class and, most importantly, who was alive and being treated in one of four local hospitals. The school had only one phone line, which seemed persistently engaged with desperate parents. Communication with the Casualty Bureau set up at Stirling Royal Infirmary was almost impossible. In 1996, those few people who had a mobile phone discovered that the Vodafone network was also overloaded.

Inside the school, the parents were in a state of purgatorial ignorance. Outside, William Wilson, the chief constable, had already announced to the world's media the grim facts as he then knew them. 'There's thirteen children dead at the moment, two adults and a number of children in hospital. We're obviously having a tremendous business sorting out who's who and what's what, and please bear with us.' When asked where the attack had taken place, Wilson said it was the gymnasium. To a follow-up question enquiring if a suspect was in custody, he replied that it was 'different to that'. He added that he could say no more until the families of the victims had been informed.

Officers at Stirling Royal Infirmary managed to use mobile phones to speak to the police at the school. The names of those injured and in hospital were fed through slowly in batches of two or three names at a time.

Kenny Ross was at work in Livingston when he was called to the site office later that morning. At first, he was told he needed to go home as something had happened to his daughter, but when he spoke to his supervisor he was told that this was a mistake, he shouldn't have been told that much, and that he needed to get back to Dunblane. Concerned Kenny might not be fit to drive, the supervisor arranged for him to be driven home. Unable to reach the school, Kenny walked the last 300 yards through the gathered crowds. At the gate he met the man for whom he had been best man at his wedding, and his wife, who said, 'We're awful sorry, Kenny.' 'Sorry for what?' he asked. At that, she led him by the arm up to a policeman and told the officer, 'This is one of the parents.' Still confused, Kenny was thinking, 'Aren't we all parents? It's a school.' He was led through the gate and up to the school, where he was reunited with Pam in the staffroom.

Kenny knew several of the parents and when he saw Willie Turner, with whom he regularly played golf, both men exchanged nods but few words. All he could do was keep an eye on the clock.

Detective Superintendent Holden had decided it was important for the wounded children's parents to be told as soon as possible. He asked for specific parents to step outside and broke the news to them, having first arranged for a police car, or in some cases an ambulance, to be waiting at the school entrance, doors open and engine running. More than one couple ran down the corridor.

In the hour between 12.30 and 1.30 p.m., all these parents were informed of their child's location and transported at high speed to either the Stirling Royal Infirmary, Falkirk and District Royal Infirmary or Yorkhill children's hospital in Glasgow. In the staffroom, those parents who remained could only wait. The exact length of time they waited would become a matter of bitter debate.

The clergy, members of school staff and the local GPs in attendance had been given strict instructions to tell the parents nothing. If anyone needed the bathroom, they were escorted by a police officer. Isabel MacBeath had baby Catherine on her lap and was concerned that she had no disposable nappies with her. At one point, she became so agitated and frustrated that she tried to leave the staffroom. A uniformed police officer said in a cold manner that if she tried to leave it would be a 'problem' and that they had the power to 'detain' her. She sat back down.

Even packed with almost fifty people, the room was silent. Hardly anyone spoke; if they did, it was in a whisper. Kathryn Morton, whose daughter Emily was close friends with North's daughter, Sophie, looked at him and thought North would be spared. He couldn't possibly have lost his daughter and his wife, she thought. Sophie would be safe, and by extension Emily would be too.

As Mick North would later reflect: 'Every parent will on occasion experience those awful sensations in the pit of the stomach when you feel there is something wrong with your child. I used to have them in the late evening if Sophie cried out from her bedroom, disturbed by a dream. I'd go upstairs in a cold sweat only to find her settling back to sleep again. There are also those heart-rending times when your child is sobbing as if nothing in the world could ever make things better. Yet somehow something always does. And then there are those other moments of more concern, instances of real danger, often over before you have had time to react, but which leave you shaking afterwards. I remember one when a waitress in a restaurant stumbled next to our table and nearly poured boiling water over Sophie. None of those experiences had equipped me for dealing with the emotion of sitting and waiting for news that could mean my daughter was severely traumatised, permanently handicapped or dead. In the end, thinking through the awful possibilities had numbed all feeling, and the fact that my friends must have been working through those same possibilities was of no help. Quite the opposite. We said supportive words to one another, but these weren't getting through to the places inside where they were needed. There was no comfort.'

The police had asked for the names of every child in Gwen Mayor's class. This list was then separated into two: the living and the dead. Yet there were problems from the beginning. The police had not stopped to ask each child's name and record it on a central list before they were taken to hospital. Like all teachers, Gwen Mayor took a morning register each day to record who was present and absent. However, as the class had been going straight from assembly to their gym hall, no register had yet been taken.

They started with the most up-to-date class register, which recorded thirty-four pupils in the class, but they did not know if it was accurate for this given day. Each child had their own school identification card with their parents' contact address and telephone number, but the cards did not include a photograph.

Each time a child was identified as either alive and in hospital or dead, their card was handed to the police officer tasked with collating the lists.

As headmaster of such a large primary school, Ron Taylor couldn't hope to know the names of every child in his care. And with Mayor dead, and Blake and Harrild in hospital, it was necessary for him to turn to other teachers for support. With the help of his deputy head, two nursery class teachers and the nursery nurse, Taylor set about the terrible task of putting names to small bodies.

After the doctors had personally examined them and confirmed the death of each child in the gym hall, Taylor and his colleagues were escorted back to see if they could recognise each child's face. They now knew that the fifteen children still in the gym were dead.

Identification was attempted by examining the name tags on their gym clothes, gently lifting the children where necessary. Unfortunately, not every child's clothes had been labelled, while the name on one girl's tag was illegible. This pushed Taylor to breaking point, and he was taken back to his office to recover.

The team were close to compiling the full list when a major problem emerged: the name of one child was on both lists. The police took the decision that this meant both lists were not to be trusted. The child's whereabouts was finally confirmed after three separate phone calls to the hospital, where doctors were able to consult a label on his shoe. He was not dead in the gym, but alive in the hospital.

At around 1 p.m., the police and teachers were finally confident they had the names of the living, dead and wounded. Taylor was too distraught, so three other teachers were joined by a senior officer and a police photographer for the final viewing, during which each person agreed on the individual identifications and watched as the bodies were labelled with a numbered piece of paper.

NUMBER 2:   Melissa Currie
NUMBER 3:   Charlotte Dunn

NUMBER 4:   Sophie North
NUMBER 5:   Hannah Scott
NUMBER 6:   Abigail McLennan
NUMBER 7:   Joanna Ross
NUMBER 8:   Emily Morton
NUMBER 9:   Megan Turner
NUMBER 10: John Petrie
NUMBER 11: Ross Irvine
NUMBER 12: David Kerr
NUMBER 13: Kevin Hasell
NUMBER 14: Victoria Clydesdale
NUMBER 15: Gwen Mayor
NUMBER 16: Emma Crozier
NUMBER 17: Brett McKinnon

Thomas Hamilton had been designated 'Body Number 1' by police.

The first family member to be informed was Rod Mayor, Gwen's husband. He had arrived at the school around 1 p.m., where he was met at the main entrance by DS Moffat, who brought him into the school library. Mayor had heard news reports on the car radio that a teacher was dead and asked if this was his wife. Moffat refused to say.

Mayor told the detective that he wanted confirmation, that he needed to call his nineteen-year-old daughter in London with an update. He said his daughter was hysterical with fear, and that she should find out what had happened from her father, not a report on the television.

Debbie Mayor, meanwhile, was in Holloway, North London, in the small room she rented in the terraced house of a Cypriot couple: a doctor and his wife, who were expecting their second child. She had been drying her hair, getting ready to go into university, when she heard the news on the radio. She had a phone in her room and called her dad. He didn't pick up. She then tried the school and was able to get straight through to reception and asked to speak to her mum, but the secretary only directed her to the helpline. When she asked to speak to her mum's friend and fellow Primary 1 teacher Claire McLeod, she was again told to call the helpline.

During the call, Debbie's landlady picked up the landline to make a call and heard the anxiety in her lodger's voice. She came upstairs to check what was wrong. They then both watched the television news coverage of panicked parents gathering outside the school gates downstairs in the living room.

For more than thirty minutes, Rod Mayor was told he would have an update in 'just five minutes'. He decided that if no one told him by 1.30 what had happened, he was leaving. He would find out himself. When 1.30 passed, he told the policeman at the door that he was going outside to speak to the media. A few minutes later, DS Moffat returned. It had taken him fifteen minutes to find and speak to DS Holden, who had the most accurate information on fatalities and casualties.

'Is it the worst scenario?' Mayor asked. The detective still refused to confirm or deny his wife's death. Mayor said again that he would leave and speak to the media. They must know by now. Only then did the detective say, 'In that case, Mr Mayor, it is the worst scenario.'

All Mayor wanted to do now was call his daughters. He asked for access to a phone but was told none were available. He said he'd go and use the phone in his car. 'In that case, there is a telephone,' the policeman said. It was in the library, a few feet from where he had been sitting.

It was 2.10 when Mayor called Debbie, and she picked up instantly.

The first word he said to his daughter was 'Deborah' – he always used her full name when it was serious. She was standing in the hall, at the bottom of the stairs, cradling a large white plastic phone. He then said simply, 'It's your mum.'

The couple's other daughter, Esther, had originally travelled to Stirling Royal Infirmary before being redirected back to the primary school, where she was waiting in the staffroom, unaware her dad was in a neighbouring room.

Between 1.15 and 1.40 p.m., Detective Holden was told that a final visit to the gym hall had been made by three teachers and a lead detective. Each child had now been named and numbered, and everyone was confident the identifications were correct. There would be no mistakes, which was everyone's gravest concern.

Holden had already planned how to break the news. Each child's parents would be appointed two police officers and the support of a social worker, which would comprise a family liaison team. Each family would be informed, in private, in a different room, which meant he had to find sixteen empty classrooms.

At 1.40, Holden briefed the assembled family liaison teams, a total of forty-eight police officers and social workers. They were to explain clearly what had happened, then take the parents home and stay with the family as long as they wanted them to, overnight if necessary. Those who wished to see their child in the gym were to be told this was not possible, that it was a crime scene and could not be disturbed. Arrangements would be made for them to formally identify their child later that day. Once everything was finally in place, Holden walked slowly down the corridor to the staffroom.

Holden knew Hamilton. For five months, between July and September 1991, as head of the child protection unit, he had been briefed on the ongoing investigation into the gunman. He had sat opposite him in his living room for more than two hours conducting a police interview. He was aware of attempts by his fellow detectives to have Hamilton's firearms licence revoked, as well as the deputy chief constable's reluctance to do so.

Now, he was seconds away from breaking the heart of every parent in the staffroom. When he arrived, he called out the name of the first parents and asked them to step outside. Slowly, the staffroom began to empty.

According to Holden's final report, the last parents were taken out of the room at 2.30 p.m. The parents said it had been 3.30 p.m.

At least North was not alone; Olwen stayed by his side. Her daughter Lowri was in Primary 4 and she assumed was safe. He asked what time Primary 1 usually finished. 'It's probably about now,' Olwen said. His watch said 2.40 p.m., and North remembers thinking that this was the time Sophie was born. For over an hour, parents had been called out one couple at a time. Then he heard a call for the North family.

Standing at the door of the staffroom were three people: Elspeth, a social worker, John, a uniformed constable, and Derek, a plain-clothes police constable. He and Olwen joined them and together they walked out of the school and across the playground to one of the wooden huts, an empty classroom, where they sat down.

'Mr and Mrs North,' said Derek in a formal manner. North interrupted to explain that he was a widower, and that his friend Olwen had kindly waited with him.

The constable began again and said simply that there had been a shooting in the school, that sixteen children and two adults had been killed. North had been expecting the word 'twelve', but when he heard 'sixteen' he knew instantly that Sophie was dead. In a final desperate attempt to play the odds he had added up the number of parents in the staffroom and taken solace in the disparity between twelve children and sixteen sets of parents. Maybe four families would be lucky. But no. Derek told them that the teacher Gwen Mayor was dead, as was the shooter, who he did not name.

North responded with devastating grief and burning anger. With controlled fury he told Derek, Elspeth and John how awful the wait had been. Both police officers and the social worker could only agree and said that they had waited over an hour after being told they would be breaking the news to the North family while the police made final preparations and secured classrooms. North's daughter had died at around 9.37 a.m. He was told more than five hours later.

Kenny and Pam Ross were the penultimate parents to be told. They were led on a circuitous route through the school to a small room resembling a store cupboard. Once seated, their family liaison officer asked if they had a preference for who should break the news. Pam, now barely able to restrain herself, simply pleaded to be told something by anyone. And so they did. Kenny couldn't believe that his daughter was gone, and so many other children too. At one point, struggling to comprehend, he said: 'Did he have a fuckin' machine gun?'

After a few minutes, the couple were taken out of the school by a back entrance and driven the short distance home. As Pam and Kenny walked up the flagstone path, their next-door neighbour came up to ask if Joanna was okay. Kenny, unable to speak, could only shake his head and look down. His neighbour collapsed to his knees.

Kenny's parents and Pam's mum were in the house. When Kenny told his dad that Joanna was dead, he feared his dad would drop dead on the spot. Grandfather and granddaughter were very close. He would take Joanna to school each morning because Pam and Kenny were usually already at work. He had been the last to see Joanna as he waved her off at the school gates hours earlier. On their daily walk, he always offered her a Polo mint and that day she had said to keep it for later. (The Polo remained with him for the rest of his life, kept in a small silver box.)

Before the couple arrived home the front door bell had rang. It was a female reporter, who Pam's mother quickly sent away. 'How could they know?' thought Kenny when told. 'How could they possibly know so soon.'

In a state of stunned bewilderment, Mick North walked the icy streets. Elspeth the social worker walked beside him, but neither spoke. When they arrived home, Elspeth put on the kettle and North checked his answering machine. There were dozens of messages. Listening to the calls of Sophie's grandparents, his sister, his friends, each message became more desperate as the news developed and 'an incident' became 'a shooting' and twelve children became sixteen. North tried to call his family, but the town's phone lines seemed to have collapsed.

The first thing Isabel MacBeath saw when she opened her front door was Mhairi's school shoes. Her daughter had worn wellingtons to school on account of the snow. She immediately picked them up, walked into the kitchen and threw them in the bin. Her family liaison police officer would later say he had never been so shocked in his life. Privately, he considered the act callous. To Isabel, it was her first conscious act of survival. She knew she couldn't look at those small shoes at the bottom of the stairs each day, knowing Mhairi would never again put them on.

George Robertson had been in a meeting at Millbank Tower, headquarters of the Labour Party, when his pager alerted him to call his office. He used the phone in the outside corridor and his staff said there were vague reports of a shooting in a school in Dunblane. His daughter attended Dunblane High School. He briefly returned to the meeting, explained what he had been told and said he was returning home.

He went downstairs to his office and tried to call his wife, Sandra, but she didn't pick up and so he called the high school. When he managed to get through, he was relieved to hear that nothing had happened there, but chilled to be told there were reports of a shooting at the primary school. After hanging up, he was beginning to organise a plane ticket when the Scottish Secretary's office called. Michael Forsyth was heading north. A car to Heathrow would be leaving from the House of Commons' members' entrance. He grabbed his papers and ran down the stairs.

At the entrance to Parliament, the chauffeur-driven, dark blue ministerial car had its engine running. The passenger door was held open and Robertson, breathless, climbed inside. Forsyth was already seated, his face grey and concerned.

An edge had long existed between Robertson and Forsyth, one regularly sharpened by verbal jousts at the Dispatch Box in the House of Commons. And as Forsyth's shadow and political adversary, Robertson's job was to spend his every waking hour figuring out ways to undermine, embarrass and humiliate both Forsyth's character and his political party. In private, Robertson had never once used his opponent's first name. After today, he would never again use his surname.

As the car pulled out past the black portcullis gates of Parliament and began the hour-long drive to Heathrow, Forsyth updated Robertson on the latest information from Central Scotland Police. A gunman had entered the school and several children were dead: at least eight or nine, with others badly injured.

At the airport, the two men, who were also travelling with Forsyth's private secretary, Michael Lugton, immediately went to the British Airways executive lounge, where their fellow passengers had gathered around the television to watch live coverage from Dunblane.

During their flight, Forsyth worked through ministerial papers as Lugton passed him regular updates. At one point, Lugton passed a folded piece of paper to Forsyth on which was written a single name: Thomas Hamilton. When Forsyth read it, he immediately felt like he had been hit with a brick. For a few seconds Forsyth thought of all their encounters over the years and what he might have missed, then the professional politician kicked in and ordered him to focus on the task at hand. He turned to Robertson and said that he was about to show him something in complete confidence, and warned him that it was 'going to come as a bit of a shock to you'. Robertson opened the note and said, 'Jesus.'

The three men were picked up by an official car on the airport tarmac. They then sped towards Stirling with two police motorbikes as outriders. On the M80 motorway, updates confirmed that Hamilton was dead, but the number of fatalities had risen. By the time they arrived in the office of Chief Constable Wilson at Central Police Headquarters, Wilson confirmed the deaths of sixteen children and one teacher. The men were briefed by the police and the procurator fiscal.

A press conference was scheduled for 3.30 p.m., but first Forsyth, as Secretary of State for Scotland, wished to visit the school with Robertson. As they arrived, Robertson focused on the sign WELCOME TO OUR SCHOOL, thinking how many times he had been through the doors for parents' evenings, concerts or the annual school fete. Today, it was a school transformed, the corridors peopled with teachers, their faces white with shock. They spoke to Ron Taylor, who gave a graphic description of what had happened and the staff's response.

Wilson asked the politicians if they wished to go into the gym. Teachers, janitors, nursery staff, paramedics, doctors and police officers had all witnessed what had been done; should the nation's elected politicians be spared? Wilson may not have thought so, but at least he offered both men the opportunity to decline. He stressed that it wasn't going to be easy, but as people responsible for shaping public policy, for writing the laws of the land, perhaps it was right. Forsyth immediately said, 'Yes, of course,' and for many years afterwards thought he had been too rash.

The men went no further than a few feet into the gym. 'It is a picture that remains etched in my mind forever,' Robertson later said. He managed to contain his emotions (he would break down later at home), but Forsyth began to weep uncontrollably, and he took several minutes to recover his composure. The sight of so much blood and small bodies, so many small bodies, would never leave him. As he looked around, he thought about the shooting at Hungerford and felt a crushing sense of responsibility.

At around 3.30 p.m., a press conference began in one of the rooms at Victoria Hall, where a hastily prepared press centre had been set up. Sitting at a table before a bank of microphones and tape recorders was Chief Constable Wilson, with Forsyth to his left and Robertson to his right. The identity of the gunman had not yet been officially released to the media. Forsyth said, 'I cannot find the words to express what has happened here today. Our thoughts are with the families of the children who have died and members of staff at the school. This is a close-knit community where everyone knows everyone else, and the impact will be felt in every household as it will across the whole country.'

Robertson was on the verge of tears as he described the shooting as 'an act of unspeakable brutality and woe ... I am bound to know many of the casualties and the parents concerned and know how devastated they are. I saw parents in grief, and I don't think I will ever forget it ... Michael Forsyth and I are used to being adversaries, but we stand totally united behind this community that has been devastated.'

Forsyth described Ron Taylor as 'a hero in circumstances which would have felled many other people', while the chief constable added that the headmaster had been 'an enormous tower of strength to staff and children in the school'.

The rest of the school's parents had waited for their children for two to three hours. The police had to coordinate the release of each class to ensure no child caught a glimpse of the crime scene. In the crush of parents, tempers flared. Parents shouted desperately for their children. Eventually they were allowed into the school and parents queued along the corridors, distracted by the paintings on the walls. A small cloakroom had dozens of jackets still hanging on the hooks.

It was mid afternoon by the time Judy Murray was reunited with her boys. She hugged them tighter than ever before. Both boys had been told to hide under their tables, and they had then been entertained with songs and games by teachers anxious to keep their pupils as calm as possible. All they had been told was that a man with a gun had got into the school.

On the drive home, Judy pulled over and turned to speak to the boys. Although it would be another six hours before the identity of the killer was confirmed and released to the media, it was already common knowledge on the streets of Dunblane. As the boys knew Hamilton, she didn't want them to hear it from anyone else.

After she broke the news, Jamie remained quiet. He would never speak of it again. Andy wanted to know why Mr Hamilton hadn't just killed himself. Later, Andy would think about how a man capable of mass murder had been in the family car, sitting next to his mum.

———

Five hundred members of the press and broadcast media had now descended on a town with a population of just eight thousand, with more arriving every hour from all over the world. At a second press conference in the evening, Inspector Louis Munn, who had been drafted in from Strathclyde Police, read out the names of each dead child and their age in a long litany many of the assembled journalists found difficult to endure.

The identity of the gunman was officially released by police at 9 p.m. When Agnes called her son, worried he hadn't called her the night before as usual, the telephone at Kent Road was answered by a police officer. Agnes's father, James Hamilton, was sitting with friends in the Thistle Centre in Stirling when he heard about the shooting, but it was not until he was visited later by two reporters asking for a photograph that it dawned on him that his grandson was the person responsible.

Thomas Watt, Hamilton's natural father, was tracked down by the *Daily Record* in Barlanark in Glasgow. A retired bus driver, he explained that he had not seen his son since he was eighteen months old. He said he was 'sorry that I planted the seed that created him'.

———

A family friend in Bridge of Allan secured Debbie Mayor a seat on the evening flight from Heathrow to Scotland. Deborah's landlord drove her, her best friend and her boyfriend to the airport. The flight was a blur. She was staring out of the window at the clouds and inky blackness of the night sky when an attendant leaned over to say that the crew were aware she was flying under 'very difficult circumstances' and to let them know if she needed anything. The two ladies sitting beside her in the row ordered her a gin and tonic. When the plane touched down, all the passengers were asked to remain seated and Debbie was allowed to disembark first. Her dad and a police officer were waiting in the reception hall.

The ancient cathedral, whose oldest stones dated back almost a thousand years, opened its heavy wooden doors in the evening for private prayers. The pews were quietly filled with residents whose heads were bowed in mourning or at times shaking with bewilderment. Lit candles flickered in the darkness of the nave.

The bodies were moved to the Stirling Royal Infirmary, where the families would identify their children. They were invited to attend from 10 p.m. onwards, with visits going on into the small hours as the same room was used for each visit.

Mick North, who had dropped off Sophie at 8.20 a.m. at her preschool club, saw his daughter shortly before midnight. He was told she had died instantly. She had been shot five times: in the head and chest, the hand, the buttock and the leg.

As Isabel MacBeath had baby Catherine to care for, her niece and nephew, who were both doctors, attended the Royal Infirmary on her behalf. After viewing the body, they advised Isabel against attending; Mhairi had been shot in the head.

When the curtains were drawn back, Kenny Ross had never seen his wife move so fast nor cry so hard. Pam seemed to pounce towards Joanna, though they had to argue in order to simply touch her.

The last family members to go into the room, after midnight, were Rod Mayor and his two daughters. His wife's body lay behind a sheet of glass, the glass covered by velvet curtains. When the curtains were opened, the first thing Rod thought was that Gwen resembled a nun. A white sheet covered her head wounds and there was a white patch on her eye. A second white sheet covered the rest of her body. Only her face was visible. Ron asked if he could go behind the glass screen. He wanted to kiss Gwen goodbye; only then could he accept that she was gone. 'When I kissed her,' he said, 'she was cold.'

A dozen wounded children lay in hospitals' intensive care units. Coll Austin had been flown by air ambulance to Yorkhill Hospital in Glasgow. Surgeons had removed four bullets from his foot, back and arm. His parents Joe and Rona were on either side of the bed, which looked so big while their son appeared so small. Each held a hand. Coll was intubated. When he woke up three days later and found himself unable to speak, he pulled one of his hands out from his parent's light grip and carefully began to curl his bottom three fingers into his palm. He then thrust his thumb upright like a gun's hammer and extended his index finger like a barrel.

He turned the 'gun' on himself, then began jabbing at his bandaged chest. The effort and the memory were too much, and he became so upset and tearful that the doctor stepped in to administer sedation, returning him briefly to a gentle sleep.

After

VI

THE CABINET MEETING

EVERY Thursday morning at 10.30 a.m., the various Secretaries of State gather in the Cabinet Room of 10 Downing Street. On 14 March 1996, there was a last-minute addition to the agenda, listed as the third item under Home Affairs: 'Shooting Incident at Dunblane Primary School'.

Over the next two hours, the Conservative government of John Major appeared to collectively agree that little, or preferably nothing at all, should be done in the light of the murder of sixteen young children and their teacher. Known as the 'party of hunting and shooting', the government's primary concern appeared to be the rights of the nation's gun owners rather than the young victims of legal firearms.

Twenty-two ministers were present, as well as the prime minister and a further six senior civil servants. Before the meeting, Michael Forsyth and the Lord Chancellor had met with Major to discuss the shootings and the recommended government response.

Forsyth was aware that under the Fatal Accidents and Sudden Deaths Inquiry (Scotland) Act of 1976, an inquiry would have to be held, but also that under such horrendous circumstances this alone would not suffice. He believed that only a public inquiry chaired by a senior High Court judge would meet public approval. In the early nineties, as Minister of State at the Department of Employment, Forsyth had been responsible for implementing the changes in safety case legislation recommended by Lord Cullen after his public inquiry into the Piper Alpha oil platform disaster of 6 July 1988, in which 167 men had been killed. He respected Cullen's calm manner and forensic mind though the final decision on appointment was made by David Hope, as Lord President and Scotland's most senior judge.

Forsyth, who had barely slept, had taken the first flight back to London on Thursday morning and was at Downing Street before 9 a.m.

In Cabinet, he began with a brief precis of the previous day's events. He also gave a short summary of Hamilton's background, describing him as a 'man of forty-three who had held a firearm certificate which included provision for the two revolvers and two pistols which were the weapons used in the incident'.

He stated that Hamilton had 'no history of mental instability', but that he had been known to the police, laying out his disputes with the Boy Scouts, allegations of improper conduct with boys, and that he had set up and run his own boys' clubs for several years. Forsyth said the gunman had also been known to both George Robertson and himself and that he had been involved in the man's 'energetic campaign to clear his name' of allegations of child abuse. The police had investigated his behaviour over many years, he said, but there had been insufficient evidence to charge him, and at the time of the shooting he had had no criminal record.

Forsyth said he and the Lord Chancellor agreed that only a public inquiry would be acceptable to the people of Scotland and

THE CABINET MEETING

Britain, who would demand answers to their questions about the current adequacy of firearms controls and security in schools. He then recommended that the government approach Lord Cullen.

Cullen would not be able to direct an inquiry himself. Instead the Lord Advocate would be responsible for leading the Crown's evidence and have an important advisory role. He would ensure that it had a clear focus and direction and help it progress as speedily as possible. With the approval of the prime minister and Cabinet Forsyth planned to announce his plans in the House of Commons that afternoon.

The subject of the shooting was then opened to Cabinet discussion, with Michael Howard, as Home Secretary, taking a vocal lead. The Cabinet minutes record a key point: 'The incident did not suggest a need for substantive change to firearms law.'

The official minutes continue: 'Although there would undoubtedly be strong pressure for a high-level judicial inquiry, there was a danger that it would become a focus for those who argued that firearms controls should be tightened further and that school security should be enhanced well beyond what would be sensible.

'The incident did not suggest a need for substantive change to firearms law. What had happened in Dunblane was the kind of tragedy against which no society could insure completely. There was a risk that the judge in charge of the inquiry would come under pressure to make recommendations which would be unwelcome to the Government but would be hard to resist. Although the incident had occurred in Scotland, the underlying issues were ones which affected the whole country.'

At the beginning of the meeting, the prime minister and many of the Cabinet were firmly against a public inquiry, but Forsyth proved persuasive. At the end of the discussion, the prime minister summed up the government's position. He believed appointing a High Court judge to lead the inquiry was 'by no means free of risk', and he shared the reservations of several of his Cabinet members, but he said that the circumstances demanded an appropriate response.

Leaving the meeting, Forsyth was relieved to have persuaded the prime minister to agree to a public inquiry but privately concerned at his colleagues' resistance to changes to firearms legislation. They had not seen what he had seen less than twenty-four hours before. For them the matter of gun control remained political; some were keen wielders of shotguns and had constituents who were avid target marksmen. For Forsyth, the tightening of Britain's gun laws and a ban on all handguns was now deeply personal.

In the pale light of a winter's morning, as George Robertson sat in the back seat of a taxi bound for Glasgow airport, he looked out at a town transformed by the arrival of the world's media. The cobbled streets were now lined by rows of trucks with external generators and satellite dishes fixed to their roof. Reporters from CNN and ABC were delivering pieces to camera to their audiences in America; NHK were broadcasting to Japan; and somewhere among the media village was the crew from Australian television who had been anxious to secure Robertson's early-morning appearance.

On the flight, Robertson began to draft a short speech to the House of Commons. Around him, businesspeople in suits wiped tears from their eyes as they read the morning newspapers. *The Herald* and the *Daily Record* had quoted the Bible in their headlines – SLAUGHTER OF THE INNOCENTS – each devoting twenty pages to the shooting. The image printed on the front page of almost every daily newspaper in Britain and around the world was the school photograph of Class 13B, a class of children smiling into a future half of them would now never see.

In the spirit of partnership developed over the previous day, Robertson met with Forsyth to show him his speech, and the Secretary of State gave him an advance copy of his own statement, which he would be making to the House that afternoon.

The prime minister had a fundraising dinner at the Hilton Hotel in Glasgow scheduled for Friday, and it was obvious he would also now visit Dunblane. Yet George Robertson, after discussions with Forsyth, was adamant that the community would welcome both leaders and told Tony Blair he should clear his diary and prepare to travel north. However, Blair was conscious not to attract accusations of 'playing politics' at such a time and insisted he would only attend if John Major asked him.

In the Leader of the Opposition's office in the House of Commons, Robertson reiterated his position to Blair, who again made the point that he did not wish to impose himself without the prime minister's consent. Robertson called Forsyth, who agreed to speak to Major. The issue was briefly set aside during Prime Minister's Questions, which focused on the response to the shooting.

George Robertson wore a black tie as he rose to speak in the Commons. 'No one will have wakened today not hoping beyond hope that yesterday had been just a bad dream,' he told the assembled Members of Parliament. 'You don't need to have lived in the town of Dunblane or to have seen three children go through Dunblane Primary School to share the grief and the horror and the sheer desolation our town feels today. You just have to be a fellow human being.' On the issue of Thomas Hamilton, Robertson said: 'Those of us who met and distrusted Thomas Hamilton – and I myself argued with him in my own home – will ask ourselves until the grave if we did enough.'

Gun laws, he said, would have to be examined, as would school security. 'But that is not for today,' he added. 'Today the nation stands beside, and with, a community devastated by a unique and terrible act of evil.'

As Secretary of State for Scotland, Michael Forsyth announced that there would be a public inquiry into the shooting.

In his statement, John Major said he would be going to Dunblane tomorrow on behalf of the whole house.

Afterwards, Blair went to see Major, and the pair spoke privately for a few minutes. Major told him that Margaret Thatcher always wanted to do these 'tragedy visits', but that he personally was never comfortable with them and did not wish to make the political circus any larger than necessary. Blair pushed back and said that Forsyth, who was after all the prime minister's Secretary of State for Scotland, was insistent that the community wanted political support. 'He really doesn't want me to go, that much is clear,' Blair told Alastair Campbell, the Labour Party's director of communications. Blair didn't want to push the issue any further, but said that if Robertson and Forsyth were adamant that he and the prime minister visit together, they should both speak to Major.

Shortly before 5 p.m., Forsyth and Robertson secured a brief slot to speak with the prime minister at Downing Street. Their joint argument was that the entire community would appreciate a joint visit, that one VIP visit would be preferable to separate visits, and that the community needed the whole nation's support. 'If my judgement is proved wrong, you can sack me,' Forsyth ended by saying. Major then pointed to Robertson and said, 'Yes, but I can't sack him.'

Finally, Major was persuaded. Arrangements were made for the Labour leader and his team to accompany Major on the government's RAF plane. The prime minister even extended an invitation for Blair to join him for dinner at the Hilton in Glasgow, but Blair politely declined, having already agreed to stay with Robertson and his wife at their family home in Dunblane.

———

In Dunblane, Ron Taylor had agreed to speak in front of the world's press and camera crews. Dressed in a dark suit and tie and visibly shaken, he spoke with a simple eloquence: 'Evil visited us on Wednesday, and we don't know why. We don't understand, and I guess we never will.' He continued: 'I can't get the images out of my head yet. That will take some time. My colleagues and I tried to do what we could and tried to stem the blood. The children were traumatised. The ones who were injured but still conscious were distressed. We managed to get those out fairly quickly because it was just an appalling scene. The police arrived very quickly, and together we tried to identify those who were still alive and whose wounds could be treated, but there were so many of them.'

He said he felt 'totally helpless ... I was not really aware of what was happening. One grasped instantly that the guy was there and it was obvious what had taken place. But I was not prepared for what we found. The emergency services were just magnificent. They, too, had not faced anything like this before.'

However, Taylor insisted he was not a hero: 'It's unjustified. We all tried the best that we could together. There were other staff doing just as much as I did. I got my strength from them, and we got our strength from each other.' He said the term 'hero' was best suited to Gwen Mayor: 'Gwen was a highly respected, very experienced, lovely lady. The kids all loved her. We have lost a super colleague and a friend.'

At Robertson's family home, Blair and his Shadow Secretary of State for Scotland spent the morning discussing the question of devolution, before joining the prime minister in Stirling. All talk of the future was set aside when they arrived at the headquarters of Central Police for a briefing by Chief Constable William Wilson. In a grim, factual manner, Wilson explained how Hamilton had shot the children one by one. Alastair Campbell, who accompanied the group, felt Major was eager to speak and later recorded in his diary that the prime minister 'couldn't really find anything to match the enormity of what he'd just heard'. He enquired not about Hamilton's access to automatic handguns and military-grade ammunition but 18-certificate videotapes. The prime minister wanted to know if Hamilton watched violent videos. The chief constable said there was no evidence of this, to which Major replied, 'I know a lot of my colleagues are worried about videos.'

Major and Blair then made their way to Stirling Royal Infirmary, where fifty of the ambulance and medical staff were gathered in the hospital's conference room. Brenda Fleming, a consultant, told them that if someone had said, 'Stop filming, this is a Hollywood set', she 'would have believed them'. She told the two men: 'As I walked in, the teacher who had died and a little girl were lying at my feet. I went from body to body feeling pulses, seeing who was alive and who was dead. I was saying to the ambulanceman, "That child, that child, that child must go to the hospital first."'

Wilma Duggan, a senior nurse who lived in Dunblane, said that when the first call had come in everyone had been desperate for it to be a hoax. Then a second call had come through to say there had been at least twelve fatalities. 'It was just so awful,' she said. 'They were so wee and pale. Nothing could prepare me for what I saw.' Then she began to cry, unable to say any more.

Major and Blair moved from group to group, shaking hands and listening. 'I can't imagine the horrors you must have seen. You must be so strong. I just want to say how proud we are of you. I am sorry we have had to meet in these terrible circumstances,' Blair told one group. Then John Major, his wife Norma by his side, added, 'The nation is proud of you, we all feel your grief.'

After visiting the staff, the men went upstairs to meet with Eileen Harrild, Mary Blake and two boys who were also recovering from gunshot wounds. Matthew Birnie was so keen to meet the prime minister he jumped out of bed to be the first in line. The prime minister asked about his favourite toy. Blair talked football. For Harrild, still on powerful pain medication, it was a strange sight to see the prime minister by her bed and the Leader of the Opposition with tears in his eyes. The prime minister's delegation was an hour late departing for Dunblane.

Isabel MacBeath was invited to attend, and a car was arranged to carry her the short way to the school gates. As there was no one to look after the baby, Catherine came too, and so, wearing her

Paddington Bear-style duffel coat, flat shoes and leggings, Isabel found herself minutes later sitting in a room with the prime minister, his wife Norma and the Leader of the Opposition, Tony Blair (she was initially surprised by how tall John Major was). Also in the room was Chief Constable William Wilson.

Isabel didn't waste any time and explained that she had had to wait almost five hours to be told of her daughter's death. 'You knew my daughter was dead and you didn't tell me – why? You put me through four hours of not knowing.'

Major remained silent, but Norma stepped into the breach and turned to address the chief constable. She asked him why that was. Wilson turned red and remained silent.

Later, the politicians were shown into the gym hall, where they saw the bloodstains and the bullet holes. Major, Forsyth and Robertson entered first. Blair entered a little after them. The short delay was because he had taken time to write a letter. He had been so moved by Isabel's story that he had felt compelled to write to her (he would have spoken to her during the meeting but had felt unable to speak there for fear of undermining the prime minister). Within thirty minutes of Isabel's departure home, an aide arrived at her door with an envelope. It contained a handwritten letter from Blair explaining how shocked he had been at the delay that she and the rest of the families had endured. The letter would mean more to the young mother than he would ever know.

After finishing his letter, Blair was led into the gymnasium. He was confronted by the large pool of blood where Gwen Mayor had lain. Ron Taylor spoke to Alastair Campbell and said the images wouldn't go away. He said he doubted they ever would.

Major turned to Ron Taylor and said, 'We must tear it down.' Taylor replied, 'Will you give us the money?' Major then looked across at Michael Forsyth and said, 'Of course we will.' Taylor said, 'That man will not kill our school. Come back in a year's time and I'll show you what we have done.'

The politicians then went outside. On one side of the road was a sea of tributes, a long blanket of flowers and soft toys, sent from all over Britain, that stretched for almost a hundred feet. On the other side of the road, television crews from all over the world had gathered – sixty yards of photographers, camera crews and print journalists.

Outside the school gate, Major praised the courage of the residents: 'We have just had the opportunity over the last hour or so to meet the headmaster, his staff and many of the other people connected with the school to express our thanks to them for the way they have handled the appalling tragedy they have had to cope with in the last few days. I don't think it would ever be possible to put into words precisely what they had to deal with, and I think the way they have coped has been quite remarkable. The community and the school will need to pull together over the weeks and months ahead. But I think the strength and resilience I found in the school today suggests that hugely difficult task can be done.'

After laying bouquets among the floral tributes, the two men stepped across the road and addressed the cameras. Blair was distraught and struggled to maintain his composure. He said: 'We have seen the enormity of the evil act perpetrated at the school, but also the quite extraordinary courage of the staff and everyone connected to the school and community. We are both absolutely proud to have been here and paid our respects to them. This community has suffered so much and yet there is so much strength in it.'

Afterwards, Campbell felt compelled to needle Blair about his Christian faith, asking what 'his God thought of all this'. How could he see what they had seen today and still believe in a divine being? Blair replied along the lines of, 'Just because the killer is bad does not mean that God is not good.'

If the visit to Dunblane by Blair and Major was a masterclass in political diplomacy, then it was left to the royal family to demonstrate their tin ear to the times. On the same day as the two men's visit, the queen was opening the Royal Armouries Museum in Leeds. In her speech, she said, 'The weapons of war, which can be as beautiful as they are terrible, are often products of the very finest design and craftsmanship.' Then, speaking of the victims of Wednesday's shooting, she said, 'My heart goes out to each and every one, especially the families of those who were killed and injured. May their courage remain undimmed.'

The royal family were not alone in their apparent insensitivity; the behaviour of Chief Constable William Wilson and the senior command of Central Scotland Police was even more indelicate. Later that same evening, there was a knock on the door of Isabel MacBeath's home. The senior police officer walked into Isabel's living room and asked her male relatives to leave. Stanley, a friend of the family, stood his ground and stayed in the room. The officer wished to speak to Isabel, a widower and young mother grieving the murder of her young daughter, to forcefully dissuade her from any further public criticism of the police service.

Isabel would later recall his hectoring tone. She reports him saying words to the effect of, 'How dare you ask William Wilson a question in front of the prime minister. Back off.'

THE CABINET MEETING

Isabel picked up Catherine and began to breastfeed. The officer immediately moved back across the room. To Isabel's mind his repulsion at her maternal instinct was evident, and all she could think was, 'Good, that worked.' She had successfully pushed back against the police's attempt at intimidation – her personal space was firmly re-established. She would not be bullied. She would not back off.

The following day, Joanna's mother Pam Ross was sitting on the living room floor, watching the news while nursing baby Alison. On the screen, a young woman was broadcasting to the nation from Dunblane, the cameras only a few hundred metres from Pam's home. Lorraine Kelly and her co-host Eamonn Holmes had arrived the previous afternoon as *GMTV*, Britain's most popular breakfast news programme, geared up to broadcast the whole show live from the town.

At one point, as the presenters were about to go into a commercial break, Kelly could feel her emotions, previously under tight control, begin to slip. Tears pricked the corner of her eyes. She willed herself to stop.

If it was a slip, it was one Pam Ross caught. Watching Kelly struggle to control her emotions touched Ross in the most surprising and profound way. In the depths of her own grief, she wanted to reach out and connect with the presenter. Then she realised she didn't want to; she needed to.

Constable Ian Hamilton, the family's liaison officer, contacted GMTV on Pam's behalf, but the team had already left town. Kelly had only just walked through the door of her family home outside London when her husband Steve said the police in Dunblane needed to speak to her. Hamilton explained that both Pam and her husband Kenny had respected how she reported on what happened and wanted to meet with her, on the understanding that the meeting would be strictly private. The couple had no wish to be interviewed. Kelly said she would do anything to help and agreed to fly back to Scotland the following day, a Saturday. She was picked up from Glasgow Airport.

It was only as the constable's car pulled up outside the Ross's semi-detached home that Kelly began to doubt herself. What could she possibly say? What if she said the wrong thing? Hamilton's advice was simply to talk to them. Kelly had brought presents: a silver picture frame for a portrait of Joanna and one of her own daughter's teddy bears for baby Alison.

When Kelly walked into the living room, both women immediately embraced, and Kelly began to cry, later saying, 'I just cried my eyes out for ages.' Then they sat down on the carpet and talked as if they had known each other for a lifetime. Kelly showed pictures of her daughter Rosie, who was two, and Pam flicked through photographs of Joanna. For several hours they chatted and drank tea.

Then Pam asked if Kelly wished to see Joanna. After identifying her body at the hospital, the couple had asked to bring their daughter home, ahead of the funeral on Monday. The hospital and funeral directors agreed, and in preparation Pam put on the radiator in Joanna's bedroom. Kenny, in a conversation he never imagined he would ever have, gently explained that the room couldn't be warm; it needed to be cold, with the windows ajar. Pam opened the windows, then stopped and stared, momentarily distracted by a mark on the glass.

Pam explained that Joanna was now back in her bedroom. Kelly climbed the stairs, walked into the bedroom, and saw Joanna, dressed in a *Pocahontas* nightgown, the open coffin resting on her bed among her soft toys and drawings. Looking at the little girl, Kelly had two thoughts: the first was that she had never seen a more beautiful child; the second was what kind of evil could have put her there, in her bedroom, in a wooden box?

Kelly spent ten minutes in the room alone, then went back downstairs, where she and Pam talked until the early hours of Sunday morning. On the dark of the doorstep, as she prepared to travel to her mother's house in East Kilbride, Kelly promised the couple that if they ever needed anything, she would be there for them. It was the beginning of a friendship that would last thirty years.

Sunday, 17 March was a Mother's Day like no other. 'It was the bleakest of Mothering Sundays, brimming with grief and bitter rain. The Queen came north, not as a monarch but as pilgrim to a town of desecrated innocence,' wrote Anne Simpson, a columnist for *The Herald* and one of an army of journalists and broadcasters encamped in the town now preparing to make a quiet retreat.

The queen's visit to Dunblane and Stirling Royal Infirmary on Sunday was to be the final media event. The temporary media facilities were closed and the press departed, leaving the town to their grief and the families to bury their children in private. Seventeen funerals were scheduled for the next five days.

That day began with a minute's silence at 9.30 a.m., observed across the United Kingdom. In railway stations, people stopped and bowed their heads; on airport runways, pilots and passengers paused. At Dunblane Cathedral, the end of the minute's silence was marked by a tolling bell. The bell rang out seventy times, one for every bullet then believed to have been fired; in fact, the bells should have rung out 105 times. Inside, the pews were packed, with hundreds more mourners gathered outside on the grass and among the gravestones. For Reverend Colin McIntosh, what to say was a struggle. There were seventeen victims: in the grim arithmetic of grief, how long could he give each child from whom all time had been taken?

McIntosh took to the pulpit and began his sermon: 'God doesn't go around this world with his finger on the trigger. In those fatal, frightening moments in the school gymnasium, God's heart was the first to break.'

Then, speaking to the pupils who were in attendance at Sunday school, the reverend said: 'Even grown-ups don't understand why this has happened ... and when we are feeling like that, we know it is not wrong to cry and not wrong to tell people how we feel. But today I want us to smile and remember all the very special things about our friends.'

He asked the congregation to hold hands as the names of each of the victims was read out, beginning with Victoria Clydesdale, whose mother was in the congregation, and ending with Gwen Mayor.

'When we cannot understand, when we cannot even find words to express the depth of sorrow, anguish and horror we feel, when we cannot answer why this should have happened, then God knows this is not the time or place for explanations,' McIntosh told them. 'We in Dunblane are beginning to find that the sheer numbness, the shock which was our first reaction is only now beginning to pass, and the bitter, dreadful reality is slowly dawning.

'The reality is that last Wednesday morning we glimpsed a facet of life that we don't ever dare to consider for too long. That what begins as an ordinary day for ordinary people, walking to the shops, meeting neighbours, taking our children to school can end in such heartache, sorrow and despair. That it can happen to innocent children in school where they always felt happy and safe.

'And that not even the strongest words of faith can bypass the pain of loss and grief or protect us from that awful sense we have that with the deaths of many of our children and their devoted teacher, something of our own life has lost its meaning.

'When our parents die, they take with them a large portion of the past. But when children die, they take away the future as well.'

In Stirling, Queen Elizabeth, dressed in heather-coloured tweeds and accompanied by her daughter Princess Anne, began their visit by disappointing two injured children. Robert Purves asked the queen where her dogs were. The queen laughed and said that she hoped someone was walking them. Amy Hutchison, whose leg was hung up in traction, wanted to know why the monarch was not wearing her crown. The queen explained that, sadly, there hadn't been room in her hand luggage on the plane. Although disappointed that the queen had arrived improperly attired, Amy agreed to show off her new silver plastic bangle. While they spoke, another child, Ben Wallace, rode around the ward on a tricycle while a detective from the queen's close protection detail pretended to catch him, his handgun discreetly hidden under his jacket.

The queen and princess also met Eileen Harrild and Mary Blake, who had come through to the children's ward. They had an emotional reunion with the pupils they had last seen on Wednesday morning, holding their hands and asking about their recovery while struggling to hold back tears.

Then, the queen and princess travelled to Dunblane and met with mothers who had lost their daughters and fathers who had lost their sons, including Pam and Kenny Ross. The queen spent time speaking to Pam and then turned to Kenny, who roused himself and announced that he had worked on her house, the Balmoral estate. The queen said that she hoped he had done a good job.

Afterwards, the queen and princess visited the school. The queen laid a bouquet of pink hyacinths, white tulips, pink lilies and lemon narcissi at the gates, accompanied by a handwritten message: 'With Deepest Sympathy – Elizabeth R'. Anne's flowers were picked from her garden at Gatcombe Park and tied with a green tartan ribbon. They were snowdrops.

VII

THE SNOWDROP CAMPAIGN

ANN Pearston returned from Dunblane Cathedral with a heaviness that would not lift. She had volunteered to help in the crèche to allow the staff to attend the church service. Now, back at home in a quiet cul-de-sac in Alloa, she picked up the *Sunday Times*. In the coverage of the shooting, one line caught her eye: the paper claimed incorrectly that a bullet hole high on the window of the hall meant a terrified child had climbed the monkey bars in a bid to escape. Such speculation was wrong, she thought, and so Ann called the newspaper to inform them. As it was early evening on a Sunday, she found herself in conversation with a subeditor at *The Times*, who attempted to defend his colleagues. He also suggested she write a letter for next week's edition. Duly placated, Ann found herself asking the subeditor what 'ordinary people' could do to help; when he suggested a petition, she initially thought something like that would be futile. The subeditor then suggested a parliamentary petition, which is recorded in Hansard, the official record of the Houses of Parliament. To Ann this sounded like something worth doing.

Later that evening, Ann's friend Jacqueline Walsh called her house. Jacqueline was another young mother and fellow member of the National Childbirth Trust, and as a resident of nearby Deanston, she knew some of the victims. The women briefly discussed the possibility of a petition and decided to continue their conversation at the next morning's NCT meeting. Ann then ironed her children's clothes, a chore she usually hated – but tonight she had never been more grateful to be able to do so.

Ann had been a shy child. The daughter of a postman, she and her elder sister had been born and raised in Bristol. A bout of glandular fever meant she had failed two of three A levels, but a medical note secured a place at Stirling University to study accountancy, economics and business law. After a spell in London, where she qualified as a chartered accountant, she worked for two years in Kenya as an auditor, where she met her husband, Doug, a fellow accountant. During an attempted military coup in 1982 they had briefly stared down the barrel of a gun. On a return to Scotland in 1992 the couple had rented a house in Dunblane, where their young children attended the nursery at the primary school. Sophie North had attended their youngest children's birthday parties.

The next morning, sitting on the carpet of a flat in Stirling, as their toddlers played around them, Ann and Jacqueline created what would become the Snowdrop Campaign, one of the most successful single-issue political campaigns in modern British history. The petition was typed on the office computer at Ann and Doug's accountancy business, based at Stirling Business Park. The twenty different lines were hand-drawn with a ruler and later photocopied.

In the ornate language of prospective legislation, the Dunblane Snowdrop Petition stated that:

Wherefore your Petitioners pray that your honourable House introduce or amend the law relating to the ownership and usage of firearms such that: —

1. *All firearms held for recreational purposes for use in authorised shooting clubs be held securely at such clubs with the firing mechanism removed.*
2. *The private ownership of handguns be made illegal.*
3. *Certification of all firearms be subject to stricter control.*

They were joined later that week by Rosemary Hunter, a member of their yoga class in the upstairs room of Stirling's Albert Halls, a concert and conference venue. Over coffee, Rosemary expressed a keen interest to help in any way; she would later turn out to be the most politically astute. The title for the group was inspired by the only flowers growing in March, which were white snowdrops. To Ann, Rosemary and Jacqueline they were a symbol of innocence lost.

The world was grieving alongside the residents of Dunblane. Leaders from across the globe – from the prime minister of Japan to the crown prince of Kuwait – sent sincere messages of sympathy and shock. 'News of the tragedy in Dunblane has provoked consternation all over Quebec,' Lucien Bouchard of the Quebec government in Canada wrote; it had reopened wounds left by the shooting of fourteen women at the University of Montreal in 1989.

'To the depth of my soul I am shocked by the tragedy,' wrote the president of Russia, Boris Yeltsin.

Václav Havel, the poet, playwright and then-president of the Czech Republic, offered the country's 'deepest sympathy to the families of the victims, even though we realise any words we might say will hardly be adequate to alleviate their pain'. As did South African president Nelson Mandela, who wrote to convey 'sympathy and dismay at the heartbreaking tragedy which took place at the Dunblane Primary school in Scotland'.

To each letter, fax or note, John Major sent a largely standard reply. 'Thank you for your kind message of support following the unspeakable events at Dunblane. I visited that shattered community shortly afterwards. The hearts of the whole nation have gone out to them in their grief. Nothing can begin to address their loss. But the process of rebuilding is now under way. The other children at the Primary School have returned to their classes, and most of the injured have left hospital.'

Over the course of five days, beginning on the Monday, there were sixteen funerals for the seventeen victims. The first was a joint service for Joanna Ross and Emma Crozier – the two girls had been baptised at the same service five years previously and had grown up as firm friends, and their parents agreed they should remain together. Each funeral was private. The press were asked to stay away, and they did. Piers Morgan, the editor of the *Daily Mirror*, called Central Scotland Police to ask if the families would consider a single photographer and reporter, with words and pictures pooled among the world's press, but the answer was no. Pam and Kenny Ross were provided with the strong sedative diazepam by their doctor, and they watched through the windows of the black hearse as hundreds of people lined the streets. Builders on scaffolds took off their hard hats and bowed their heads.

At the funeral of Brett McKinnon, a verse by A. A. Milne, author of Winnie the Pooh, was read to the congregation:

When I was one, I had just begun
When I was two, I was nearly new,
...
Now I'm six, and as clever as clever,
So I think I'll be six now, for ever and ever.

———

Thomas Hamilton was cremated at Dundee Crematorium on Tuesday night. His mother Agnes and grandfather were the only mourners in attendance. His ashes were handed to the police for disposal.

———

On Thursday night, council workers began to clear up the 400-metre-long carpet of flowers which bloomed out from the school gates, sent from across Scotland, Britain and the world. Under cover of darkness, and assisted by volunteers, each bouquet was carefully transported to the cemetery and laid on the graves of those newly buried, blanketing the surrounding grass for almost an acre. Visitors to the graves forever remembered a curious sound: the riffle of so much cellophane flapping in the chill wind.

———

After a week of funerals, Dunblane Primary School reopened on Friday, 22 March. Ron Taylor was there to greet the pupils. 'As you can imagine this has been a long, dark week full of tears,' he told them. 'However, the evil that came last week has gone. The children return to school today, and this is a very important day for us because it marks the beginning of our recovery ... Mark my words, we will recover. I promise you that.'

The choice of Lord Cullen as chair of the public inquiry into the shooting at Dunblane was popular, but the manner in which he chose to begin was not – at least not with the press. Supported by Michael Forsyth, Cullen believed the inquiry should be set up under the Tribunals of Inquiry (Evidence) Act 1921. The Act required the consent of both Houses of Parliament and was favoured by Lord Cullen because witnesses would be required to testify under oath.

As Forsyth wrote in a letter seeking support, 'A further important advantage of the 1921 Act is that it attracts the provisions of the Contempt of Court Act 1981. This should exercise a moderating effect on the media, help to protect prospective witnesses and restrain speculation on the incident.'

Yet for the press the implementation of the Contempt of Court Act was baffling. The culprit was dead and there were no obvious co-conspirators. Rightly or wrongly, the question this triggered in the nation's newsrooms was 'What are they hiding?'

At the second Cabinet meeting after the shooting, Forsyth updated his colleagues on his plans to announce the terms of the public inquiry later that afternoon. Cullen hoped to begin taking evidence in June and deliver the final report by end of September.

On Thursday, 21 March, a meeting was held in the House of Commons so Forsyth and Howard could brief the opposition parties of their plans. In attendance were George Robertson and Shadow Home Secretary Jack Straw, as well as Alex Salmond, representing the Scottish National Party, and Dafydd Wigley, representing Plaid Cymru, the Welsh nationalist party.

During the meeting, Michael Howard said that he and Forsyth had initiated a joint review of firearm controls, which they would send to Cullen as a submission. The paper would outline the background to the current law, include key statistical information on the number of guns in circulation as well as licences and gun crimes, then set out the various options for change. The Home Secretary invited the opposition parties to cooperate with the review, allowing the government to incorporate any suggestions each party might have. While George Robertson empathised with the desire for swift action, he knew it was crucial to get the law right. Hungerford had prompted legislative change, but it had still left room for tragedy. At the end of the meeting Alex Salmond criticised the suggested timetable, which would result in little action before the end of the year.

Forsyth met with Lord Cullen in the evening of 21 March to present him with the written agreement, now authorised by the Houses of Parliament, for the inquiry to proceed. In newsrooms across Britain, all stories concerning Thomas Hamilton or the shooting were now potentially subject to contempt of court. The Law Lords believed this would put the press on a tight enough leash, but it would not stop reporters straining in pursuit of the story. Less than two weeks later the Lord Advocate, Lord Mackay of Drumadoon, felt it necessary to bring them to heel. In early April he issued an official note to the editors of Scotland's newspapers threatening contempt of court proceedings if they continued their own independent investigations of the shooting. There was pushback by Scotland's editors, but coverage lessened.

After some confusion between Forsyth and the school's board about who would fund the destruction of the gym hall in Dunblane, demolition began on 10 April. A mechanical digger tore at the 1960s structure and loaded the bricks and rubble onto a fleet of trucks that shuttled back and forth to an undisclosed landfill site. By 12 April, when a small group of journalists were invited onto the site, all that remained was a blue wall with five exposed radiators. What had been the inside wall of the gym was now the gable end of the school assembly block. Over the next few days the radiators were removed, the wall painted and the landscape smoothed over with golden gravel and dotted with tubs of flowers.

The question of what to do with Britain's guns was now a matter of national debate.

David Mellor was the first Conservative MP to come out strongly in favour of a complete handgun ban, in a column in the *Mail on Sunday* four days after the shooting. The following weekend he wrote for the Scottish paper the *Sunday Mail* as part of their new campaign, arguing that 'There is no place in Britain for the handgun. Handguns are part of American culture, not ours. If we want to import the American way of life, we will also have to endure the American way of death.'

The Monday after Mellor's initial column, Alastair Campbell wrote in his diary: 'David Mellor was doing a big number on gun law. I thought we were terribly weak. I felt we should be calling for a ban on guns. It was the right thing to do anyway but after Dunblane even more so. I was pointing people to George Robertson's remarks at the weekend that it should be necessary to prove a need to own a gun, rather than the police prove unfitness to hold one. Otherwise, Mellor was making the running on this one.'

Two days later, at Prime Minister's Questions, Tony Blair hardened Labour's stance.

VIII

THE GUN LOBBY

ONE week after the shooting, on a morning when two more children were buried, Boris Johnson wrote an opinion column in the *Daily Telegraph* mocking the idea of tightening gun controls. The future prime minister, then considered a comic and controversial columnist, argued that such legislation would be pointless, ineffective and an affront to an Englishman's personal liberty. Because the legislation introduced after Hungerford had failed to prevent another fatal shooting, he said, the answer should be *less* legislation, not more. He also mocked Conservative MP David Mellor for what he described as an 'ecstasy of politically correct sycophancy'.

There were many who agreed with Johnson. In the Home Office there was no sense of mea culpa; instead, civil servants and ministers such as Ann Widdecombe held the view that further legislation was unnecessary.

In 1996, the gun lobby in Britain was an army of different divisions. Little connected the owners of the nation's great estates and the predominantly male readership of magazines like *Handgunner* beyond an interest in firing guns of different size, cost and calibre, and a firm belief in defending their right to do so. At the time, there were around 174,000 firearms certificates and 722,620 shotgun licences active in Britain. Only 950 licences had been revoked and 250 refused, and gun crimes had doubled between 1979 and 1994.

There were as many as eight bodies articulating the rights and views of the nation's one million shooters, including the Shooters' Rights Association (SRA) and the British Shooting Sports Council (BSSC). There were then more than two thousand individual shooting clubs across the United Kingdom and Northern Ireland. Since Hungerford, shooting's fastest-growing trend was powerful handguns. The Palace of Westminster did not yet have a crèche, but it did have its own two-lane shooting range. The Westminster Rifle Club had been in operation since 1875. The majority of the thirty-five MPs who listed 'shooting' among their interests were Conservatives, but three sat on the Labour benches.

Among the most influential figures defending the right to bear arms was Sir Jerry Wiggin, MP for Weston-super-Mare and both a member of the Westminster Rifle Club and chair of the BSSC. In 1988, he led the revolt against the firearms bill introduced after the Hungerford shooting. He threatened to do the same with any future bill brought before the House, saying, 'I am opposed to legislation on this issue. You can't legislate against a madman, and that is what happened in Dunblane.'

The most controversial and vocal wing of the gun lobby was the Shooters' Rights Association, which was founded in 1984 and whose secretary Richard Law had built a membership of six thousand gun enthusiasts. He and his wife ran firearms training courses and a shooting range from their rural farmhouse at Llanfyrnach in south-west Wales. The SRA was set up to lobby against police prejudice and inconsistencies in the application of existing laws, and each committee member had personal experience. Law and his wife had been convicted in 1989 of the illegal ownership of a Bren-type sub-machine gun, while Law alone had been convicted of the illegal ownership of a Thompson self-loading carbine and a Mossberg 12-bore pump-action shotgun, weapons banned after Hungerford. The couple's convictions were later quashed on appeal. The chair of the SRA was Jan Stevenson, an American born in Alabama who had worked for the Pinkerton detective agency and shot for Oxford University. In Britain he also ran a training course for professional bodyguards. In the late 1980s, Stevenson had been fined £500 for a contravention of the Firearms Act 1968 when a trainee was accidentally shot dead. The director of the SRA, Guy Savage, had been banned from owning or trading firearms on the grounds that he was a danger to the public, following a raid on his premises and the seizure of a substantial cache of banned weapons.

Richard Law was in a gun shop when he heard the news of the shooting at Dunblane on a radio news bulletin. By midnight he had conducted five TV interviews and asked Scottish members of the SRA about Thomas Hamilton. Six days after the shooting, Jan Stevenson was quoted in *The Observer*, defending his sport: 'We have never seen such a frenzy of media backlash. This is a lynch mob, a psychic need for revenge now Hamilton has taken himself out of the picture.' He argued that even current firearms legislation had gone too far, and the government ran the risk of pushing law-abiding owners to the point at which they would 'no longer comply with gun controls'.

In the aftermath of Dunblane, the media's spotlight turned on Britain's gun culture. Reporters visited the Mayfair Gun Club, which had been featured in the lads' mag *Maxim*. Under the headline WHO NEEDS PROZAC WHEN YOU'VE GOT A MAGNUM?, the article stated that 'A growing number of young professionals and execs are bringing a gruelling day to a close with a stress-busting session at their local gun club.' *Men's Health* published an article on alternative methods of stress relief and declared, 'Happiness is a warm gun.'

The Mayfair Gun Club, set up in 1988 by two brothers, Andrew and Peter Dickson, after they left the Parachute Regiment of the British Army, operated from premises under the railway arches on Druid Street, south of Tower Bridge. Observing a growing trend, Andrew Dickson said that 'when members fire a gun, they're not thinking about their mortgage. They're not thinking about the hassle at work. They're concentrating on the bull's eye. So it's a release.'

The sport attracted different characters, all of whom were looking for different things. There were those who enjoyed the quiet discipline of target shooting, and other, younger enthusiasts who preferred the illicit excitement of 'run-roll-fire' in 'combat shooting', where the preferred weapon was a Uzi converted to single fire or the Magnum revolver. When *The Observer* investigated gun clubs in southern England in 1993, one member was overheard telling a prospective member, 'You'll dream of killing people tonight.' This was exactly the image Mike Yardley, a journalist and shooting instructor, was anxious to dispel. A regular guest on *BBC News*, in the wake of Dunblane Yardley became an eloquent and measured spokesman for the sport of shooting. A graduate of both the Royal Military Academy at Sandhurst and the London School of Economics, he had worked as an author and safari guide, and had been a photographer for *Time* magazine. During his media appearances and interviews Yardley sought to strike a balance by advocating for the rights of innocent, law-abiding shooters.

The week after the shooting, the chair of the Home Affairs Select Committee decided it would be an appropriate time to examine the issue of firearms in Britain. Sir Ivan Lawrence was a colourful figure, a Queen's Counsel who had defended the Kray twins and the serial killer Dennis Nilsen while also acting as the MP for Burton. Lawrence called each of the other members of the committee – five fellow Conservatives and five Labour MPs, including the former journalist and diarist Chris Mullin – to recommend that firearms rise to the top of their agenda.

Lawrence was well aware he was treading the same path as Lord Cullen, but also that his committee's report would be published before the end of the parliamentary session in July. It would preempt Cullen by several months, and it had the potential to set the political agenda.

IX

THE THURSDAY NIGHT GROUP

A TWO-STOREY stone building, Scottish Churches House in Dunblane was an ecumenical centre and community space. On the evening of Friday, 22 March, the first meeting of the bereaved families took place, organised by a member of the Central Regional Council's social work department. After introducing everyone, now seated in a circle in an upstairs room, he asked if the group wanted him to stay. The new group's first decision was unanimous: they wished to be alone.

Mick North was among the last to arrive. No one outside the room could imagine what each person had endured, but within these four walls were everyone who could. Over the next year, the bereaved families group became a source of strength and solace.

The first meeting began with each parent identifying themselves with who they'd lost: Sophie's dad, Megan's mum, Joanna's dad. Then Hannah's mum, Karen Scott, asked if anyone was angry. The answer might have surprised outsiders. The answer, again unanimously, was no. The parents were stunned, numb, bereft and in the deepest anguish, but not angry. They spoke briefly about Thomas Hamilton, who no one seemed to have recognised beyond the odd flyer. A longer conversation concerned the behaviour of Central Scotland Police.

Abigail's dad, Duncan McLennan, was the first to raise the issue of the upcoming public inquiry and suggested that they would need their own legal representation. None of them wanted to be marginalised, and it was crucial the group had their own voice. McLennan recommended a solicitor in Glasgow, Peter Watson of Levy & McRae, who had worked on previous public inquiries, including Piper Alpha. When North offered to record everyone's name, address and telephone number he became the de facto group secretary, and each week he typed up a summary of discussions, which he circulated as a newsletter. It was agreed that Thursday was the best evening to meet, and so they became the Thursday Night Group, gathering in either the centre's formal conference room or the lounge, depending on the topic of discussion.

One week, John Crozier arrived carrying a cardboard box filled with bottles of red and white wine, whisky, gin and tonic. Over time, they began to end meetings by going across to the Tappit Hen, a pub across the street. At first, they felt awkward. Pam Ross said it was like having BP, 'bereaved parent', stamped on your forehead. The parents felt judged for going out, judged for having a drink, judged for laughing. But going to the pub was a small island of normalcy in a time when nothing was normal.

The group's first newsletter was dated 9 April and included the new meeting times; a copy of the *Sunday Mail* petition against handguns; and an invitation to Michael Forsyth to meet with the group and with Peter Watson, who had agreed to act for the families at the upcoming public inquiry.

On High Street, a drop-in centre appeared. For the next six months, this centre was staffed by trained counsellors offering stunned residents a safe space to sit, drink tea and look through a book of condolence. Gifts and tributes continued to arrive from around the world; perhaps the most touching was sent by the village of Aberfan, scene of the 1966 mining disaster that had killed 116 children and 28 adults. It was the miner's lamp to guide the town out of the darkness.

———

The Snowdrop Petition was first pitched to the public on Saturday, 30 March. Out of respect for the traumatised residents of Dunblane, Ann Pearston and Jacqueline Walsh opted to set up in Stirling. The local council refused permission to operate from inside the local shopping centre, but offered the doorway of an empty shop. Jacqueline bought disinfectant and a brush to scrub away the smell of urine, and together they put up a collapsible pasting table and a handmade sign propped up with runner bean canes from Ann's garden. Slowly, the public began to pay attention.

A meeting with Ann's local MP, Martin O'Neill, prompted the idea of 'officially' launching the campaign at the Scottish Grand Committee in Inverness on 22 April. The meeting of all fifty-five of Scotland's MPs had been due to take place on 15 March but had been cancelled in the wake of the shooting. Traditionally the committee met in London, but under Michael Forsyth's leadership, government ministers were expected to travel north.

Ann and her husband Doug retreated to their office in Stirling to draft the press release. Ann had arranged to meet Mick North on Sunday afternoon, in what would be their first encounter since

Sophie had attended her children's birthday parties, and she was nervous. But all concerns about what to say dissolved as soon as North opened the door of his cottage and then his arms. Later, in the living room, where Sophie watched from the mantelpiece and tabletops, North agreed to endorse the group and accompany them to Inverness. He made it clear he had no wish to speak to the press, but his presence would confirm the families' tacit support for the burgeoning campaign. On 21 March North had released his own statement, initially blocked by the police as 'too political', in which he had asked, in the name of Sophie, her fifteen classmates and their teacher, for 'please no more guns and certainly no more worship of guns.'

The next day, North travelled to Inverness by train, while the Pearstons sped up the A9 in a second-hand red Saab, the family's ten-year-old car. They were joined later by Rosemary Hunter and Jacqueline Walsh. During the Grand Committee meeting, Labour's George Robertson, the SNP's Alex Salmond and the Liberal Democrats' Jim Wallace all signed the petition. Politely, Michael Forsyth refused, on the grounds that it would be improper to publicly favour one position over another before Lord Cullen's recommendations had been published.

If Snowdrop was only beginning to bud, by this time another campaign was in full bloom.

In just over four weeks, the *Sunday Mail* had collected almost half a million signatures, which they planned to present to Westminster. The paper's editorial staff recognised the power of persuading the parents to participate, but were worried about the emotional cost. A few parents had assisted with interviews, comments and quotes, but this would mean a trip to London and a potentially arduous day in the spotlight, only seven weeks after the shooting. When asked if anyone wished to accompany the petition, however, Mick North, John Crozier, Willie and Kareen Turner, Kenny Ross and his parents, Jimmy and Betty, agreed to go, along with Gwen Mayor's daughter, Esther, and her partner Mark.

On 24 April, a minibus collected the group in Dunblane for the drive out to Edinburgh airport. Joining them on the coach was the feature writer Melanie Reid, who was wracked with doubt about how best to respond to the parents, whose pain she could scarcely imagine.

The trip offered Reid profound lessons in each individual's varying coping strategies. An indescribable sense of loss had not dulled Kenny Ross's wit and humour. When the journalist, who stood at over six feet tall, was accidentally addressed as 'sir' by a waiter, Ross didn't let her hear the end of it. Reid listened discreetly as one group of parents, who had each lost a daughter, discussed their child's daily presence in their lives: a shared fantasy or a glimpse behind the veil: 'I saw her last night, you know. She showed herself to me.' 'Did she turn round? Have you seen them? Are they growing? My little one's wings are quite big now.'

When they arrived in London, the group's first meeting was with the Labour Party at Millbank Tower. George Robertson had arranged for the group to meet with Tony Blair and Jack Straw, the shadow Home Secretary. Labour's position on firearms legislation was still flexible, but it already promised to be more proactive than the Conservatives'. It was clear that while sympathy with the parents was abundant, the decision would have to be a political one. Blair knew that to win the next year's general election, Labour needed to convince large swathes of traditional Conservative voters to change their allegiance.

A similar atmosphere prevailed at their next meeting: on one side of the table were John Major and his wife, Norma, and Michael Forsyth. The parents, across five feet of polished oak, sat opposite. Five weeks before this meeting, Major had reacted as a parent; today he was a politician. While sympathetic to what the families continued to endure, the prime minister was adamant that the government should wait for the conclusion of Lord Cullen's inquiry. Firearms weren't the real problem, he explained. He represented the large rural constituency of Huntingdon, and gun control was not something his constituents had raised as a concern. Motivated killers could always choose other methods of murder. After all, hours earlier the IRA had attempted to destroy Hammersmith Bridge; Major said that if Hamilton had not had access to guns he might have tried to blow up the school with Semtex.

But their children had not been killed by Semtex, Kareen Turner said; they had been killed by a legally owned and licensed handgun. They were all here in this room because of the consequences of an evil man pulling a trigger on powerful guns, legally owned and licensed by the state. They all believed handguns should be banned, and so did everyone who had signed the petition.

On the way back to Dunblane from Edinburgh airport, Reid spoke to North. She could see the pain in his eyes. Earlier, he had spoken about losing his wife and daughter and the loneliness of his life, saying, 'There is no one to tell me not to bite my nails now. Sophie used to sit beside me in the car and tell me off.' On the bus, the energy and distraction of an important task had begun to wane, and as the light faded over the hills north of Stirling the mood grew darker. But the trip had taught the group some valuable lessons. The media could potentially be trusted. If they were to make progress, they would need to find a way to speak with a unified voice.

This, however, would prove more difficult than first thought.

Four days after the Dunblane parents met with John Major, twenty-eight-year-old Martin Bryant entered a cafe at the site of the historic penal colony at Port Arthur in Tasmania. He ate lunch, pulled out a semi-automatic rifle from his bag, and started to shoot. By the time he was arrested the next morning, Bryant had murdered thirty-five people and wounded twenty-three more. He had paid in cash at a local gun dealer, and had later told his psychiatrist he was partly inspired by news footage of Dunblane. Within two weeks John Howard, the Conservative prime minister of Australia, introduced the National Firearms Agreement, legislation that outlawed automatic and semi-automatic rifles and pump-action shotguns. He spoke to a crowd of 3,000 anti-reform protesters while wearing a bulletproof vest under his shirt and tie.

In Britain, the pace of reform, if there was to be any, was considerably slower. The Home Affairs Select Committee was in a curious bind. Having decided to run a parallel investigation, Sir Ivan Lawrence opted to hold a single day of oral evidence from a narrow band of largely pro-gun contributors, including the Association of Chief Police Officers and the Home Office minister David Maclean, who was strongly opposed to reform. The committee had a Conservative majority of six MPs, and Chris Mullin, one of the few Labour MPs on the committee, suspected that their goal was to provide the Home Secretary with a mandate to maintain the status quo. Mullin, a former journalist whose diligent campaigning had led to the release of the Birmingham Six, innocent Irishmen convicted in 1975 for murders committed by the IRA, wrote in his diary of the day: 'Jerry Wiggin gave evidence for the gun lobby. His line was basically that most gun-related crime involved unregistered weapons, and that little or nothing could be done about anything ... I suspect Dunblane is going to make very little difference.'

At the headquarters of Central Scotland Police, the atmosphere was grim. That so many police officers had had personal knowledge of Thomas Hamilton or encountered him during their professional careers cast a pall of unexpressed guilt over the building.

Any evidence of culpability by Central Scotland Police would be uncovered by Chief Inspector John Ogg, who was tasked with mounting a swift and extensive investigation into every aspect of the life and death of Thomas Hamilton. Ogg was given a team of more than sixty detectives and police officers, with Ogg himself directed by John Miller, the procurator fiscal at Stirling, who had overall responsibility for the investigation on behalf of the Crown Office. Over an eleven-week period, the team worked around the clock seven days a week, compiling witness statements and documenting a trail that extended back into the history of Hamilton's family.

A key objective of any investigation would be to assess police conduct during their investigations of Hamilton, as well as the authorisation of his firearms licence. There was then the question of the procurator fiscal's conduct. On 22 April, Alfred Vannet, the regional procurator fiscal of Grampian, Highland and Islands, began to review the four historical reports about Thomas Hamilton made by Strathclyde Police and Central Scotland Police to the procurator fiscal. By early June, Vannet had submitted an eighteen-page report which set out the interaction between the police and the procurators fiscal in relation to Thomas Hamilton. He said that one section of paperwork was missing. The decisions not to charge Hamilton had been based on the fact that the children at his camps had been precognosced – interviewed a second time – with this process highlighting further discrepancies. Unfortunately, none of these precognition statements could be found. The missing paperwork, said Vannet's report, had been '"weeded", in accordance with office practice'.

X

THE CULLEN INQUIRY

Lord Cullen displayed an openness and an even temper throughout the inquiry, and he felt a responsibility to be prepared before proceedings got under way. He educated himself on the intricacies of the firearms community, attending Pistol '96 at the shooting ranges in Bisley in Surrey, a visit facilitated by the British National Rifle Association. He also visited the gym hall in Dunblane.

The hardest aspect of his preparation took place on 23 May. Lord Cullen and the Lord Advocate arrived at Church House in Dunblane with the intention of preparing the families for what was to come. Both men were aware of the parents' specific concerns about the court's identification of individual children and the display of their injuries. The Lord Advocate explained that evidence involving their children would be kept to a minimum, and that each child would be anonymised by the application of random letters.

Lord Cullen acknowledged that Thomas Hamilton would have to be the centre of the inquiry. Hamilton's life and death would be examined in forensic detail, he said, not just for hours or days, but weeks. Despite this, the parents must never think that their children, who had lost their lives or been badly injured, had been forgotten by him or anyone else in the room.

THE CULLEN INQUIRY

By the time the men said their goodbyes, the mood among the parents was positive. Their minds had been put at ease, and all expected the inquiry to be fair and open.

Over the next few weeks, the families were also engaged in their own kind of preparation, debating the issue of gun control among themselves and trying to establish a unified position independent of any other party, political or otherwise.

Three months before their conversations, no member of the group had had any interest in or understanding of muzzle velocity, calibre or barrel length. Now, increasingly, many spent their evenings scrutinising international firearms legislation or debating the idiosyncrasies of British law. Inevitably, tensions developed within the group. Mick North was part of a small group that examined the Labour Party's submissions to the Cullen Inquiry with a group of parents, which included those with children injured, stating, 'Our feeling is that there should be a total ban on the private ownership of handguns. Of those handguns held in authorised clubs, only single-shot handguns of 0.22 calibre and below should be allowed.'

A sharp division began to grow between the pragmatists and the absolutists; between those who favoured a ban on handguns and those who insisted that all guns, including shotguns and hunting rifles, should be banned.

As the opening of the inquiry approached, the solicitor Peter Watson felt it appropriate to make a limited comment to the press on behalf of the parents, who under the legal terms of the inquiry were prohibited from talking to the media. In Watson's words, he believed that 'radical reappraisal' was required to 'the present law in relation to firearms and ammunition', and he acknowledged the families' support of Lord Cullen's key areas of concern.

The sun did not shine on Stirling on 29 May, and a filter of clouds cast a grey shadow over the opening day of the public inquiry at the Albert Halls into the shooting at Dunblane Primary. The Albert Halls is a neoclassical building of weathered grey stone, designed in 1881 by William Simpson and used for decades as a concert and conference venue. Lord Cullen set the tone sartorially when he arrived promptly in a sober grey suit, white shirt and dark blue tie. He took his seat alone on the raised stage. The rows of chairs reserved for the press were packed, in contrast to the eerily empty public benches; it was as if the nation had felt it proper to turn away.

At 10 a.m., the families were guided to their private seating area on the balcony. When all were settled, Lord Cullen gave a nod to the Lord Advocate and began to speak. 'Ladies and gentlemen, this is the opening of the Dunblane Public Inquiry.'

The first witness to testify was James Lister, a police constable with Strathclyde Police Air Support. He had photographed the school from 5,000 feet and now testified to the pictures projected on the screens positioned around the hall.

Eileen Harrild, the second witness, had been much closer. She walked into the hall wearing a bright red, short-sleeved jacket, a thick scar along her arm clearly visible. There was silence as she led the inquiry through her memories of the day. 'I saw a man coming through the door and I turned,' she said. 'It was quite normal for people to come into the gym. He was wearing a woollen hat and earmuffs. He was holding a gun in his hand, extended, and he immediately began to shoot.' After completing her testimony, Harrild was led back to the balcony by a phalanx of officials.

The written statement of Mary Blake was then read: 'He was shooting constantly. I could hear the children screaming.'

Malcolm Chisholm, a ballistics expert, was next to testify, aided by a series of diagrams projected on the public screens which showed a small red figure, designed to represent Thomas Hamilton, from whom emanated long black lines depicting bullet trajectories. Hamilton had arrived at the school with 743 rounds of ammunition, he explained, and fired 105 bullets. Over the course of his testimony, Chisholm was restrained and articulate. Only once did he seem lost for words; when he was asked why bullets designed to maximise damage to the human body were legal in Britain, he replied, 'I can't say,' shaking his head. 'I can't understand it myself.'

At one point the small red figure was replaced on the public screens by a police photograph of Thomas Hamilton lying dead, in a pool of blood, beside his guns. In the balcony Mick North, still in pain from a bout of sciatica that had left him bed-bound for a weekend, was furious that such an image was now being shown in public, though he was later relieved to learn that the Crown Office refused to release it to the media. This was the only time the photograph was shown in public.

In the afternoon, Detective Chief Superintendent John Ogg laid out the events of 13 March under the guidance and questioning of Iain Bonomy, the lead Queen's Counsel for the Lord Advocate's office. Ogg's tone was flat, neutral and focused, honed by hours of testimony in criminal trials and designed to project authority and accuracy. If there was a point when the families' faith began to crack, it was when Ogg stated that all parents had been informed of the deaths of their children between 1.30 and 2.30 p.m. There was an audible groan from the gallery.

At the end of the first day, North was so disturbed by Ogg's testimony and what he felt was the gross insensitivity of broadcasting a photograph of Hamilton's body that, after being driven home by his social worker Elspeth, he drove out alone to Backwater Reservoir in Angus. Sitting on the grassy banks overlooking the still waters, North sought to find peace by conjuring memories of a picnic there with Barbara and Sophie three years before.

Ann Pearston, Rosemary Hunter and Jacqueline Walsh had spent the day at the inquiry, sitting a few rows from the front. Ann had taken roughly twenty pages of notes over the course of seven hours. After the children were put to bed that evening, she told her husband Doug that something was telling her to attend every day, that she needed to hear what was going on. They had been married for eleven years; Doug knew how stubborn and persistent his wife could be. If he needed to work, shop, cook, clean and look after the kids a little more than usual for a few weeks, then so be it.

In Dunblane, Isabel MacBeath was nursing her infant daughter. Each parent wanted answers from the inquiry, but for Isabel police incompetence might have been the difference between life and death. She was the only parent whose child had left the school alive; Mhairi had been declared dead on arrival at Stirling Royal Infirmary. The knowledge that she had been in the crowd gathered at the school gates when an ambulance carrying her dying daughter had left the school by the rear entrance was a persistent physical pain. As Mhairi's mother, Isabel should have been with her to hold her hand, to kiss her goodbye, to tell her everything was going to be okay, even if it never would be. For weeks, Isabel had wanted to know everything about her daughter's final moments; she had asked to speak to the ambulance staff who treated Mhairi

THE CULLEN INQUIRY

but had been told this wouldn't be possible until after the inquiry. Contempt of court protocols prevented the 'collusion' of witnesses. Instead, Isabel planned to speak to anyone she could as soon as they testified. She would chase them down the street if she had to.

In the end, Isabel did run down the stairs from the courtroom balcony to corner two members of the ambulance crew. They were startled at first, and it took Isabel a few minutes to convince them she wasn't a ghoulish spectator. Isabel's greatest fear was that her daughter had been calling for her. But when she finally convinced them of who she was and asked if her daughter had been conscious at any point from the gym hall floor to the casualty department, the paramedic shook his head. No, Mhairi's wounds had been so traumatic that there had been no possibility of her being conscious at any point.

Her daughter hadn't died calling her name or wondering why her mother had abandoned her. Isabel's relief was profound.

At the beginning of the second day, Ogg returned to the stand. After the Crown Office had completed their questioning, Laura Dunlop, junior counsel for Colin Campbell QC, who was acting for the families, took over. 'Might it be the case that parents were still waiting to be told by half past three?' she asked.

'I don't think so,' Ogg replied.

'Well, might you be wrong about that?'

'I am only going from the information that has been given to me. Superintendent Holden was dealing with that. According to the victim profiles we drew up and from the information we had, 2.30 was the last.'

'You suggest that Superintendent Holden would be in a better position to explain about the times?'

'He will know first-hand.'

'But if parents were to say that some of them were not told until 3.30,' Dunlop said, 'you are personally not in a position to contradict that?'

'No.'

'So, at that stage it follows that some parents had been waiting for around five hours for news?'

'I find that difficult to believe.'

On the stand, Ogg insisted that he had only learned two or three days ago about any complaints, and that the police had offered to meet with the families to explain the complexity of the identification process, an offer that had not yet been accepted. Watching from the balcony, Kenny Ross was so angry that he considered moving into Ogg's eyeline.

The next witness was Ron Taylor, the headmaster of Dunblane Primary, whose testimony lasted seventy-five minutes and left much of the room in tears. At one point, he said, 'The air seemed to be thick with bluish smoke and the smell of cordite was very strong ... it was a scene of unimaginable carnage.' He was followed by Agnes Awlson, who spoke of her attempts to assist a group of children lying together on the gym floor. 'You can't help them, Mrs Awlson, they are gone,' she had to be told by the school janitor.

In the afternoon, the first witness arrived accompanied by her friend. Hamilton's mother, Agnes Watt, wore large, round glasses, a straight black skirt and a white cardigan decorated with bright flowers. She walked to the stand without once looking up at the families of her son's victims and answered questions for roughly fifteen minutes, replying, 'Yes' or 'Dinnae know' in a neutral tone.

Watching from the eighth row, Ann, who had attended every day, surprised herself: she felt only compassion and pity for a mother whose son had committed such evil.

———

By the seventh day, Mick North needed a rest. After the day's testimony, he climbed into his car and drove south.

North had been contacted by Gill Marshall-Andrews, who was establishing a political pressure group to reduce the number of firearms in Britain, along with Tony Hill, whose daughter had been murdered by Michael Ryan at Hungerford. Marshall-Andrews, an educational therapist, had been depressed by an interview with Paul Condon, then commissioner of the Metropolitan Police, in which he predicted that the UK would embrace US levels of gun ownership.

In the lush, semi-tropical garden at Marshall-Andrews' home in Richmond, North met to discuss the new organisation's immediate and long-term objectives. They decided to launch the Gun Control Network (GCN), as it would be called, after Cullen had completed his evidence but before Parliament broke for summer recess.

———

The first person who had truly recognised the danger Thomas Hamilton posed was Doreen Hagger, who had tried to stop him in 1989. And yet she and her family would become one of the victims of the public inquiry, in a drama that played out inside the Albert Halls and outside on the streets of Aberdeen. In the days immediately after the shooting, the world's media was anxious for every detail about the life and crimes of the shooter. In an interview with *The Sun*, Hagger confirmed that Hamilton had threatened her with a handgun, an incident she said had been reported to the police. For John Miller, the procurator fiscal in charge of the investigation, and Chief Inspector John Orr, it was imperative they discover the truth behind Hagger's claims.

Doreen and her neighbour Janet Reilly were interviewed by police in the run-up to the inquiry. As Hagger recalled, Hamilton arrived on her doorstep in Bridgend to question her about what she had told the police about him threatening her with a gun pointed through his jacket pocket and describing his guns as his 'friends'. By this point Hagger believed that she had then sent her son Andrew to fetch her neighbour Janet, who had witnessed Hamilton's threats.

When questioned now, Janet distinctly remembered Victoria Hagger, then eight years old, arriving at her door, rather than Andrew. Janet said she had seen Hamilton's hand in his pocket but that she hadn't seen it pointed at Doreen. It was only when Hamilton had left that day, she said, that Doreen had claimed he had threatened her with a gun. Janet couldn't recall if they had reported the incident to the police, but she was convinced that officers had attended the house and taken a statement.

Although all records in Linlithgow, Livingston and Bathgate Police Stations were searched, no statement was found. The personal notebooks of all officers at Linlithgow were examined for any supporting reference, without success. Officers remembered Doreen and Janet as 'persistent complainers of trivia', but no officers recalled any complaints relating specifically to Thomas Hamilton or any allegations regarding a gun.

A second incident involving Doreen, in April or early May 1989, was also far from clear-cut. She said Hamilton had arrived at her house in his van and rested the short barrel of a gun on its open window. Again, he had said the gun was his 'friend', who didn't like people talking about him. Though her mother said she witnessed it, Victoria didn't recall the incident and Janet only remembered Hamilton visiting in his van. She also thought it had happened six months earlier than Doreen did and couldn't be sure Hamilton had had a gun. Once again, there was no supporting physical evidence of a statement made to police.

However, evidence was eventually discovered of a call received from Doreen Hagger by Central Scotland Police on 20 May 1989. The message said that Thomas Hamilton possessed firearms and had taken them by train to show to a family in Linlithgow, adding, 'The caller considered Hamilton could become violent and could use the weapons against her due to the nature of her complaints against him.'

This makes Doreen the first person to have voiced concerns about Hamilton's possession of legal handguns. If she expected this to be recognised at Lord Cullen's public inquiry, however, she would be bitterly disappointed. She was instead subjected to a lengthy and at times persistent cross-examination by both the Lord Advocate's office and the QC working on behalf of Central Scotland Police, who were determined to underline her inconsistencies. It was their belief that no such incidents had taken place.

The Crown Office made it clear they also wished Victoria Hagger to testify, and she responded by running away from school.

On 4 June, Victoria wrote a letter to Lord Cullen: 'Eight and a half years ago I, my mother and many other children [spoke out] about a very evil person. It would seem, as children, our word was not enough for our [older] peers ... He struck fear and terror into us, so much so I had nightmares about this camp and Hamilton for months after. Then when he murdered these children, the nightmares came back and I'm too distressed about those children. I could not and did not want to believe it was the same man.'

A friend of Victoria passed a message to her mother, explaining that Victoria couldn't face her after the inquiry. She felt responsible for Doreen's treatment. Her mother said she didn't blame her for any of it and simply urged Victoria to phone home so they could talk. Victoria eventually called Doreen on the evening of 13 June. She was picked up the next day in Aberdeen city centre and taken to Bucksburn police station, where she was reunited with Doreen. Hours earlier, the Crown Office had announced that Victoria would no longer be compelled to testify.

Victoria Hagger was ultimately to have a brief and troubled life. She would die of a drug overdose in 1998, at the age of eighteen, leaving behind a young child.

Chief Inspector Paul Hughes took to the witness stand to verify the memo he had written in 1991 as a detective sergeant with the child protection unit, in which he had claimed Thomas Hamilton was an 'unsuitable person' to possess a firearms certificate. He also confirmed that it had been returned marked 'no action'. Hughes was aware that his memo was now the single most damning piece of evidence against the institution of which he was now a senior figure: 'I never imagined at all that anyone would have been capable of doing what happened on March the thirteenth, and I would like it to be seen in that context.'

Hughes had drafted ten charges following his investigation into Hamilton's behaviour in 1991, which included physical assault of children and inappropriate photography. He explained that when he had asked for the reasons why it had been decided not to charge Hamilton, he was not provided with a clear answer. He believed Hamilton was a paedophile and a schizophrenic (though Lord Cullen eliminated the latter, believing there was no evidence of schizophrenia).

On day twelve there were tears. For Douglas McMurdo, the deputy chief constable, the weight of what had happened was too much. Over the course of two days of testimony and cross-examination, McMurdo said he probably knew Hamilton better than anyone else. He knew his behaviour among young boys was disturbing, but he 'never dreamt for one moment that he would be dangerous with a firearm', later adding, 'There was nothing I knew about Thomas Hamilton that prevented me from signing the certificate.'

McMurdo said he had not looked at Hamilton's file when he had approved his firearm certificate, because he knew what it contained and believed his fellow officers would have notified him of any major concerns. However, he did say that 'With hindsight – which is a great thing – Hamilton should not have had firearms.' When asked if Central Scotland Police had failed to identify Hamilton as an unfit person, he agreed that they had.

Colin Campbell, who was acting for the families, could not understand why McMurdo had failed to use his discretionary powers to refuse the application. He wanted to know if McMurdo had signed the certificate for the sake of an easier life. With Hamilton placated, he had been less likely to wage another campaign of complaints against him and his officers.

McMurdo argued that Hughes's memo had simply been insufficient: 'The whole memo was an impression, a gut feeling, a sixth sense … A gut feeling would not be enough.'

―――

The relationship between the legal teams was largely constructive, and never fractious. The solemnity of the subject and the weight of the task at hand was a natural barrier to bad behaviour. The closest the inquiry came to open hostility was over the decisions made by the procurators fiscal in relation to Hamilton and the question of how they should be scrutinised in public.

To the external world Cullen's inquiry seemed a strange affair. As Scotland's senior legal figure, the Lord Advocate was responsible for leading the evidence and deciding what should be put before the judgement and scrutiny of Lord Cullen. Now, on the nineteenth day, Iain Bonomy, on behalf of the Lord Advocate, was arguing that the decisions of procurators fiscal were legally protected and 'accountable only to the Lord Advocate'. How the decisions were made, and the decisions themselves, should not be subject to scrutiny by the inquiry or criticism by Lord Cullen in his final written report, Bonomy claimed. The Lord Advocate's staff, and only his staff, were off limits, a long-established legal boundary that applied throughout the United Kingdom.

The Lord Advocate was aware of the 'exceptional circumstances' of the inquiry, however, and felt it appropriate for police reports, which in normal circumstances would remain strictly confidential to the Crown Office, to be made available to the inquiry, as well as the reasons for the decisions taken. Nevertheless, these were not to be questioned.

Lord Cullen considered both arguments but ultimately decided, unsurprisingly, to agree with the Lord Advocate, saying, 'I am satisfied that it would not be proper for this inquiry to require the prosecutors to justify their decisions, or to entertain submissions concerning the sufficiency of those justifications.'

———

Michael Forsyth and George Robertson testified on the same day and arrived at the Albert Halls accompanied by their wives, Susan and Sandra. Over the years, the MPs had kept in touch about Hamilton's increasing volatility, but the severity of his crimes had come as a devastating shock to both. As Forsyth said, 'There was nothing about him that would have led me to conclude in any way he would have been capable of doing what he did.'

Why Hamilton did do what he did was considered closely, during the inquiry, by a forensic psychologist and a forensic psychiatrist, both of whom were provided with access to Hamilton's photographs and videotape collection, as well as to all witness statements. Professor David Cooke's conclusion was that Hamilton was not psychopathic, scoring only six points out of a possible twenty-four on a diagnostic scale whose threshold for psychopathy was eighteen. Instead, he concluded, Hamilton was a paedophile and sexual sadist, who derived sexual pleasure from dominating young boys. The gym classes provided him with the opportunity to touch and hold children performing sit-ups or assist them onto wall bars while also dominating them by dispensing orders and instructions. His videos 'gave the impression of being fantasy material', featuring lingering shots of boys' torsos.

As Cooke observed, 'He was taking photographs and videotapes, presumably to look at later, of children who seem to be suffering. They seem to be cowed – they seem to be in distress when they're doing certain of the exercises. He may well have gained pleasure from the suffering of others.'

Cooke believed the shooting had been planned for months and was directed at the community as an act of revenge: 'One of the most powerful ways of getting back at people is to kill their children.'

The Dunblane Snowdrop Campaign made its own submission to Lord Cullen. The eleven-page document, written with the assistance of Charles Coull, a veteran of both the Royal Navy and the Argyll and Sutherland Highlanders, argued for handguns to be made illegal while all other firearms used for recreational purposes should be safely stored at authorised sports clubs, with their firing mechanism removed.

On the evening of 2 July, the lawyers Peter Watson, Colin Campbell and Laura Dunlop met with the families with a view to reaching a broad collective view. Lord Cullen had requested the families put together a letter stating how they wanted the law to change; this letter would then be passed on to other interested parties.

A clear majority wanted to focus their argument on a handgun ban. They believed there was a strong, clear case to be made and that pushing for a ban on all firearms, including shotguns and hunting rifles, was impractical and unrealistic. No one believed it would succeed, and some were concerned it would drain public support. Emma's father, John Crozier, however, was adamant and eloquently forceful that their position should be stronger: all or nothing. In the wrong hands, a shotgun or hunting rifle was just as lethal as a .357 magnum. During the discussion, Emily's father, Les Morton, sided with Crozier, and neither man was prepared to compromise their firm belief. It was Campbell who fashioned a workable solution: they would present a primary and a secondary submission, which led with Crozier and Morton's total ban and suggested the majority view as a back-up.

Each morning of the inquiry, Campbell and Dunlop met at Edinburgh's Waverley station to catch the early train to Stirling. On board, they spent the hour looking over papers and preparing questions for the day's witnesses. As the inquiry drew to its conclusion, their conversation turned to their closing address.

On Tuesday, 9 July, Colin Campbell rose to his feet and in a strong clear voice began to eviscerate Central Scotland Police. The facts, laid out over the past twenty-four days, were clear: the police had failed in their duty to protect the public and failed to prevent the shooting at Dunblane Primary. 'But for the firearms department's culpable failure to remove his weapons,' he said, 'this terrible tragedy would not have occurred.' He reminded the inquiry that Central Scotland Police had rejected a detective's recommendation that Hamilton should not have guns, and that a senior official had disregarded a female police constable's intuition. It was remarkable, said Campbell, that Douglas McMurdo had told the inquiry that Hamilton's firearm applications had prompted no alarms. This was evidence of a department that discouraged officers from acting on instinct. The police had refused to exercise the discretion entrusted to them by Parliament. He then explained what the families wished to see happen, saying, 'Dunblane will happen again, unless decisive action is taken.'

He continued: 'The carnage in that gymnasium was horrendous, an evil crime of the very worst kind. However, when considering the need for any law reform, it is as well to bear in mind that Hamilton might have murdered hundreds of children and their teachers that day. Had he arrived when the assembly hall was full, or had he not killed himself when he did, there is no knowing what might have happened.'

Turning to Lord Cullen, Campbell said, 'It is the cry of the families of the dead and injured children that never again should we tolerate the possibility of crimes such as this being carried out by lawfully held weapons. Their aim is that never again should anyone be murdered by a lawfully held weapon. Hence the call for a complete ban on the civilian ownership, possession and use of all types of guns.

'This is the families' plea – that the death and injury of their children be not in vain, and that, in future, government will act to remove the potential for murder by the use of guns lawfully held under the civilian firearms licensing system.'

And then, after twenty-six days, 178 witnesses, 123 written submissions and more than one million spoken words, the inquiry was over.

XI

THE PRINCESS

As the public inquiry was ending, the Snowdrop Petition ramped up. In the previous four months, thousands of petitions had been posted across Britain to volunteers who had been canvassing in villages, towns and cities from Cornwall to Cromarty. One technology-savvy volunteer posted the petition on the new World Wide Web so it could be printed off, filled out and posted back. Over weeks and months, the boxes of paperwork in Doug and Ann Pearston's office multiplied exponentially.

While Ann focused on attending the inquiry, Doug and Charles Coull worked on the logistics of transporting the boxes, the Dunblane parents and the Snowdrop team down to London. An approach to Virgin Atlantic based on a rumour that Richard Branson had said he was eager to help was rejected on the grounds that paying for flights would be 'too political'. British Midland also declined a request for twenty-four free return flights. To afford the journey, Doug agreed an extension on the couple's mortgage and business overdraft, and Charles said he would put some flights on his credit card. (Since Snowdrop's inception, the group had steadfastly refused to accept any cash donations, asking only for donations of stamps and envelopes. All three women had agreed it was preferable to be out of pocket than to raise even a hint of financial gain.)

The breakthrough came from Snowdrop's unofficial archivist, Marion Miller, a mother of four who lived next door to Ann and Doug. She suggested they contact Princess Diana.

Miller had read in the newspaper that Diana had wanted to visit Dunblane in March but had been blocked by Buckingham Palace. The princess had separated from Prince Charles in 1992 and since then had operated an alternative royal court from Kensington Palace, the two-storey red-brick Jacobean mansion in the grounds of Kensington Gardens. In January, her private secretary Patrick Jephson had stepped down after eight years. In June the queen had applied pressure on Charles and Diana to clarify their personal lives and divorce, and a financial settlement was currently being negotiated. It was amid this personal tumult that the Princess of Wales and her small staff received a phone call, out of the blue, from a dental hygienist in the small Scottish town of Alloa.

Miller had called directory inquiries to get the correct phone number for Kensington Palace, then cold-called the most famous woman in the world. A member of staff was polite enough to explain that the princess was 'unavailable', but when Miller explained that she represented the Snowdrop Campaign and that the Dunblane families were coming to London to present a petition to Parliament, the palace doors began to creak open.

By early evening, Miller was back on Doug and Ann's doorstep with the news that Princess Diana had invited the Dunblane families and Snowdrop to tea at Kensington Palace.

As a courtesy, Jacqueline Walsh and Ann met with Michael Forsyth at a constituency meeting in Stirling. He offered to host the families for lunch at Dover House, the Secretary of State's lavish Georgian mansion on Whitehall, and would invite Home Secretary Michael Howard to give the group the opportunity to lobby him in person. The *Sunday Times* came on board as a key sponsor, securing return flights and transportation, and the Labour Party, through Ann's local MP, Martin O'Neill, arranged to have the petition detailed in Parliament and read into Hansard.

On 3 July, during a week's adjournment in the Cullen Inquiry, the party of parents, campaigners and press, represented by Jenny Shields for the *Sunday Times*, met at Edinburgh airport. Their 'secret' visit with Princess Diana was splashed across the front page of the *Daily Record*. The media leak annoyed a few of the parents, who were suspicious of Diana's personal agenda, and Mick North and Kenny Ross decided on the flight that they would not attend the morning meeting at Kensington Palace. Both fathers were dropped off near Kensington Park and walked to a pub in Whitehall, preferring a pint there to tea with a princess.

The rest of the party, which included Eileen Harrild, Pam Ross and John and Alison Crozier, who were travelling with their young son Jack, drove down the Mall in the summer sunshine towards Kensington Palace. On arrival they were escorted to the first floor and into a sunlit drawing room with yellow satin wallpaper and ochre silk curtains, a lime-green sofa and elaborate fireplace. The windows looked out onto the courtyard and beyond to the blossoms of the gardens. The group were served tea and sandwiches.

A minute or two later, Princess Diana appeared. Dressed in a navy-blue suit jacket trimmed with white piping and matching waistcoat and skirt, she broke into a beaming smile as she approached the group, shaking hands and glancing at the parents' ID badges before smoothly addressing them by their first names.

At five foot nine and taller in heels, the princess towered over Pam and Alison. She ushered the mothers over to the sofa and sat beside them on a small green armchair. Diana began by apologising; she said she had wanted to travel up to Dunblane in the immediate aftermath but that the palace had prohibited her from doing so. She was delighted to see them now. And then they spoke mother to mothers. Pam talked about Joanna, her love of fun and attention, while Alison talked about Emma. John came over and crouched over the princess to show her a photograph of his daughter.

Ann was sceptical of Diana. Raised by parents who had a genuine deference to the queen, she much preferred Princess Anne. However, everyone in the room was aware of her charisma and presence. Ann and Doug kept to the sidelines with Rosemary Hunter and Jacqueline, appreciating that this meeting was for the parents and not an opportunity to advocate for their cause. John Crozier had no such qualms, and asked Diana if she supported Snowdrop. Though the princess attempted to sidestep the issue and maintain her neutrality, it was apparent she was firmly on the families' side.

When Pam needed a comfort break, she was directed by a lady-in-waiting to the downstairs toilet. On her way back upstairs, she was surprised to bump into a tall, blonde-haired boy in tennis whites, cradling a racquet. She soon realised this was a young Prince William, back from Eton.

At one point Jack Crozier, who was three years old, presented Princess Diana with a posy, and asked, 'Where's your crown?' 'Everyone asks me that,' the princess replied. 'I didn't bring it with me … it's in the car.'

At the end of the meeting Diana came down to the courtyard to see off the party. Before boarding the minibus, John Crozier took the opportunity for a cigarette break and Diana joked about joining him for one. The meeting had been a success. The families felt the princess had a genuine concern for their suffering and grief and was quietly supportive of their cause and campaign.

After collecting Mick and Kenny, the group headed to Dover House and the Scottish Office. Listening to the effusive praise for Diana rolling around the minibus, Mick North began to think he might have made a mistake.

There would be no such praise for Michael Howard, whom they met over a buffet lunch of tea, sandwiches and mini meringues. The parents wanted the Home Secretary to agree with their demand for a total gun ban, including rifles and shotguns, or at a minimum the powerful handguns that had killed or seriously injured their children. Howard was against a blanket ban on any weapon, though he continued to hold up the fig leaf of Cullen's impending report as a way to remain non-committal.

John O'Donnell, whose son Andrew had been wounded, said to Howard that his son often asked if something like it could happen again. 'What should I tell him?' he asked Howard. The Home Secretary said he found it difficult to separate the personal from the political on the issue, but he added that the petitioners had certainly made their case 'strongly'. O'Donnell, who was now on the verge of tears, homed in on the minister's choice of adjective and pressed Howard to answer straightforwardly. O'Donnell asked if they had been 'persuasive'. Howard, who was a trained barrister and visibly uncomfortable at such raw emotion, managed again to evade the question, but he did promise O'Donnell that when Lord Cullen's report was published, he would remember their conversation.

The meeting after the one with Howard proved even more combative. The group left Dover House and walked to Parliament, Jack Crozier riding high on his father's shoulders. They posed for photographs outside the main gates with the petition, all 705,000 signatures, bundled into twenty-nine white cardboard boxes, and went up to the public gallery to listen to a debate about the Scottish Grand Committee. They had hoped to hear Martin O'Neill read the petition out to Parliament, but he was not called until after they had left.

This final meeting, on a long and hot day, was with Tony Blair and George Robertson. The group gathered in a long wood-panelled meeting room. When Blair addressed the parents, Jacqueline Walsh noticed that he was in tears. But Kenny Ross soon became annoyed with what he viewed as a lack of commitment from the Labour leader. Deeply frustrated, Ross said: 'Excuse me, Mr Blair, do you have a daughter?' Blair replied that yes, he did. 'And how old is she?' asked Ross. Blair said his daughter, Kathryn, was eight years old.

'Well, I had a daughter. She was five years old and now she's six feet under the ground in a wooden box and she was put there by someone with a legally held weapon. Can you imagine your daughter in a box six feet under the ground?'

Ross demanded a complete ban on all guns, a position Blair said that Labour could not support. The Labour leader said he knew how Ross felt, likely empathising with his desire to secure a complete ban on all guns, but that it sounded wrong in the room.

There is confusion on who said what next. Ross remembers replying to the Labour leader, while Ann Pearston remembers saying, 'With respect, you don't know how they feel. *I* don't know how they feel.'

Pam, standing in the crowd, felt a mixture of shock that her husband had caused such a scene and pride that he was speaking their personal, agonising truth to power.

In the tinderbox atmosphere, a match had been struck, and it took George Robertson to douse the flames. 'Clearly emotions are high at the moment,' he said. 'Why doesn't Tony come up to Dunblane?'

Looking back, Ann and Snowdrop felt that Ross's emotion had struck a nerve among the Labour leadership.

Behind the scenes, Forsyth was courting his colleagues, determined to achieve a ban on all handguns despite the Home Secretary's resistance. Having worked as a deputy to Howard, Forsyth was aware of how difficult it could be to change his mind. Forsyth's position was not popular in the Conservative Party, and in the corridors of the House of Commons he had been the recipient of several heartless comments from colleagues who insisted he was simply trying to save his own seat.

On 16 July, Mick North returned to Westminster for the official launch of the Gun Control Network. In preparation, Gill Marshall-Andrews secured pro bono media coaching from Sarah Macaulay, the founding partner of Hobsbawm Macaulay Communications, who was then dating Gordon Brown, the shadow Chancellor. The new campaign would support the Snowdrop Campaign in also demanding a ban on the private ownership of handguns, but with an exception for single-shot .22 calibre pistols. (Their position would later tighten to also include a ban on .22 pistols.) All rifles used for recreation and competition shooting should also be restricted to approved gun clubs. The Gun Control Network had two slogans: 'Towards a gun-free environment' and 'Bite the bullet. Ban the handgun.'

A motion sponsored by John Heppell MP and supported by fifty-eight signatures from fellow MPs was amended by Martyn Jones, with the support of William Ross of the Ulster Unionist Party, before being corrected by two other GCN supporters. The final text read: 'That this House welcomes the launch of Gun Control Network which has been established to pursue a goal of a gun-free environment; [and] supports the measures it proposes to outlaw the most dangerous kinds of guns, to reduce gun ownership and to eliminate gun culture.'

It was not always easy to recognise those with poor intentions. In June, an American called Tobias Elias Bernstein had asked Ann Pearston if she could arrange an introduction to the Dunblane parents. Bernstein had lost his family in a car crash and as the beneficiary of a large trust fund had founded an organisation called SAGE (Society Against Guns in Europe). He had hosted a benefit event in Dunblane during the Cullen Inquiry. Colin Campbell attended, reporting later to Laura Dunlop that something hadn't seemed right about the evening. Marshall-Andrews was also quietly concerned. She met Bernstein for lunch and was surprised an affluent philanthropist was so keen for a fledgling campaign to contribute to his costs. Nevertheless, to others, Bernstein seemed both sincere and motivated. He even asked John Crozier to be president of SAGE.

In August, SAGE launched a new advertising campaign to coincide with the Home Affairs Select Committee report. The advert, which first appeared in *The Independent*, featured a photograph of Emma Crozier alongside the text: 'No more picnics, no more days on the beach, no more butterflies, no more chockie cake, no more bedtime stories, no more teddy bears, no more kisses goodnight ... No More Guns.' Crozier, who had accepted the position as president of SAGE, said, 'What does it need for people to act? It takes something like this.' Billboards would also carry a direct appeal from Crozier to parents: 'Your child's right to life is greater than anyone's right to own a gun.'

Unfortunately, the SAGE campaign was brief. Ten days after the first advert ran in the national press, another newspaper, the *Glasgow Evening Times*, uncovered a disturbing lie at the heart of the charity. Tobias Elias Bernstein was not who he claimed to be; his real name was William Bernson, and he was a convicted fraudster who had been in jail on 13 March.

This was a bitter blow for John Crozier. When the families met on the following Thursday night, they agreed to be stronger and more cautious. Bernson fled the country but was cornered in Holland by a reporter who quoted him saying, 'I don't know what these people of Dunblane are upset about. I'm out £15,500.'

During the daily proceedings of the Cullen Inquiry, the British Shooting Sports Council had remained largely silent, instead allowing their detailed written submission to speak for their members. The umbrella organisation claiming to represent over one million 'shooting sportsmen' prepared a lengthy document arguing for judicial passivity. Britain required neither new laws nor any new gun bans to be safe, merely for elected officials to do their job with the powers currently at hand. As Patrick Johnson, secretary of the BSSC, said, 'We have made a number of positive proposals to Lord Cullen for increasing public safety – largely through more effective practice of the systems and safeguards which already exist – without putting a complete ban on possession of firearms of one sort or another. The current laws and rules should not be dismissed out of hand as ineffective.'

The BSSC had a close and integral tie to the Conservative Party through its chairman, Sir Patrick Lawrence, who was also vice chair of the National Union of Conservative and Unionist Associations, the voluntary wing of the party. In mid July, to coincide with the launch of the GCN and act as a rebuttal to the new organisation, the BSSC launched an appeal seeking £25 per member to finance a new £500,000 PR campaign to protest against any handgun ban. Speaking at the launch, Mike Yardley dismissed the GCN as a naïve organisation whose proposals were unworkable and where emotion replaced reason, with potentially dangerous results, telling attendees that 'You could see non-compliance with the new legislation on a massive scale.' The collected funds paid for a series of newspaper adverts which ran in both *The Times* and the *Daily Telegraph* and sought to place the responsibility for prevention on the police.

The advert ran:

The shooting sports community did not go to Dunblane on March 13. Thomas Hamilton did alone.

The shooting sports community did not have the power to issue or revoke Thomas Hamilton's firearm certificate. The police did.

> *A democratic society should not punish its law-abiding citizens for the misdeeds of an individual.*
>
> *The time to pass judgement is when the facts have been established and properly considered by an impartial, qualified inquiry. Lord Cullen has held such an inquiry.*
>
> *The British Shooting Sports Council is pressing for safeguards to ensure that the tragedy of Dunblane can never happen again.*

Other publications refused the ads, while the *Daily Mail* ran the advert in England and Wales but not in their Scottish editions.

At this time, the Shooters' Rights Association (SRA) reasoned that attack was now the best form of defence. Guy Savage, the association's chair, dismissed the SAGE campaign and the emotive use of Emma Crozier as 'disgusting', saying, 'I think it is an affront to the dignity and memory of that child.' However, the target at which they took aim was Central Scotland Police, whose negligence, according to the SRA, had resulted in the collapse of both businesses and sales. Richard Law, the association secretary, who compared shooters in Britain to the persecuted Jews of Nazi Germany by saying, 'We might as well wear a yellow star,' said members' business income had dropped by 64 per cent; another member of the association reported a 70 per cent drop in gun sales.

The SRA announced that they were preparing a lawsuit against Central Police. As Law explained, both gun owners and dealers and the parents whose children had been shot dead had more in common than they realised: 'It's not our fault that Central Scotland Police gave Thomas Hamilton a licence, and it sure as hell shouldn't be us that pays for it. The parents of Dunblane are considering the same action, aren't they? They think they have a claim against the chief constable of Central Scotland arising from his negligence – the difference with us is that we can quantify our loss.' The SRA said they would seek as much as £250 million in compensation for the nation's gun dealers. Then there was the British Association for Shooting and Conservation who, in early September, advised their 112,000 members to no longer cooperate with the police, who were now making random spot checks on how safely guns were stored at home.

The atmosphere became increasingly hostile to Snowdrop. Jacqueline and Dave Walsh handled most of the death threats to its members. The couple looked after the campaign's PO box and separated the hundreds of letters of support from the not infrequent hate mail posted by anonymous gun enthusiasts. The police were informed about several suspicious packages which turned out to be benign, and the couple kept copies of the worst letters in case they were required as criminal evidence.

Both Rosemary and Ann were targeted at home, while Jacqueline was stalked in public. Ann received a letter from an anonymous sender in Glasgow who said that if Snowdrop took his guns, he would go to B&Q, buy a hatchet and come to her house to kill her and her children. She tried to shrug it off, but at night she dreamt that a faceless intruder was in her house. It was a dream so vivid she could remember it frame by frame many years later.

For Rosemary the death threat came not by mail but over the phone. As the group's media contact for radio appearances, it was not uncommon for her to come home to twenty or more messages flashing on the answering machine. The death threat was message number fourteen, and she listened as a man with an English accent aggressively threatened to kill her and her family. As BT were able to provide both the exact time and the telephone number from which the call had been made – a payphone in a shopping precinct in a northern town – Central Scotland Police began an investigation. By examining the CCTV in the area they were able to source a picture and, eventually, an identity, followed by a successful prosecution and prison sentence.

Jacqueline also began to notice the same individual turning up to Snowdrop events. On one occasion she was due to give a live interview to the BBC in Dunblane when she spotted the same man. She spoke to the producer, who immediately called off the interview, escorted her to their broadcast van and called the police.

On 1 August, just three weeks after the end of the inquiry's public hearings, *The Sun* ran a front-page story: DUNBLANE JUDGE'S NO TO GUN BAN. The story, attributed to sources at the Home Office, seemed to confirm that 'an all-out ban on handguns' was off the table. Existing gun laws would merely be tightened. George Pascoe-Watson, the reporter, quoted an 'insider' as saying, 'We don't believe he will go as far as people want and recommend the complete handgun ban. He's being very dispassionate. He's convinced if police chiefs aren't calling for a ban, then he shouldn't either.'

According to *The Sun*, Lord Cullen would insist that owners of handguns keep their firing pins in the secure premises of gun clubs. The article also claimed that Cullen would ban storing ammunition at home and insist that anyone applying for a gun must have adequate reasons to do so.

Cullen was at home in Edinburgh when he was informed of the newspaper's access to his private thoughts, and he was understandably angry. He immediately asked the Lord Advocate to investigate possible sources of the story and to write to Michael Howard and Michael Forsyth. He also instructed the clerk to the public inquiry to write directly to the editor of *The Sun*. 'Since the close of the Inquiry, Lord Cullen has had to consider many issues arising out of the Dunblane shootings,' the letter said. 'He has not yet reached conclusions as to his recommendations, let alone committed them to writing or communicated them to anyone else.' He continued, 'You will appreciate that a serious view is taken of the publication of information which is unfounded in fact and is used as the basis for highly critical comment. I trust that you will make this correction known to your readers.'

The Sun was not intimidated by Lord Cullen's 'serious view' and had no interest in correcting a story it believed to be accurate. Pascoe-Watson and the newspaper's editor, Stuart Higgins, expected the eventual publication of Cullen's final report to vindicate their story.

And what was the story's genesis? If Cullen is to be believed, and had not yet decided his views nor communicated them to the Home Office, was it an exercise in 'kite flying', the standard practice by which governments clandestinely brief journalists about new policies in order to gauge the public's response? The newspaper's claims clearly corresponded with the Home Secretary's favoured approach.

If the story's publication was a subtle attempt to use *The Sun* to indicate to Lord Cullen the Home Office's preferred outcome, a more obvious approach arrived less than two weeks later. The

Home Affairs Select Committee arranged for the publication of their report to be officially published around 12 August – the 'Glorious Twelfth', as the official opening of the British grouse shooting season was known. It would prove a comforting read for any marksman taking a break from bagging a brace on the grouse moors of Perthshire or Yorkshire.

The draft report had been debated by the committee's eleven members on 17 July, and Labour MP Chris Mullin was bitterly disappointed by their conclusions. 'Apart from a bit of tinkering it proposes to do nothing about anything, despite Dunblane,' he wrote in his diary. 'I am beginning to realise the extent to which the Tories are in hock to the gun lobby. It is becoming clear that Michael Howard wants to use our report as a cover for inaction.' The select committee met again on 24 July to finalise the report, with five dissenting Labour MPs overruled by the Conservative majority.

The Guardian published a leader on 14 August headlined GUN LOBBY WINS, LOCK, STOCK AND BARREL. It read: 'No wonder the gun lobby was celebrating last night. The final report from the Conservative-controlled select committee looking at gun controls was even better for gun freaks than earlier leaks suggested; not only a rejection of a ban on handguns but the repudiation of a host of other ideas including partial bans, calibre controls, and new restrictions on the number of guns that an individual could hold. It is as though Dunblane never happened.' Sir Ivan Lawrence was mocked by the paper as 'Sir Ivan Lapdog'.

In the same edition, Mullin, one of the outvoted Labour MPs, contributed an article with the headline GUN LOBBY ON THE RUN. He suggested that one of the most disturbing revelations of the committee's investigation was the sheer quantity of legally held handguns, rifles and shotguns in Britain (1.9 million) and that there had been a 'vast explosion' in the popularity of handguns over the previous twenty-five years. His conclusion struck a defeated note: 'Given the massive vested interests involved, it was never very likely that the Tories could take on the gun lobby – despite Dunblane. We can be disappointed, but we should not be surprised.'

The *Daily Telegraph*, which was largely sympathetic to the gun lobby, initially prepared a leader to attack Mullin. A lobby correspondent got in touch to ask his opinion about IRA decommissioning. It would be convenient if the MP, in their view an 'incorrigible leftie', was happy for IRA killers to keep their Kalashnikovs while law-abiding British citizens lost their .357 Magnums or 9 mm automatics. In the end the story never ran, but the *Daily Telegraph* did publish an opinion column by Sir Ivan headlined WHY I SAID 'NO' TO A BAN ON HANDGUNS in which he said, 'No one could give our inquiry any assurance that it would prevent another Dunblane massacre.'

That evening Mullin wrote in his diary, 'The Tories have dug themselves into a great big pit. No doubt Ivan Lawrence thought he was doing Howard a favour by concluding that nothing could be done about anything only to find that the Home Office is rapidly back-pedalling, leaving Ivan and friends gently swinging in the wind.'

The Sun, meanwhile, put the names and photographs of each Conservative MP on the Home Affairs Select Committee in the paper along with their constituency telephone numbers, and invited the public to let them know how they felt. 'Being monstered by *The Sun* is a new experience for the Tories,' Mullin later wrote. 'They must be cursing Ivan for getting them into this.'

THE PRINCESS

———

When the BBC's *Newsnight* contacted the families with an invitation to contribute to a studio discussion about the select committee's report, Pam Ross accepted the challenge. Mick North was unavailable and no one else seemed keen. Ross had doubts about performing on live television, but her confidence was bolstered by a journalist with *The Independent* who had helped her craft an article advocating a gun ban. The presenter was Jeremy Paxman, known for his bullish approach to questioning, and not the more genial Kirsty Wark, a fellow Scot. Settled in the small studio in Glasgow's Queen Margaret Drive, Pam stared into the camera lens and steeled herself for battle. As the programme's familiar theme played over her earpiece, she heard Paxman's introduction: 'Tory MPs on the Home Affairs Select Committee reject calls to ban private ownership of handguns ... do they care more for the gun lobby than public opinion?'

'Good evening,' Paxman went on to say. 'It's been a disappointing day for families of the children murdered by a suicidally deranged gunman at Dunblane. The Conservative majority on the Home Affairs Select Committee has ignored public appeals and come out against banning the handgun. The mother of one of the murdered children joins us to speak of her sadness at the MPs' conclusion.'

Prior to Ross's contribution, there was a video package which showed Ann Pearston reading a picture book to her youngest daughter, before then reading the equivalent of the Riot Act to the government: 'If the government doesn't ban handguns, they will be seen as the party that is supporting the gun lobby.' In the studio, Paxman hosted a brief debate between Conservative MPs

Sir Michael Grylls, who defended the select committee's report, and David Mellor.

Paxman then turned to the camera. 'We are joined now from Glasgow by the mother of one of the children murdered at Dunblane,' he said. 'Can you tell us your feelings, Pamela Ross, when you heard the Home Affairs Select Committee's recommendation?'

Ross: 'First of all, we are outraged and very disappointed by the stance taken by the committee, particularly before Lord Cullen makes his recommendations. What has been said and the weight of public opinion in support of a ban, I just can't and don't think this can or should be ignored. How can we assure our children with any confidence in the future that this won't happen again? We have to expect the people who govern our country and make the laws to have the interests of public safety as the main priority. Radical action has to be taken, and if it isn't they will have failed … failed us and the memory of our children and their teacher.'

Paxman: 'Are you not prejudging the Cullen Inquiry?'

Ross: 'Well, we hope Lord Cullen will make the recommendations that we would like to see, and the minimum we would like to see is a ban on handguns.'

Paxman: 'What do you make of the argument that was advanced to the committee of MPs about freedom of choice?'

Ross paused, looked to the side and replied with force, 'I don't think people have the right to hold a handgun for sporting purposes. I don't think that takes priority over the lives of our children. The right to live … is much more important than the right to a sport.'

On 29 July, Michael Forsyth wrote to the Home Office laying out a suggested road map for the government's response to the imminent publication of Cullen's report. Forsyth, the son of a garage mechanic, had been raised in Arbroath and educated at the University of St Andrews, where he had been president of the university's Conservative Association. He was a devotee of former prime minister Margaret Thatcher, and comfortable in a political fight. By the time he was appointed Secretary of State for Scotland in 1995, he had a reputation as a political pugilist. John Major said that Forsyth 'suffered from the fact that he always looked as if he was plotting ... he was no peacemaker'. And yet, in 1996, Forsyth was to be an essential bridge between opposing parties while also plotting how best to undermine his own party's resistance to firearms legislation and secure a comprehensive handgun ban. To address a range of potential government responses, he recommended bilateral meetings with Gillian Shephard in the Education Department, Stephen Dorrell (the Secretary of State for Health) and William Hague (the Secretary of State for Wales).

In the nation's capital, Max Hastings, former editor of the *Daily Telegraph* and now editor of London's *Evening Standard*, himself a keen shot who enjoyed stalking stags across the gorse and heather of Highland estates, decided now was the right time to nail his paper's colours to the shooters' mast. In a long editorial on 18 September, his publication argued that the existing legislation was already among the toughest in the world, and that the police had had the authority to stop Hamilton if they had wanted to. 'The most important message for all of us, as we read Lord Cullen's judgements upon horrifying events,' the paper stated, 'will be to respond with reason, and not with unthinking demands for new regulation which would bear hard upon a large and law-abiding section of the community, rather than upon criminals or madmen.'

Hastings' editorial was suspiciously well timed. On the day of publication, key members of the Conservative Party met at the Home Office to discuss their response to Lord Cullen. The minutes state that the attendees had 'no knowledge of Lord Cullen's likely recommendations', but all agreed that it would be 'extremely difficult, although not necessarily impossible, to reject any recommendations'. The group was divided into two camps, one heavily outnumbering the other. The first, 'with a clear majority', was led by Michael Howard, who preferred not to ban handguns but to confine all privately owned handguns to club premises. The second camp was led by Forsyth, who wanted to ban high-calibre handguns while allowing .22 handguns to be kept on club premises. All agreed that financial compensation would need to be paid to gun owners for the state's confiscation of personal property. This would require careful presentation because many would oppose the use of taxpayer funds to do so.

In mid September, Robertson began to press Forsyth to delay the publication of the Cullen Report until after the party conference season. The Labour-supporting *Daily Record* was suitably briefed, and a story, which also appeared on 18 September, read, 'Scots Secretary Michael Forsyth has been warned not to score political points on the Dunblane tragedy … Publication of the Cullen report during the Labour conference would be seen as a ploy to blitz Tony Blair off the front pages. By waiting until the second week of October the government would be accused of giving John Major a Tory conference platform for a popular announcement on gun law reform.'

Forsyth's initial suggestion to John Major to delay the report's publication was met with rejection by the prime minister, who scribbled in a memo that this was 'outrageous behaviour'; if the Labour Party wished to put their party conference ahead of the report's publication, it would 'be v. petty'. In the end, however, Major did agree to delay delivery of the report from the end of September to 14 October. In a draft copy of a letter to Lord Cullen, Forsyth made clear that the delay was at his request, and that the judge had fulfilled all aspects of his role. At this point, Cullen also agreed to the delay.

If Michael Forsyth hoped this would ensure all parties agreed to leave the issue out of party debate, he was mistaken. Following Lord Cullen's agreement to the delay, George Robertson called the Pearston household on the evening of Sunday, 29 September. Doug answered the phone and Robertson asked to speak to Ann, who was sitting at the dining table reading submissions made to the public inquiry. Robertson introduced himself and asked if Ann would like to address the Labour Party conference in Blackpool. She was quick to say yes.

Ann set aside what she was reading and began to make notes for her speech. Over the next few days, an outline evolved into a rough draft, and when she was happy, she read it out loud, standing at the back of her living room while Doug listened on the sofa. She then delivered it until she was 'off book', the speech firmly memorised.

Rosemary agreed to accompany Ann, and together they took the train from Glasgow to Blackpool. The Labour Party had organised a hotel room on the seafront, and shortly after their arrival Ann was photographed in front of a grey Irish sea, gulls diving in the background.

As Ann had left the house, Doug's last words had been, 'And don't let that bloody speech out of your sight!' She had a printed copy and a floppy disc containing the speech, but the couple were paranoid that the Labour Party would try to make edits. When Ann handed these over, however, the party's only addition was a brief introduction for herself and Rosemary, who would be joining her onstage. The next day, after a fitful night's sleep, eased by a single glass of wine, Ann put on her pink and grey Richard's dress and prepared herself for the largest audience of her fledgling career as a public campaigner.

At the conference centre, Ann and Rosemary were escorted backstage for a brief rehearsal in front of shadow Home Secretary Jack Straw and shadow Secretary of State for Northern Ireland Mo Mowlam. When the Labour staff asked how long the speech was, Mowlam advised Ann to remember to build in time for people to applaud. Ann was quietly pleased when she had finished her rehearsal, because Mowlam's eyes were damp with tears.

As Ann approached the podium with Rosemary, she focused on the task at hand. 'The only reason I am speaking to you is because the pistol Thomas Hamilton used on his victims was legal,' she opened by saying, before laying out her reasons why she felt a 'complete handgun ban is the only answer to Dunblane'. She ended by saying that 'Dunblane paid the price for compromise after Hungerford. Yesterday was a little girl's sixth birthday. She got cards and flowers, but she wasn't there to blow out the candles on her cake. She was Sophie North. Compromise cost her life.'

The audience was completely silent during the speech, but as Ann sat down the delegates rose from their seats and delivered a rousing ovation. Gerald Kaufman, a veteran MP who had attended the previous forty party conferences, said there had 'never been anything like it'. Though both Robertson and Straw spoke later, the afternoon belonged to Ann and Snowdrop. In the taxi to the railway station, even the driver said he'd heard the speech on the radio.

Back in Parliament, a clear gulf had formed between the Conservative Party in government and New Labour on the issue of firearms legislation. While the prime minister stuck rigidly to his decision to make no announcement ahead of Lord Cullen's report, Michael Howard firmly opposed any ban on handguns and Michael Forsyth quietly tunnelled under his own party's defences, Labour had seized the opportunity to promote a total ban on all handguns, including .22s. Jack Straw had been partly persuaded to go further after meeting with Mick North and Gill Marshall-Andrews of the GCN on 26 September, a week before the Labour Party conference. Any hope of a political consensus had been shattered.

In public, Conservative Party chair Brian Mawhinney accused Labour of undermining the House's position when Blair had invited Ann Pearston to speak at the Labour Party conference. In private, John Major was furious at what he saw as a betrayal by Robertson, Blair, Straw and the whole of the Labour leadership. Hadn't they approached Forsyth with concerns that Cullen's inquiry would overshadow their party conference? And hadn't the government, in the spirit of cross-party consensus, appreciated these concerns and asked Lord Cullen to delay his report? In the prime minister's opinion, this was a classic example of Westminster opportunism.

When it came time for Blair to speak at the conference, he strengthened his party's position: 'I believe that we should ban the private ownership and possession of handguns ... Conservative

MPs complain that our response has been emotional. Well, if they had been in that gym, if they had talked to those parents sitting on those tiny chairs where once their children had sat, they would have been emotional too.'

―――

On Wednesday, 9 October, a memorial service for the victims of the shooting was held in Dunblane Cathedral, an intimate service with the minimum number of dignitaries. Prince Charles, the Prince of Wales, agreed to represent the queen. The only politicians invited were Michael Forsyth and George Robertson. Black was banned in favour of the brightest colours, and each parent wore a tartan ribbon as a symbol of solidarity. The BBC organised a national television broadcast.

The service began with the hymn 'All Things Bright and Beautiful' and closed with 'Shine, Jesus, Shine'. Lorraine Kelly's friendship with Pam Ross had deepened in the past six months, with the presenter inviting Kenny, Pam and baby Alison down to stay with her in August. She had also spoken at one of the Thursday Night Group's meetings and had been invited to participate in the service. At the rehearsal the night before, however, Kelly had been unable to read the poem or the children's names without crying so hard her words were inaudible. As she was staying with Kenny and Pam, she asked if she could rehearse in Joanna's room, imagining her audience was not a nation but instead a single child.

On the day, a solitary piper played 'Lament for the Children', a piece written by Patrick Mòr MacCrimmon in the seventeenth century after smallpox had killed seven of his eight children. Kelly then flawlessly read out the names of the dead, each family coming forward to light a white candle on which their child's name was printed in gold.

Pam Ross maintained a firm belief that each day she pulled herself through was not only a day devoted to baby Alison, but also a day closer to some distant future in which she would again hold Joanna. As an atheist, Mick North could take no comfort in thoughts of a distant reunion, but at times like this a flickering candle was enough: a brief light, all too soon extinguished.

After the service, North, who had regretted his decision to snub Princess Diana, found himself in conversation with her former husband, Prince Charles. The heir to the British throne was asking North if he'd been born in Dunblane, a question that annoyed him more than it should have. The formality of the occasion was a straitjacket he was keen to escape, and North persuaded Willie Turner to join him in the Tappit Hen across the road for a pint.

All were content for their children to be remembered today by words and songs. Most of all, they wanted their children remembered by legislation that would protect future generations.

XII

THE CULLEN REPORT

THE Conservative Party conference in Bournemouth had started on 8 October. The party had been in power for seventeen years, and almost all in attendance knew the government had entered its final months. Apart from a brief answer to a question during an informal question and answer session, the prime minister made no comment on either Dunblane or the question of firearms legislation.

If there was a feeling of end times around the salt water and sea spray of the fading seaside town, Forsyth, who returned to the conference after attending the memorial service at Dunblane Cathedral, kept his eye on the prize of a radical ban on powerful handguns, regardless of what Cullen had already decided and committed to paper and which would soon be made public.

At Dunblane Primary one autumn morning, worksheets were passed out to the children. Each contained outlines of familiar objects yet to be coloured in, with incomplete accompanying words. Amy Hutchison's object was painfully recognisable. She refused to colour in the shape or add the missing letter to the word 'G_N'.

This was an unfortunate oversight, and the worksheets were quickly removed from all Scottish classrooms. Occurring the same week as the publication of Lord Cullen's report, the incident posed a fitting question: how 'everyday' should handguns be in modern Britain?

The parents made their views clear on Sunday, 13 October, when the final proof checks were being made to the report ahead of its being delivered to the Secretary of State for Scotland. They gathered in the glass conservatory in John and Alison Crozier's house in Dunblane and spoke eloquently to a conveyor belt of camera crews from Britain's broadcasters.

Mick North was busy writing an article for the *Sunday Times*, with the headline 'DON'T PUT SPORT BEFORE SAFETY'. 'If we can't guarantee the behaviour of handgun users,' he said, 'there is only one course of action and that is to ban their weapons and to ban them completely. It is too late for Sophie and the other victims of Dunblane, but it is not too late for everyone else.'

The goal was to apply maximum emotional pressure on the government, which would provide Forsyth with leverage in his upcoming discussions with Michael Howard and the prime minister. Ann Pearston hinted in a newspaper interview that unless a complete handgun ban was introduced, a member of Snowdrop would stand against Forsyth in his constituency. As Forsyth prepared for what he understood to be the most consequential week of his political career, he did not know if it would end in success or the ignominy of a public resignation.

ONE MORNING IN MARCH

The elegant streets of Edinburgh's New Town were silent except for a light drizzle. Shortly before midnight, a civil servant from the Scottish Office arrived at Lord Cullen's townhouse to collect the report. In the forthcoming days Cullen would make no public comment, opting to let his inquiry's written words speak for themselves.

At St Andrew's House, a couple of miles away, a team of civil servants worked through the early hours of Monday, 14 October to produce an accurate precis of the document's key points, ready for Forsyth and his senior staff to read over breakfast.

The key point was to be found on page 150 of the report. In the summary of recommendations, under the heading 'The Availability of Section 1 Firearms', Cullen wrote at 9.112, 'Consideration should be given to restricting the availability of self-loading pistols and revolvers of any calibre which are held by individuals for target shooting. Preferably this should be done by their disablement while they are not in use, by either (i) the removal of the slide assembly/cylinder, which is to be kept securely on the premises of an approved club of which the owner is a member or by a club official: or (ii) the fitting of a locked barrel block by a club official.'

He did, however, append one final point: 'If such a system is not adopted, by the banning of the possession of such handguns by individual owners.'

As regards school security, he stated that local authorities 'should prepare a safety strategy for the protection of the school population against violence, together with an action plan for implementing and monitoring the effectiveness of safety measures appropriate to the particular school'.

THE CULLEN REPORT

To prevent individuals such as Thomas Hamilton from having unfettered access to young people, Cullen recommended 'a system of accreditation', the main purpose of which would be 'to ensure that there are adequate checks on the suitability of the leaders and workers who have substantial unsupervised access to [children and young people]'.

Doreen Hagger, the first person to recognise the danger of Thomas Hamilton, was dismissed by Cullen as having not told the truth: 'Mrs Hagger is lacking in both reliability and credibility.' Although those that knew her preferred to recall Colin Campbell's closing comments when he described her as a 'brave and determined lady'.

Forsyth spent Monday in discussion with his officials at St Andrew's House. Privately, he was disappointed with Cullen's final report. Forsyth had hoped for a ban; the report had now made that goal much harder.

Most of the report's criticism was directed at Douglas McMurdo, and Forsyth felt it only fair that the former deputy chief constable be allowed to read the criticisms ahead of publication. The pages were faxed to McMurdo's office at Scotland HMIC, and shortly afterwards the two men spoke on the phone. It was an emotional call. McMurdo said he would resign immediately as assistant inspector of constabulary. Forsyth said he would include this in his statement to the House of Commons on Wednesday.

In the late afternoon, Forsyth left St Andrew's House to catch a flight from Edinburgh to London. He wanted to secure a ban on all handguns, something Cullen had *not* recommended. He spoke to the press on the way to his car, insisting that the government would respond quickly and decisively to the recommendations.

At the Home Office, the Forensic Science Service had examined Lord Cullen's suggestion that handguns could be disabled, and they concluded that it would be impractical to devise a gadget that could not be circumvented by a reasonably competent enthusiast.

Around 9 a.m. on Tuesday, 15 October, Michael Forsyth and Michael Howard arrived at 10 Downing Street to discuss the government's response with the prime minister. Forsyth knew the Home Secretary was against any kind of gun ban, but that the fervour of his position had begun to erode as public opposition had grown more vocal. He also knew Howard hated to feel forced into any decision. John Major, meanwhile, was only too aware of how unpopular any ban on firearms would be among many in his party, and he had hoped Cullen's report would provide political cover. Instead, the prime minister found himself being pushed by the Scottish Secretary to go far beyond Cullen's recommendations.

Forsyth had come prepared for a fierce debate and had the threat of resignation in his back pocket. But the meeting between the men was cordial, measured and relatively brief. Forsyth explained privately to Howard that if the government opted for anything less than a ban on the most powerful handguns, he could not remain in government. Howard thought for a second and replied, 'Okay. I'll go with you as far as .22, but this is going to be really difficult, and we will have to impose a whip.' Forsyth tried to push Howard further, to include .22 handguns and match Labour's position, but Howard refused. This was as far as the Home Secretary would go.

Forsyth returned to Dover House and drafted a letter to be included with a copy of the published report, as well as a slimmer document detailing the government's response, to be made available to the Dunblane parents three hours before its official publication at 3 p.m.

In his letter, Forsyth confirmed that the government had accepted all twenty-eight of Lord Cullen's recommendations, clarifying that in the case of 'recommendation 24, which deals with restricting the availability of self-loading pistols and revolvers, we have carefully considered all the points Lord Cullen has made. We have reached the view that the suggestions he makes for disabling weapons of this kind would not be effective in protecting the public. We have therefore decided that the private ownership and use of all handguns of over 0.22 calibre will be prohibited. Those of less than 0.22 calibre will be banned except in clubs which can meet the highest standards of security.'

The letter continued, 'You may recall that in the aftermath of last March's tragic event I said that I found it obscene that Thomas Hamilton or any private individual could have in his home the armoury and ammunition he possessed. The measures which the Government have announced today mean that guns of the type Hamilton used will never again be legally held or used by private citizens. I hope you will agree that this does indeed represent a firm and decisive response.'

Forsyth signed thirty-seven individual letters, one for each parent of those killed or wounded. Then he put down his pen. In the face of virulent hostility from his own party and sackloads of hate mail from both pro- and anti-gun campaigners, he had done what he could.

On 16 October, the parents gathered in a conference room at the Dunblane Hydro Hotel for the publication of the Cullen Report. Civil servants were present with envelopes addressed to each family. A television was set up so the group could watch Forsyth and Howard present Cullen's findings and the government's response. A second room was prepared for a press conference.

The families' responses were varied. Some stopped reading after a few pages, pushing the report away in disgust. Mick North felt it was important to understand Cullen's arguments if he was expected to oppose them on live television. He concluded that Cullen had 'failed to look at the broad picture of firearms use'. He had wanted the judge not only to make target shooting safer but to grapple with the wider question of 'whether target shooting of any kind was an acceptable pastime'. In North's eyes, Lord Cullen had concluded that it was.

At 3.30 p.m., Michael Forsyth rose in the House of Commons to address Parliament. The government would be accepting all of Lord Cullen's recommendations, 'and in some respects intend to go further'. In a single powerful paragraph, Forsyth described the events of nine months before: 'The gunman, Thomas Hamilton, entered Dunblane Primary School shortly after 9.30 a.m. and made his way to the gymnasium armed with two 9 mm Browning self-loading pistols and two .357 Smith and Wesson revolvers, together with 743 rounds of ammunition – all of which he lawfully held, and which he legally kept at home, together with more than 1,000 further rounds of ammunition. Within three or four minutes, he fired 105 rounds with the 9 mm Browning, resulting in the deaths of Mrs Gwen Mayor and 16 children, and injuring a further three teaching staff and 14 children. He then used the .357 Smith and Wesson to take his own life.'

Forsyth highlighted the dedication of Ron Taylor and his staff, who, as Cullen said, 'did everything that they possibly could to assist, far beyond what might reasonably have been expected of them'.

Cullen had considered in detail the question of Thomas Hamilton's firearms licences, said Forsyth, adding that 'He points to the weaknesses in the system used by Central Scotland police for the carrying out of inquiries and the making of decisions about firearms applications. In particular, the report is critical of the former deputy chief constable of Central Scotland police, Mr Douglas McMurdo, who was appointed earlier this year to Her Majesty's Inspectorate of Constabulary for Scotland. I thought it right that Mr McMurdo should have sight of the relevant paragraphs in the report, and he has today offered his resignation, which I have accepted. He has informed the Scottish Office that he also intends to resign from Central Scotland police. The House will respect his decision.'

After a few more minutes, Forsyth concluded: 'The whole country has been struck by the courage and dignity with which the community of Dunblane has worked together in the aftermath of this terrible atrocity. That community now looks to the House for rapid and united action.'

As the Secretary of State sat down, George Robertson stood up and extended his gratitude to Lord Cullen, and added, 'I also express my personal gratitude and thanks to the Secretary of State for Scotland for the genuine kindness and consideration that he has shown to myself and to my wife during and after the tragedy – a tragedy that took place in the small town of Dunblane, which he represents and where I and my family have lived for over twenty years.

'On 13 March, we were two rival politicians with politics utterly forgotten in the shadow of unspeakable evil and tragedy; two fathers united in total grief at the horror that we were to witness, and perhaps recall for ever, in a school that we both knew so well; two men, members of the human family, united then and now in an overriding conviction that this massacre, involving 16 tiny children and their brave, dedicated teacher, or anything like it, must never, ever happen again.'

Robertson did admit that 'mistakes were clearly made', the most serious one of which 'was the treatment on the day of the parents of the dead and of the injured. Lord Cullen says that this was unacceptable. Central Scotland police and the chief constable have acknowledged that fault, and have apologised to those who were concerned, but it is a lesson in human handling which must never be lost.'

As far as the families in Dunblane were concerned, there had been no apology from Central Scotland Police.

It had just gone 4 p.m. when the Home Secretary, Michael Howard, began his address to Parliament: 'Among all the words that have been written since that dreadful event at Dunblane, there is one irrefutable fact. The crimes that were committed on 13 March were committed with a gun that was legally bought and legally possessed. Those facts place an extremely onerous duty on the Government to consider what controls there should be on the ownership and possession of guns.'

Howard went on to tell them that, having looked at the practicalities, they could not recommend Lord Cullen's suggestions for disabling handguns. He added, 'I therefore come to Lord Cullen's alternative suggestion of banning multi-shot handguns from individual ownership. I propose to go considerably further than Lord Cullen has suggested in two respects. First, we shall ban all handguns from people's homes. I do not agree with Lord Cullen that it would be safe to allow single-shot handguns to remain in the home. I believe that they should be subject to the same controls as those imposed on multi-shot handguns.

'Secondly, we shall outlaw high-calibre handguns of the kind used by Thomas Hamilton. Low-calibre handguns – .22 rimfire handguns – will have to be used and kept in licensed clubs.'

Howard then acknowledged that these proposals would mean that at least 160,000 handguns, roughly 80 per cent of those in legal possession, would be destroyed, and that appropriate compensation would be paid. Any breach of the new legislation would be a criminal offence, with a maximum penalty of ten years.

The country, he said, would now have 'some of the toughest gun control laws in the world. We shall ban all handguns from the home. We shall outlaw completely higher-calibre handguns such as those owned and used by Thomas Hamilton. We shall require .22 rimfire handguns to be kept in gun clubs under conditions of the most stringent security. And we shall drastically strengthen the rules under which firearm certificates are granted.'

Howard concluded by urging the opposition parties to support the bill, saying, 'I am confident that if they do, it could have Royal Assent by Christmas. The country expects nothing less.'

At this, shadow Home Secretary Jack Straw, who sat on the front bench opposite Howard, rose to reply that the country should expect a good deal more than 'nothing less', adding, 'With respect, we do not believe that his proposals go far enough.' The compromise would still leave 40,000 handguns, including many

.22 semi-automatics, in private ownership. 'Nine years ago, our nation was similarly repulsed by the consequences of the slaughter of innocent people in Hungerford by a lawfully licensed gunman. Our actions then failed to match what was needed. Is it not the case that today we owe it to the victims of both Hungerford and Dunblane not to fail again?'

The significant achievement of Michael Forsyth's quiet diplomacy in getting the Tories to agree to a ban was quickly lost and scarcely recognised. The Secretary of State for Scotland had delivered what the Snowdrop Campaign had first requested back in early April, and what Mick North had passionately recommended, but times had changed – and so had the demands of the campaign group and the families. When Les Morton read out the families' statement at a press conference in Dunblane, it did not praise the Conservative government and instead condemned what they viewed as another unacceptable compromise: 'Any decision to continue to permit lawful possession of firearms implies a willingness by this government to tolerate gun crime. It also implies a willingness to tolerate another Hungerford or Dunblane.'

Privately, Ann Pearston, who appeared raw and overworked during her speech at the press conference afterwards, was impressed by how far the Conservatives had gone, saying later that she had been 'overwhelmed by what Howard did', having believed the government would only ban home storage, the Home Secretary's favoured response.

For many of the parents, the press conference was the beginning of a treadmill of live radio and television interviews. On two occasions, North was directly followed by Michael Howard, who was also touring the news studios promoting the government's compromise.

Later that evening, Mick North, Les Morton and David Scott travelled to the Glasgow headquarters of BBC Scotland, where *Newsnight* was hosting a live studio discussion chaired by Jeremy Paxman. Ann Pearston was also in attendance, as well as representatives of Britain's now incensed shooting community. In the green room before the discussion, one of the shooters complained loudly about the financial cost of the government's handgun ban. North seethed and chose to leave the room.

For *The Scotsman*'s columnist Ian Bell, who had taken offence to the Crown Office's attempts to silence his profession's public duty to investigate Hamilton, Lord Cullen's report was a disappointment. 'It offers compromise in a matter that will only be exacerbated by compromise,' he wrote. 'It encourages the Government, having done "more than Cullen", to dig in its heels and refuse to take the final, rational step.'

Other newspapers were more supportive of the government, but the *Daily Mirror*, *The Sun* and the *Sunday Mail* all relaunched campaigns to secure a total ban on all handguns, including the .22.

―――

Ann, Rosemary Hunter and Jacqueline Walsh of Snowdrop now had to learn how the Houses of Parliament worked. The bill's title would first be read out in the House of Commons (known as the first reading). Then it would be printed for MPs to read, from which there would follow the second reading, during which the bill would be debated in the Commons for the first time. What followed next would be the committee stage, where the bill would be scrutinised line by line and any amendments proposed. If an amendment was proposed, it would trigger a debate and subsequent vote on whether the amendment should be accepted. A report stage would then be followed by a third – and final – reading, offering the opportunity for further minor changes.

After going through the House of Commons, the firearms bill would be passed to the House of Lords, where it would go through the same individual stages. If there were any amendments from peers, it would trigger a back-and-forth between both houses until differences were resolved. Although the House of Commons eventually always triumphs, the House of Lords can delay the government. When the bill was finally agreed, it would be sent to the monarch, usually in monthly batches, for her approval (known as royal assent), at which point the bill would be transformed into an Act of Parliament, with a specific date on which it would become law.

The weekend after the publication of Cullen's report, a war council assembled in Bisley in Surrey. The village had long been home to the National Shooting Centre, and around six hundred enthusiasts had gathered to calculate their next move. For those who arrived with .357 Magnums or 9 mm Browning pistols in their locked gun cases, it was with the almost certain knowledge that this would be their final legal competition.

Among the attendees was Albie Fox, a former helicopter pilot, who ran a machine embroidery business in Shropshire. As the chair of the Sportsman's Association of Great Britain and Northern

Ireland, he declared that if Snowdrop could secure 750,000 signatures, they would trump them by seeking one million in defence of guns. 'We have maintained a dignified silence out of respect for the families of Dunblane,' said Fox. 'But that dignity has been abused by single-issue campaigners and cynical politicians.' If their campaign failed and the legislation passed, Fox vowed to set up a new political party and field candidates at next year's general election.

The Shooters' Rights Association, based in Wales, decided to pull the trigger on plans to field political candidates. In a deliberately provocative move, Richard Law, the SRA's secretary, chose Michael Forsyth's constituency of Stirling and Dunblane as their principal target. Elizabeth Law, his Scottish wife, would consider standing against the Secretary of State for Scotland. Over the next few days, Elizabeth gave media interviews in which she posed in the family armoury: a room with a steel window shutter in which the couple's sixteen licensed guns were locked. She believed the government was acting 'like a dictatorship', and that it was time for all shooters to stand up and be counted at the ballot box. In the end, though, after a week of television and press interviews, Elizabeth decided against standing.

In the town of Arnold, the Nottingham Shooting Centre had had an estimated value of £400,000 before the government's announcement, but according to owners Bruce Rainford and Brian Phillips it was now virtually worthless. Staff had been made redundant and the pair feared losing their homes, as both properties had been put down as security for the centre. 'We set out to run a friendly, family social aspect of the sport,' said Rainford. 'Anyone with a violent history or an inclination to violence just wouldn't be here. These are not weapons, they are firearms. To call them weapons is an insult.' As few of the centre's 900 members, which included 120 police officers, used .22-calibre firearms, the centre was no longer sustainable, according to the co-owner: 'I am facing financial ruin. Closing my business and putting me out of work won't stop another tragedy and won't guarantee to save another life. It makes me terribly bitter,' he said.

Rainford and Phillips were not alone in their concerns. Brian Carter, the director of the Gun Trade Association, said the industry was collapsing: 'My members are losing their businesses and their homes because the venom that should have been directed at Thomas Hamilton and at Central Scotland Police is being directed at them ... I hope the people who campaigned for a ban on handguns are happy.'

The government's gun ban attracted the attention of the world's media. On 21 October, CNN ran a segment headlined 'Bloodbath triggers drive to take guns away from every home in Great Britain. Could the same thing happen here in the US?' The debate, hosted by broadcast journalist Mary Tillotson, featured Gill Marshall-Andrews representing the Gun Control Network and Guy Savage from the British Shooters' Rights Association.

Marshall-Andrews argued that Britain was anxious not to repeat the same mistakes: 'We had a disaster in this country in 1987 when Michael Ryan killed seventeen people with a mixture of handguns and other weapons. If at that point we had banned handguns, Dunblane might not have happened.'

Savage, on the other hand, was intent on blaming the police for failing to act: 'There have allegedly been seven separate investigations into Thomas Hamilton. On more than one occasion, junior police officers asked senior officers to revoke his gun licence. On every single occasion that any kind of police intervention could have been undertaken, those items that were brought to their attention were ignored or blocked and nothing was ever done about him. Shooters are being pilloried for the failures of a police department to actually administer the legal process ... The terrible acts that happen all over the world have nothing to do with individuals like myself. I'm not responsible for the deaths of those children. I don't see why I need to be put out of a job. I don't see the reason why I should have my property confiscated.'

Privately, there were tensions between the 'hot heads' of the SRA, always quick to fire off a provocation, and the cooler heads of the Sportsman's Association. Mike Yardley stepped in to assist the organisation's bid to secure a million-strong petition. The new application form was headlined: 'They thought there was a gun lobby & there is now'. An accompanying leaflet stated: 'Keeping a low profile, turning the other cheek has failed. All shooting sports are on the line and, whilst the anti-campaign relied on children signing something they may not have understood we have far greater credibility. For a paltry £5, you can add your voice to this swelling body of very angry people.'

The strategy would be two-pronged: a public campaign designed to overthrow the planned legislation through 'people power' would act alongside a private lobbying campaign that would push to drastically increase the compensation available in the event of failure.

On 23 October, the Firearms Consultative Committee met for the first time since the Cullen Report publication and recommended the Home Office extend compensation to a wider cross section of shooting-adjacent businesses. The next day, the secretaries of the National Pistol Association, NRA and the

British Shooting Sports Council met civil servants at the Home Office in Whitehall to insist on adequate compensation for legal, law-abiding businesses.

One week later, the big guns were drawn. Sir Jerry Wiggin led a delegation of seventeen Conservative MPs and one Ulster Unionist MP to meet with Michael Howard. The delegation not only pushed against the ban but insisted that, should it go through, funded compensation should be fair. The government had been planning to recompense handgun owners at a price pegged to the weapon's value on the day prior to the announcement of their ban; Wiggin, however, argued that it should be pegged to a date prior to the shooting and that there should be financial compensation for holsters, cases and specialist security cabinets. He then warned that 'this was just for the individual', and that businesses required a bespoke compensation package commensurate with their needs.

Target Gun magazine delivered a petition to the prime minister protesting that 500 businesses and 16,000 jobs were in jeopardy and stating that the December issue was their last, as advertising revenue had collapsed. The editor said that this final issue would 'provide its distraught readers with information for our final "push" against this unjust and almost insane piece of legislation'.

In the fledgling world of the internet, gun enthusiasts also rallied to the cause and urged different shooting disciplines to set aside 'internecine bickering', which was damaging a collective campaign. An email circulated that suggested an intelligence-gathering operation on their 'enemies', including Snowdrop: 'We need to know as much about our enemies as we can. From the figures and politicians who oppose us, to details about Snowdrop. The latter is the most vociferous and it is important for us to dig up any facts that can be used to question the integrity of those who run, front and contribute to that organisation.' One contributor to the online discussion offered his assistance: 'As a professional communicator, I know how to distort information and manipulate facts.' Ann Pearston was branded as a 'non-poll-tax-paying IRA sympathiser', all of which was untrue.

To capture the public's imagination and highlight the lethality of a .22 handgun, Snowdrop and the Dunblane families rebranded the weapon as the 'assassin's choice'. The gun was small, easily concealable and demonstrably lethal, as illustrated by the assassination of Yitzhak Rabin, the Israeli prime minister, the previous year, while a .22 handgun had also been used in the attempted assassination of Ronald Reagan in 1981 and Pope John Paul II the same year. The justification for not banning the firearm was that it was used in target shooting in the Olympic Games, but as Mick North argued in an article published in *Scotland on Sunday*, 'It is time to ask why the Olympic Games, a Celebration of Life, should include a sport which involves instruments of death.' Defenders of the sport could argue that such a strict view would also strip out javelin and archery from the competition.

For Snowdrop, the next objective was to persuade enough Conservative MPs to defy their party's whip and vote for the bill's amendment, which would include .22 handguns. In late October, Mick North and Les Morton flew to London to attend meetings in Westminster. The most important of these was organised by Robert Hughes, the Conservative MP for Harrow West, who had arranged for them to meet with backbench Conservatives. Only two MPs attended: Hugh Dykes and Terry Dicks, both of whom had previously committed to the cause. Morton and North returned to Parliament a week later to meet MPs Phil Gallie and Bill Walker. Walker took a superior tone. He told the grieving fathers it was not the means that had been important, but the intent. Thomas Hamilton could just as easily have killed their children by driving an articulated lorry into the gym hall, he said. Neither of the second two MPs was prepared to consider stepping beyond the government's current path.

When the bill reached the committee stage, where amendments could be proposed, Hughes attached a document that would include all lower-calibre handguns including .22 firearms among those to be prohibited. The bill's vote was scheduled for the evening of 18 November. It was time to rally as many supporters as possible for a final push.

On 1 November, the new Firearms (Amendment) Bill went before the Commons for the first time, and again Michael Howard defended the right of shooters to own .22 handguns.

In the following day's edition of *The Independent*, Ann criticised the government for leaving 40,000 lethal weapons untouched: 'Lord Cullen's condensing of the inquiry evidence was excellent. But his recommendations were narrow, vague and legalistic. The government has converted them into a bill in a narrow, blinkered way.'

To the four hundred enthusiastic shooters who gathered on 5 November in the Grand Committee Room just off Westminster Hall with its ancient hammer beam roof and worn flagstones, a handgun ban was repellent. They listened to several Conservative MPs who believed their government was overreacting. Sir Jerry

Wiggin was preaching to the converted when he described shooters as law-abiding citizens being demonised by a virulent media. It was a line that earned warm applause.

During that month, the Dunblane parents were persistent in lobbying politicians, organising multiple trips to Westminster. There was initial hope that the amendment for a total ban on all handguns might be supported by the Ulster Unionists representing Northern Ireland. However, the party's leader, David Trimble, argued that it was wrong to make a 'fetish of small arms': a sawn-off shotgun could easily be concealed and was 'just as dangerous'. Rather than ban handguns, it was wiser to increase school security. There would be no question of a vote to support a total ban on handguns; it was only a matter of whether the party might abstain.

Snowdrop had more success with the smaller Democratic Unionist Party (DUP). Their leader, Ian Paisley, had spoken eloquently in the aftermath of the shooting and urged the party to put their three votes behind the amendment. Leaving the DUP's office, Rosemary had a strong feeling they could add the party to their tally.

The Gun Control Network, meanwhile, had organised another private meeting in November with Conservatives who were considering voting against the government. The event coincided with the second reading of the Firearms (Amendment) Bill and was attended by Rod Mayor, the widower of Gwen Mayor.

During Prime Minister's Questions, John Major was again asked and again refused to permit a free vote on banning handguns. It was a position he repeated at his next meeting, during which Major and Forsyth met with John Crozier, Les Morton and Martyn Dunn, each of whom had lost a daughter. The fathers wanted to know why the prime minister had allowed a free vote on corporal punishment in schools but refused to do so on the issue of handguns. Major explained that he could afford to be more relaxed in the former case, which was less important. Crozier told Major that there were hundreds of MPs who backed a total ban. The prime minister pushed back, arguing that they 'weren't flooding into his office'. Major had agonised over the decision but could not agree to a free vote, he said. Morton understood that politics was the art of compromise, but he argued that this issue was a matter of life and death: 'Compromise will cost lives.' The meeting lasted forty minutes, but despite the fathers' persistence, Major refused to budge. So unpopular had the gun ban become that Major had to whip his own MPs to stop them voting against it.

Afterwards, speaking to reporters, the three men praised Major's courtesy and generosity with his time, but said his stance was wrong and that he would have to consider who would be to blame should another atrocity take place: 'We are nine months away from the deaths of our children. I would be interested to hear what the prime minister could say to future families that were so affected as we have been,' said Morton, who then went on to urge voters to lobby their MP. 'Do they want to live in a society where people can quite legitimately have handguns?' he asked. 'Do they want to take the chance that one day their children, their father, their mother, their brother, their sister could be murdered like our children were? Everyone else in the country will think this could never happen to them. We thought it would never happen to us.'

Earlier in the day, under less emotional circumstances than at their previous meeting in July, the parents had met with Tony Blair and George Robertson. The Labour leader said he would continue to press for a free vote and that the party's policy was that public safety could only be guaranteed if there was a total ban on the civilian use of handguns. If the Conservative Party refused a free vote and Labour should win the election next year, Blair would ensure a ban on .22 calibre handguns.

Both the pro and anti-gun lobbies agreed on the necessity of a free vote. Michael Yardley, now the official spokesman for the Sportsman's Association, argued that only a free vote would create the opportunity for wide-ranging debate: 'By denying a free vote,' he said, 'the government is also denying an opportunity to Parliament to explore this legislation and its flaws in detail.'

During the debate that accompanied the second reading, two MPs opposed to any ban on handguns described the abuse they had endured in recent months. John Carlisle, MP for Luton North, said, 'I received hate mail and death threats – so it isn't all one-way.' However, Dame Jill Knight, the MP for Edgbaston, who was a member of the Home Affairs Select Committee, accused the tabloid press and public of whipping up a bitter campaign of 'hate and vilification such as I have never seen before: *The Sun* newspaper and a rag called the *Daily Record* gave out our addresses and phone numbers and urged their readers to write or phone and condemn us. As a result, I had a number of death threats. I was sent photographs of myself with a bullet hole through the centre of my forehead. Parcels of excreta were sent to me, and worst of all there were threats that people intended to lie in wait outside the schools my grandchildren attend and shoot them.' Dame Jill insisted that those in opposition to tighter gun controls were not 'bloodthirsty savages', and ended with a lament: 'I never thought I would see the day when a Conservative government would rush to deprive such people of the opportunity to pursue their chosen sport.'

ONE MORNING IN MARCH

The Home Affairs Select Committee had agreed collectively to send a letter of complaint to the Press Complaints Committee about how their members had been treated. As Labour MP Chris Mullin wrote in his diary, 'The truth is, of course, that most Tories aren't used to being on the receiving end of the sort of hate campaign that is usually reserved for the Arthur Scargills and Peter Tatchells of this world.'

London was colder than usual on 18 November. The light rain falling held a hint of snow. Later that evening, MPs would vote on the bill's amendment.

Members of the gun lobby had gathered early and were outside waving placards such as '57,000 SHOOTERS ARE BEING PUNISHED FOR ONE MAN'S ACTION'; one protester wore his National Pistol Association sweater amended with the single word: 'INNOCENT'.

Passing the protesters on her way into Parliament, Eileen Harrild felt little sympathy for them. The gym teacher, who was still recovering from her wounds, had agreed to lend her support to the families' final hope to secure a total ban on all handguns under the present government. Speaking at a press conference beside Rod Mayor, Harrild spoke in a soft, emotional voice. 'I am down in Westminster to shame MPs into doing the right thing,' she said through rising tears. 'It seems no more than common sense to me to ban all handguns. It just seems ludicrous that the government are thinking of retaining .22-calibre handguns in the name of sport. This is just not an argument.'

The line-by-line committee stage of the Firearms (Amendment) Bill commenced later that night. In the debate preceding the vote, Conservative MP David Mellor said that for the first time in his political career he would defy the government's three-line whip and vote to ban .22 handguns. He joked at how 'craven' and 'snivelling' he must have been not to have defied the government over the past seventeen years; those opposed would have to ask how they would be able to look the electorate in the eye if someone 'creeps out of the woodwork of the latest little loophole that we have left, and does something awful'.

He said, 'If ... we trust the very people that let us down before, we will not have made adequate redress for the ghastly tragedy that hit the community of Dunblane back in March.' He took time to praise the Snowdrop Campaign for 'the measured manner in which it has insisted that the issue will not go away' and said that one parent had told him today: 'If we do not achieve a complete ban, I do not think I shall ever be able to get over it.' Mellor said MPs had run out of road as far as the public was concerned, and it was time to ban all handguns.

George Robertson stood to address the House. He first posed a question: if a gunman had killed seventeen MPs instead of young children and a teacher, would the Commons 'have waited eight months to discuss a partial ban on the very instrument that killed so many legislators of this land?' This was an echo of a question posed by Pam Ross on a front-page article in *The Independent* in the summer.

This inflammatory start prompted an immediate interruption from the Home Secretary. Michael Howard rose to criticise Robertson's 'absolutely outrageous suggestion', then pointed out that both he and the Labour Party had agreed to the timetable associated with the Cullen Inquiry and demanded he apologise to the House.

Robertson insisted that he wasn't criticising the government but taking collective responsibility for the House of Commons.

The Secretary of State for Scotland, Michael Forsyth, then interrupted and also insisted Robertson clarify his position: 'Surely he is not for a moment suggesting that the reaction of the House of Commons to the murder of 16 children and their teacher would be any different if a crime had been committed in the House involving 17 Members of Parliament?'

When Forsyth had concluded his point, Robertson looked across at him and replied, 'The right hon. Gentleman and I have stood side by side during the whole episode and I do not regret that for a moment, but we have arrived at a different conclusion at this stage and that is the point that I make solemnly and seriously to the Committee.'

Once Robertson had finished Forsyth responded, 'The hon. Gentleman is right to say that we have stood side by side on this issue, and I am grateful for the way in which he has done that, but it is important that he should make it clear that the House of Commons is not treating the events of Dunblane any less seriously ... We may disagree on the appropriate response, but it is wrong to suggest that the response would have been different if those events had happened here in Westminster and not in my constituency.'

A few minutes later, as Robertson closed his argument, he made one last emotional plea: 'There were snowdrops growing in Dunblane on that awful day in March this year. That is why the grassroots campaign – with hardly any money, but with conviction and common-sense arguments on its side – set out to make sure that no similar tragedy could affect any other small community in this country. The snowdrops will be back in bloom in March next year and the memories, which are still so fresh to so many people, will flood back to remind us and the world of what happened so close to us.'

In the Strangers' Gallery, the public terrace above the debating chamber, the wounded and the bereaved looked on. Eileen Harrild had stayed to watch the debate and was joined by Rod Mayor and John Crozier. Ann Pearston was also present and, at one point, walked past Guy Savage of the Shooters' Rights Association. At 9.19 p.m. the Speaker of the House, Betty Boothroyd, called the House to order and announced that the votes would now take place. The MPs came down from the green leather benches and filed into their chosen lobby: 281 MPs into Aye; 306 into No. The amendment to extend the ban to all handguns was defeated by twenty-five votes.

The partial ban was eventually passed 306 to 281. As the vote was announced, a shout of 'Shame' was heard in the House. The last opportunity to secure a complete ban on handguns during the current parliamentary session had passed.

There was nothing else they could do – for now.

For the Dunblane families each failure of the police was a single frame of film; these frames laced together unspooled into the gym hall: the officer who had assisted Hamilton in obtaining the licence for a second 9 mm semi-automatic handgun and a second .357 revolver, the empty intelligence file, the disregarded warnings, the failure to recognise police powers, the 'rubber stamp' firearms licence renewal. Then the grim coda: the callous delays on the day, the bullying of the bereaved, the doctored timeline, the lies. As an institution, the principal duty of Central Scotland Police seemed to be to protect itself. In times of crisis, it has been said, 'deputy heads must roll'. In the case of Deputy Chief Constable Douglas McMurdo, as the named individual most criticised by Lord Cullen, his resignation was expected. But William Wilson, chief constable since 1990, managed to insulate himself from direct criticism with opaque, generalising assurances. As Wilson was keen to point out, he lived in Dunblane and was 'one of them' – but for many parents and the wounded, his presence only made life more difficult. To see the man they held partly responsible for the death of their son or daughter going through life as usual, laughing at the bar of the golf club, was hard to take. If there was anything to apologise for, Wilson said, he would do so. In time, it became apparent he never would.

Central Scotland Police was technically 'answerable' to the Central Scotland Joint Police Board, a panel made up of local councillors, but they appeared more concerned with how the force felt than holding senior officers to account. When the board met in July, its members did not bring up the shootings.

One week after the Cullen Report was published, the board met to question Wilson and Detective Chief Superintendent John Ogg. The first item on the agenda was a vote to hold the meeting behind closed doors. They did ultimately agree to hold a post-meeting press conference, where the board's convener, Jeanette Burness, insisted both officers had received tough questioning and had nothing left to answer. The following year, Her Majesty's Inspectorate of Constabulary (HMIC) reviewed Central Scotland Police's conduct and concluded that the force was to be commended for adapting quickly to Cullen's criticisms. As regards the excruciating delay in informing the parents, the report stated that 'the procedures were applied with the best intentions, but the force now recognises their shortcomings and has acted appropriately.'

The question of whether to take legal action against Central Scotland Police dominated Thursday Night Group meetings during the autumn of 1996. Peter Watson, though no longer paid by the government to act for the families, continued to give legal advice. A lawsuit for wrongful death and the physical disabilities of the wounded would be expensive to mount, would possibly last for years and had no guarantee of success, and in the end, they decided against pursuing one.

Despite external appearances to the contrary, however, the shooting weighed heavily on Chief Constable Wilson. One evening before Christmas, Wilson and his son Ewan, a young probationary officer at Central Police, went for a pint at the Tappit Hen. He was aware the pub was popular with the bereaved parents, a few of whom were seated in the corner when they arrived. As they waited at the bar, one of the parents began to shout and swear at Wilson, who told his son not to react: the parents had suffered an unimaginable loss. They finished their drinks and left.

Wilson would always defend the police in public, but privately he felt tremendous guilt. Arguably the worst crime in Britain in the twentieth century had happened under his watch. In the new year, he met with the force psychologist, where he was joined by his wife Catherine and Ewan, who had never seen his father so upset. Until Wilson's death, a teddy bear from among the donations left outside the school sat in a chair in the conservatory of the family home, a memory of a day he could never forget.

A request by the Thursday Night Group had been made in early October to Stirling Council to put a Christmas tree in Dunblane Cemetery, and the families had taken the lack of response to mean they could go ahead. The tree they chose was a six-foot Norwegian fir, decorated with seventeen white lights. Then, in early December, their request was refused. After several phone calls it was revealed that objections had been raised in the local community. In the season of goodwill, an exception had been made for the most brutally bereaved.

The Thursday Night Group wrote to the council: 'The tree was to symbolise peace and hope and to help our families through this first Christmas without our children. However, we would not want our wishes to be fulfilled at the cost of dividing the community.'

When news of the cancelled tree broke in the media, Ann Dickson, the local councillor for Dunblane East, was interviewed on the BBC's *Reporting Scotland*: 'We've got a division. It had to happen. And it's regrettable that it's happened over a Christmas tree. But I would say that the Christmas tree is a symptom of what is wrong in Dunblane.'

What was wrong in Dunblane was that a portion of the town had run out of patience with the parents. On 13 March they put their grief on a clock and deemed their time to have elapsed. For nine months, certain people within the community had become increasingly resentful at the black cloud that hung over the town, at the press reports, at the Cullen Inquiry, at the campaigning, at what they saw as a need to always defer to the parents of the deceased. An unnatural hierarchy of need had been created, they felt, with the apex occupied by the parents of a dead son or daughter. The editor of the

Stirling Observer, Alan Rennie, supported Dickson's stance: 'What she has said is what I have heard on countless occasions since about May or June this year.' Then the floodgates opened, with newspaper reports about the bereaved parents' concerns about the school board's fundraising and even their voluble behaviour in the Tappit Hen.

For North, the backlash against the Christmas tree severed another thread tying him to the town. He had only just summoned the strength to arrange Sophie's headstone and now he was being lectured by strangers on how to grieve. He took comfort in C. S. Lewis's *A Grief Observed*, in which the author states that 'an odd by-product of my loss is that I'm aware of being an embarrassment to everyone I meet ... Perhaps the bereaved ought to be isolated in special settlements like lepers.' Before Christmas he wrote an article for *Scotland on Sunday*, in which he said, 'The public deaths of our children, followed by the public inquiry, made it inevitable that grieving privately would be difficult. It has been suggested that we should have left the issue of gun control to others and that we have delayed our grieving process as a consequence of our involvement. This again presumes there is a normal grieving process. I, along with other families, knew that the death and injuries in the gym that day were the result of poor gun laws. We were in a unique position to be heard. But such is the fickleness of public opinion that I doubt we would have received such wide attention had we grieved in silence for a year and then taken up the gun issue in 1997. We believe we have done what we had to do to prevent others having to grieve over the loss of their loved ones in such a massacre or gun incident.'

Yet Dunblane would be a part of the nation's Christmas, as a protest song was released and narrowly missed becoming Britain's Christmas number one.

Ted Christopher owned a record and musical instrument shop in Stirling and as a musician played pubs at night and weddings at the weekend. In the wake of the shooting, he adapted a song from his regular repertoire, Bob Dylan's 'Knockin' on Heaven's Door', adding an extra verse: 'Lord put all the guns in the ground / we just can't shoot them any more / it's time that we spread some love around / before we're knocking on heaven's door.' John Crozier, who had had the musician play at his own wedding, brought a rough tape recording to the Thursday Night Group, who agreed to seek its release as part of their campaign. For the first and only time, Dylan agreed to an adaptation of his original lyrics, and when the story broke in the press of the parents' plans, Paul McCartney's manager Geoff Baker secured the free use of the Abbey Road studio, while Mark Knopfler of Dire Straits volunteered to play session guitar. Christopher organised a choir of children from the town, including siblings of those killed or injured. The cover of the single was a drawing by Emma Crozier, and when Christopher and the children's choir first performed on *Top of the Pops* they were greeted by the Spice Girls, while Robbie Williams played football in the car park with the children. The single went to number one the week before Christmas and sold 673,000 units, with Midge Ure sending out hundreds of copies instead of Christmas cards.

As expected, the bill's passage through the House of Lords was not smooth. The second chamber of the Houses of Parliament applies rigorous scrutiny to prospective legislation, but most members in 1996 were hereditary peers who had earned their seats through birth rather than personal achievement or public election. The bill was first debated on the evening of 16 December, shortly before Parliament broke for Christmas. Eight members, all of whom were life peers – a non-heritable title appointed by the monarch – voiced their support for the bill or encouraged even tougher measures. Yet the majority of speakers were harshly critical of any measure limiting the rights of recreational shooters. Nine members had attended Eton, which offered marksmanship as part of its curriculum. The Earl of Shrewsbury, the former chair of the Firearms Consultative Committee, an organisation established in the wake of Hungerford, said, 'It is a very great pity that Thomas Hamilton and Michael Ryan committed their atrocities with legally held weapons. The problem does not lie with those who legally hold guns. The problem lies with the millions of illegally held weapons which are cheap and freely available.' The Earl of Haddington, a member of a gun club, prefaced his comments with a note that, as a father of three young children, he felt 'appalling shock' at what had taken place in Dunblane. He then said that as a young boy his father's gamekeeper had taken great care in teaching him the safety aspects of handling a gun. Writing his report on the debate, Donald Macintyre, the political editor of *The Independent*, quoted Walter Bagehot, the nineteenth-century essayist, who quipped that 'the cure for admiring the House of Lords was to go and look at it.'

XIII

THE PRINCE

PRINCESS Diana had attempted to make clear her private support for the Snowdrop Campaign during their visit to Kensington Palace. Her former father-in-law Prince Philip, on the other hand, was eager to make his support for the gun lobby public. In the week before Christmas, he said on BBC Radio 5 Live, 'I sympathise desperately with the people who are bereaved at Dunblane, but I'm not altogether convinced that it's the best system to somehow shift the blame onto a very large and peaceable part of the community ... I mean if a cricketer, for instance, suddenly decided to go into a school and batter a lot of people to death with a cricket bat, which he could very easily do, I mean are you going to ban cricket bats?'

An editorial in *The Guardian* was quick to criticise Philip's clumsiness, calling the prince's remarks 'wrong, ill-judged and inappropriate'.' Ian Bell said in *The Scotsman* that this 'latest piece of freelance sagacity was timed precisely to coincide with the rearguard action being mounted in the Lords against the Firearms (Amendment) Bill. It was, equally, a public gesture of solidarity with his fellow shooters in the middle of a fierce debate at a time of horrible symbolism and intense emotion for the families of

Dunblane.' He also pointed out the redundancy of the Duke of Edinburgh's analogy: 'When a maniac entered a Wolverhampton infant school in July with a two-foot machete, he dealt, inadvertently if psychotically, with the duke's arguments. This was something more than a cricket bat; four adults and three children were injured but no one died. A teacher's bravery had something to do with it, but the limited technology available to her attacker mattered more.'

The next day, Buckingham Palace issued a rare public apology: 'Prince Philip had no intention whatsoever of causing offence or distress to anyone and he is sorry if he has done so.'

Ann Pearston heard the prince's comment while Christmas shopping in Edinburgh. She was quick to respond: 'To think of the queen coming up here and laying a wreath at our school and then hearing her husband say something like this sickens me. I certainly cannot remember the last time a tennis player walked into a primary school and massacred sixteen children and their teacher.'

Rosemary Hunter was by no means a royalist, but she was exhausted, emotionally and physically, by the continuing tension, and wished to return to her family. For her, Snowdrop had achieved its primary goal; tough new legislation was being introduced by the Conservative government, and while Snowdrop had failed to secure the prohibition of .22-calibre handguns, the Labour leadership had promised it would be a priority should they gain power next year. What more could be done? Rosemary and Jacqueline thought it best to let Snowdrop go, for its petals to be cast into the wind.

Jacqueline Walsh and her husband Dave were more critical than Rosemary of Ann's statements about Prince Philip. They too wished to end Snowdrop. In early 1997, they delivered a letter to that effect to Ann. The couple were upset that the campaign had become involved in what they viewed as media-fuelled hysteria. In their opinion, the attention was doing Snowdrop no good – in fact, judging by the correspondence received, it had done considerable harm.

On 14 January, Dave Walsh wrote a long letter to Ann which articulated the Walshes' feelings about Snowdrop and Pearston's continued role. He claimed that Pearston's speech at the Labour Party conference had been praised by a colleague, a university lecturer, who had also suggested that Ann was now using her position for personal gain. Dave said that this belief – that Ann was taking the moral high ground and attempting to tell the community what to do – was understandable. He then wrote that taking the moral high ground on her own was dangerous when the Dunblane community did not recognise her as one of their own.

The Walshes had recently moved into the town, across the road from John Crozier, and were perhaps more aware of the town's compassion fatigue. Dave said that the fallout from Pearston's comments about Prince Philip had landed on both him and his wife; they had received more hate mail, and Rosemary, he wrote, had received abusive phone calls. He closed the letter by saying that it had not been written in bitterness and that Ann's interests and those of Snowdrop were his primary concern.

The couple's letter came as a shock to Ann, and her husband Doug was furious. Snowdrop had reached a crossroads: Jacqueline and Rosemary wished to stop, but Ann was adamant they continue to the general election. Though deeply hurt, Ann refused to stand down and, as January progressed, was more intent than ever on pursuing new media opportunities, notably the advertising agency Delaney Fletcher Bozell's offer to create a press and cinema campaign.

Earlier that month Barry Delaney, founder and creative partner of Delaney Fletcher Bozell, had contacted Pearston at Snowdrop and offered to create a poster and cinema campaign. The work would be pro bono and serve to attract attention to the agency; it would, as the agency stated, 'mark the anniversary of the tragedy', with a view to maximising pressure on politicians of all parties in the run-up to the election.

On 17 January, three days after her husband's letter had arrived, Jacqueline faxed Delaney Fletcher and said that the press release should not be put out, 'or at least do not include my and Rosemary's names on it.' She explained that Ann should have shown her the press release before it was passed to the advertising agency, that she did not agree with the contents, and that 'we do not agree to anyone exploiting the anniversary in any way – it should be a time for reflection, prayer and peace – not to be used for political (or any other types of) gain.'

A meeting for the members of Snowdrop was set for Wednesday, 22 January. The previous Friday, Jacqueline had sent a short fax to Ann requesting she bring a record of her unpaid expenses: winding up Snowdrop would include closing its bank account. 'Let's not spoil a good thing,' she wrote. 'We can then all join Gun Control Network or whatever.'

At the meeting, the women's disagreement was total. Because the group had not been established as a formal organisation or licensed charity but as a loose agreement between friends, there was no official mechanism to bring it to a close. Ann argued that

Snowdrop should continue to highlight the issue until the general election. Her now former colleagues strongly disagreed.

In the meantime, Delaney Fletcher Bozell had drafted a range of ideas and approaches to the campaign, and Ann spoke with Mick North to set up a meeting with the Thursday Night Group. The meeting proved an awkward one for Ann. Not everyone spoke to her, and for the first time she could feel a chill. Her relationship with some of the parents had become strained.

On Saturday, 11 January, a crowd of 10,000 protesters marched through the streets of London. The protest was organised by the Sportsman's Association, and protesters waved banners declaring 'WE'RE NOT THE GUILTY' and 'UNFAIR, UNETHICAL AND UN-BRITISH'. As part of the protest a note of thanks was delivered to Prince Philip in recognition of his vocal defence of shooters' rights. A separate petition, signed by 64,000 supporters – considerably less than their target of one million – was delivered by Michael Yardley to 10 Downing Street.

In the House of Lords, peers voted 158 to 135 for an amendment to increase compensation for those gun clubs forced to close because of the new law. The cost of compensation would likely rise to upwards of £500 million. In early February, the Lords then attempted to dilute the bill by voting to permit disassembled .22 handguns to be kept at home, a recommendation the government had already deemed unworkable.

Jacqueline Walsh, though resolved to disbanding Snowdrop, was incensed enough to comment to the press that this development was 'unacceptable'. The government agreed and stated that the amendment attached by the Lords would be reversed when the bill returned to the Commons. George Robertson criticised the peers' actions as 'disgraceful'; Jack Straw accused them of representing 'no interest but their own'.

The government was determined to get the bill passed before the first anniversary of the shooting. It returned to the Commons on 18 February, where several pro-shooting MPs argued that the government should trust law-abiding shooters to keep their disassembled .22 pistols at home. This stance was supported by ninety-five Conservative MPs, including six former cabinet ministers.

However, this was not enough. The Commons voted by a majority of 160 to scrap the peers' amendments. The single amendment the government did accept stipulated the creation of a national database for firearms licences. The total amount of compensation to gun owners and businesses would be £87 million.

The Firearms Bill was given royal assent on 27 February. The document was taken to Buckingham Palace where it was read by Queen Elizabeth, who would not have forgotten her emotional visit to Dunblane on that most desolate of Mothers' Days almost a year earlier.

The following day, Guy Savage wrote to the Cybershooters online community with a message from the Shooters' Rights Association. They were to now write to the queen to ask for a Royal Commission on firearms which would establish 'the facts behind Hungerford and Dunblane'. Savage insisted the monarch paid attention to her 'mailbag' and asserted that 'you haven't anyone else to write to now except the media!' He had spoken with the National Pistol Association's Fighting Fund and the Sportsman's Association the previous day, and all three groups had agreed that it was time to take the on 'fight'; this would require 'money and hatchet burying'. In the message, Savage said: 'Our sport is being banned because of the same prejudices that promoted inaction or apathy amongst a bitterly divided sport', and he called for a 'national truce', urging the shooting community to 'stop sniping at each other' and saying the government had grown to rely on 'the divisions between the different groups'. In an impassioned lament at the weapons prised from their hands, he wrote: 'A hundred years of division has cost us SLRs, Pistols, Shotguns and rights to firearms for self-defence. Enough is enough, it has got to stop now and shooters have GOT to show their teeth and be able to bite the hand that beats them.'

As March approached, the Thursday Night Group issued a statement requesting that the anniversary be left unmarked by any press, memorial event or religious service. Members of the community were instead invited, if they wished to remember the victims, to place a single lit candle in their windows at 7 p.m. It was an idea that caught fire in the national press, which urged the country to illuminate their windows. The *Daily Record* gave away free candles to readers, and *The Sun* ran a front-page picture of Sir Paul McCartney with the candle he and his wife Linda intended to light. On the evening of the anniversary, Pam Ross went to a church service to light her own candle, while her husband drove round the town and took comfort in the blaze of candles illuminating every window.

Also on 13 March 1997, Tony Blair used his first question in the Commons to ask John Major if he would 'join me in recalling that it is a year to the day since the terrible event in Dunblane? We remember the little ones who died, and we grieve with the parents and their friends. They will not be lost to the nation's memory.' Major replied by saying that the Leader of the Opposition had spoken eloquently for everyone in the House: 'Clearly, this will be a very difficult and emotional time for the bereaved and for the entire community of Dunblane.'

On the eve of the anniversary, Mick North had received a letter from Princess Diana. He may have snubbed her, but she hadn't forgotten him. Addressed in Diana's hand to 'Dear Dr North', she had written: 'It is hard to believe that it is already a year since the tragedy at Dunblane Primary School which scarred so many lives. The loss of a child is impossible to overcome, but with the support and courage of the whole community in Dunblane, the memories of warmth and love will, I hope, be of some comfort as you shoulder the difficult task of journeying on through life.' Then she had added, 'As a mother myself, my enormous admiration for you all grows stronger. Your dearly loved children will always be greatly missed, especially today as we remember ... My thoughts and prayers are with you.' Then, in thick black pen, the letter had been signed 'with love from Diana'.

At the end of March, a fortnight after the first anniversary and almost exactly a year since the three women had met to form Snowdrop, Jacqueline Walsh invited a journalist to her home with the intention of making public her disagreement with Ann Pearston. The last straw had been listening to Sean Connery in a Snowdrop advert in the cinema. She didn't believe the adverts were necessary: 'It isn't the Snowdrop we helped start. That was a petition which then turned into a campaign. But we have achieved 90 per cent of what we set out to accomplish. We got all the handguns banned from people's homes – a lot of people just wanted that – and all the handguns over .22 calibre are to go. The gun lobby says a lot of gun clubs will close. We've come a long way.'

Since the formation of Snowdrop, she told the journalist, the women had operated as a trio, and added, 'It used to be a democratic group where we all respected the majority view, but now Ann tries to dictate what is happening. Ann and I have been friends for years, but I am unhappy with her continuing to use the Snowdrop name.' There had been arguments, and Walsh was aware that speaking publicly might mark the end of their friendship, but she could not sit back and watch as the campaign imploded. Her view was simple: if Ann wished to continue, she should do so without the Snowdrop name.

A private letter was hurtful enough, but a highly critical public interview felt to Ann and Doug like betrayal. Above all, Ann was frustrated that Snowdrop had given the gun lobby the opportunity to push back in light of all the negative publicity. Yet she was also aware of how it would look to continue in the face of public and internal opprobrium. Eventually, she concluded it was time to lay down her banner. The battle had been fought and, in large part, won.

On 24 April, at a London reception hosted by the Gun Control Network, Ann announced the end of Snowdrop. It was exactly a week before the next general election. To provide the electorate with clear guidance on who supported a total ban on handguns, the GCN had surveyed the nation's political candidates. Labour made a commitment to put aside parliamentary time for a free vote, while the SNP, who were numerically unable to form a government by themselves, said they would introduce a total ban on handguns. In her farewell speech, Ann said, 'We promised we would campaign up to the election, and we have. Now is the appropriate time for the more formal organisation of GCN to be the single voice to carry the debate forward. I hope that the electorate remember the victims of violent gun misuse when they vote.' She thanked the media and the MPs who had voted for a total handgun ban, and 'the parents of Dunblane, who gave themselves so wonderfully in support of the campaign at a time when they were living a parent's worst nightmare'. Then she said some final words: 'Lastly, I would like to thank Rosemary Hunter, Charles Coull and Jacqueline and David Walsh, the core members of Snowdrop. Without their selfless commitment and enthusiastic dedication, Snowdrop would not have stayed the course. I don't think they, like myself, will ever be the same people we were on 12 March 1996. We are going back to our families and domestic routines. We are able to, and we are ever thankful that that is the case.'

After her speech, Ann looked around the room and felt a strange loneliness. Gill Marshall-Andrews was in deep conversation with fundraisers. She had an ease with politicians, (her husband Robert, a leading barrister, would soon be elected a Labour MP) that Ann did not. While she appreciated that the GCN was in capable hands, she felt a slight sadness that her campaigning days were over. Then she returned home. A pile of ironing awaited.

The general election was held on Thursday, 1 May 1997, and just under two weeks later the Dunblane families and other guests, including Eileen Harrild, were invited to meet the new prime minister. Tony Blair wanted to tell them in person that one of his first acts of government would be to fulfil his electoral promise – and his promise to each of them – that the ban on handguns would be extended to .22-calibre weapons.

On 1 July of the same year, the public were required to surrender all high-calibre handguns. On 27 November, the second Firearms (Amendment) Act received Royal Assent. And by 28 February 1998, two weeks short of the second anniversary, all lower-calibre handguns had to be surrendered to the police. All handguns were now illegal in Britain.

In the garden of 10 Downing Street, Kenny Ross was briefly reunited with Tony Blair. Looking out at the white and red roses in bloom, at the azaleas and the long, immaculate lawn, the two men stood side by side in silence for a second or two, then Ross apologised for his emotional outburst at their last meeting. The prime minister waved away his apology. Then Ross asked if it had made a difference, if it had helped get them here, to this point, with a complete ban on the horizon. Blair smiled and said he hadn't forgotten their meeting. It had always been in the back of his mind.

One Afternoon in July

At the top of High Street in Dunblane, near Churches House and a few hundred yards from the grounds of the cathedral, stands a gold Royal Mail postbox, repainted in recognition of the town's most famous son and his triumph in London's 2012 Olympic Games.

Less than a month after Andy Murray collected his gold medal, he won the US Open, his first Grand Slam title, for which Dunblane threw a parade attended by thousands. After the parade, Murray paid a visit to his grandparents' house, near the golf course, for a cup of tea and a slice of cake.

On 7 July 2013, Murray was in the final of Wimbledon, the world's most famous tennis tournament. The broadcast trucks had been to Dunblane the year before, too, when he had reached the final only to lose tearfully to Roger Federer. Today, his opponent was Novak Djokovic.

On this sunny afternoon, Chris Griffin, an ornithologist, was in the middle of a twelve-hour, 670-mile drive from Somerset to Thurso, at the northerly tip of Scotland. He had been listening to the match on the car radio when Murray won the first set. Griffin decided he had to watch the rest of the match on television. He had just passed Stirling on the M9 and when he spotted the sign for Dunblane, he thought it the perfect place to pull over. Dunblane, home of Andy Murray.

Griffin parked and followed the crowds into a long, oblong building with a vast glass frontage and walls of orange brick. Inside, several hundred people had gathered to watch the match on a giant screen. Saltires were flying, children wore cardboard Andy Murray masks and there were excited chants of 'Go, Andy, go!'

The structure Griffin found himself in gave a respectful nod to what lay behind its construction. The building had seventeen windows, each with a unique sandblasted design representing the character of each of the people absent that day. For Gwen Mayor, a hedgehog; for Victoria Clydesdale, a clematis; for Emma Crozier, her own clown; for Melissa Currie, a dove holding ballet shoes; for Charlotte Dunn, a carnation; for Kevin Hasell, Batman; for Ross Irvine, a fox from Farthing Wood; for David Kerr, a butterfly bearing his initials; for Mhairi MacBeath, a ladybird; for Brett McKinnon, a Power Ranger; for Abigail McLennan, a squirrel; for Emily Morton, a narcissus; for Sophie North, Kit-Kat the cat sitting on a Kit Kat bar; for John Petrie, a tractor; for Joanna Ross, an azalea; for Hannah Scott, daffodils; for Megan Turner, a curly-haired angel on roller skates.

On the north-facing windows, which looked out towards the cathedral, a bunch of snowdrops was engraved, each flower subtly different to reflect each wounded survivor. Then, on the walk down the ramp towards the sports hall, words had been written in the hand of Mick North: Dunblane ... Forever Remember.

For most parents, the Dunblane Centre was a physical, living memorial to their child's life; a community centre, available to all and dedicated to fun, health and learning, where children could run and play and exercise in safety and security. It was Fiona Eadington, the deputy head of Dunblane Primary, speaking outside one of the children's funerals, who had sparked the idea. 'We must not let "him" win and destroy our town,' she had said. 'There should be a place for children to play and feel safe.'

In March 1998, two years after the shooting, the resources of the two largest remaining funds – the Dunblane Fund, set up by the local authority, and the *Stirling Observer* Fund – were combined to establish the Dunblane Charitable Trust (DCT), with a view to constructing a community sports centre. From the beginning, Stirling District Council was clear that it would refuse all funding requests and that any centre built would need to be self-financed.

Among the parents who lent their early support to the centre was Mick North, who, having left the town for a detached cottage north of Loch Tay, remained a frequent visitor. North had later declared the centre open by releasing a pair of symbolic white doves, which soared into the sky only to then take up a comfortable perch on the roof. Steve Birnie, whose son Matthew had been wounded, attended the opening and shortly afterwards became the chair of the board of trustees.

On 7 July 2013, Birnie was trying to keep an eye on the big screen while he dispensed orange juice to thirsty children. North was driving between friends in London and Cambridgeshire, listening to every stroke and volley on the radio.

Over the past seventeen years, North had continued to support the GCN and travel the world to promote gun control. He had attended the Million Mom March for stricter gun control in Washington in the year 2000, a symposium on individual disarmament in Istanbul, and conferences in Rio de Janeiro and Geneva. In the wake of the brutal shooting at Sandy Hook Elementary School the previous year, in which twenty children and six adult staff had been shot dead, North had been invited to speak at Johns Hopkins University in Baltimore on ways to reduce gun violence in the USA.

Kenny Ross wouldn't step inside the Dunblane Centre, but his wife Pam had started to work there, and she found it a surprising pleasure. The years since the shooting had been more difficult than she could ever have imagined. Had she known what lay ahead, she never would have believed she could cope. She and Kenny didn't want Alison to grow up an only child, so they began trying for another. Andrew was born in July 1998. Joanna's imaginary friends, Boy and Sister, now had names.

In March 2001, Kenny returned home from work complaining of pain in his arm. Eventually he was admitted to Stirling Infirmary and later Glasgow Royal Infirmary, where he was put on a ventilator. He had somehow contracted necrotising fasciitis, the so-called 'flesh-eating bug'. The build-up of toxins in his body left him in a coma, and the medical staff were doubtful he would survive. Pam barely left his side for weeks. The worst day came when the staff performed a tracheotomy so the ventilation tubes could be removed from his throat. Afterwards, lying in the bed, Kenny looked so peaceful that Pam was briefly reminded of Joanna after her death, and she became terrified of losing Kenny too, of having to break the news to Alison and Andrew about the death of their father. She began to think: 'You are not going to die ... you are not going to do this to me.'

Later that day, for the first time in almost two months, Kenny opened his eyes. He would remain in hospital for two more months, spend a further two years in recovery and never work again. Yet his stoic humour remained. When showing people his gouged left-hand side, he would explain that he had needed to lose a bit of weight.

———

Isabel was always aware of a gap, the absence where Mhairi should have been. She felt anger at having been deprived of her daughter, that her infinite love for Mhairi had become an ocean of grief she could never hope to swim across. Reflecting on the Thursday Night Group, the nights when all she could manage was to sit and listen to the talk and the laughter, she had little doubt that it had helped save her life. She loved the laughter; it was the sound of a future she one day hoped to reach.

For Isabel MacBeath, the future arrived with Guy. As the son of a good friend of her late husband Murray, he was always around. She can remember him on the day of the shooting, still in his Arnold Clark uniform, leaning against the radiator in the living room, his face white with shock but still somehow a solid presence. It was not until three years later, after Guy had broken up with his girlfriend, that they began to hang out as friends. Isabel invited him to a play; Guy took Isabel and Catherine on a day trip to Deep Sea World in North Queensferry. When Mick North invited Isabel and the other parents to a barbecue at his new home, she asked Guy to come along with her. Over burgers and beer in the garden overlooking the soft greenery of the Perthshire hills, many of the other parents thought they were a couple. On the drive home, Guy asked Isabel why she was so resistant to romance. To him the age gap of thirteen years was an irrelevance; to Isabel it was a barrier that would surely lead to a break-up, which she couldn't countenance with Catherine. But Guy would not be put off, and in time they fell in love, got engaged and married within a year. Guy legally adopted Catherine, and over the years he became the rock around which their new family was secured. In 2006, Isabel felt it was time to leave Dunblane, and they moved to Torphins, a small town in Aberdeenshire. She returned to teaching religious studies and slowly, over time, what had been an intellectual passion evolved into a profound Christian faith.

Ann Pearston wasn't a tennis fan and didn't watch the match; it was a beautiful day, and the garden beckoned. For many years after the Snowdrop Campaign there was little contact between Ann, Jacqueline Walsh and Rosemary Hunter, except for the occasional Christmas card. Yet in the future lay a long lunch, a warm reunion where old tensions were forgotten and the only thing that would remain was pride in what the women had achieved.

Deborah Buchanan was still haunted by her mother's last seconds. Gwen Mayor had been shot six times and had wounds which the family believe suggested a struggle with the gunman. They also had no doubt she would have tried to protect Emma Crozier, the child who died by her side. Yet their attempts to have Gwen recognised for any of the nation's civilian awards for bravery were unsuccessful. It was not until 2025, nearly thirty years after the shooting, that she was posthumously awarded the Elizabeth Emblem for public servants who have died in the line of duty. Inspired by her mother's dedication to others, Deborah would train as a nurse, and later worked in the hospital where she had last seen her mother.

For George Robertson and Michael Forsyth, that day was never forgotten. Robertson would go on to become the nation's Defence Secretary and then Secretary General of NATO, a position he still held on 11 September 2001. Michael Forsyth retired from politics and entered the world of banking. When he was made a life peer, he was standing in full ermine robes when, from the back benches, he heard a comment: 'That's the chap that took my guns.'

Both George Robertson and Michael Forsyth agreed to be patrons of the Dunblane Centre.

Andy Murray looked down. His left hand began to shake violently. He had collected the balls to serve when he noticed his body was beginning to react to the pressure. Over the years, he had always developed painful mouth ulcers in the week before Wimbledon, but he had never experienced anything like this. Then again, he had never been two sets up and leading the third of the men's final at Wimbledon. The score was 40–40 at 5 sets to 4: deuce. He needed two more points.

In the crowd, he heard his mother Judy shout, 'You're all right.' He tried not to look up. He knew, his family knew, how close he was to achieving his childhood dream.

Over the next few minutes, the country would have to endure three match points. Then, on the fourth, Murray served a ball he couldn't have played any better. Djokovic managed to return the serve and Murray played a forehand return that he quickly realised wasn't one of his best. The question was: would it still be enough? Djokovic prepared his backhand and struck the ball. The ball hit the net.

Murray let go of his racquet, which dropped to the grass, and flicked off his cap. He looked up towards the BBC commentary box, moved forward to hug Djokovic and then sank to his knees, taking a series of deep breaths. He had just won Wimbledon, the first British man to do so since Fred Perry in 1936.

In the Dunblane Centre, everyone leapt to their feet. The din was incredible. Across town, Eileen Harrild rushed down to the tennis club. From the earliest, drug-filled days in Stirling Royal Infirmary, Harrild had refused to be defined by her wounds, which in time she would overcome. She had taught both Andy and Jamie Murray, and when she found and hugged the boys' grandparents, who were still stunned by the result, her joy in Andy's success was absolute.

In the days that followed, Pam Ross wrote a letter to Andy Murray, explaining what his victory meant to her and the town. Though he rarely spoke about what had happened at his former primary school, Murray knew his victory meant even more to his hometown than it might otherwise have done. That day in 1996 had left a mark on him. Whenever people, particularly in America, spoke of how 'things happen for a reason', he would think back to his school and silently disagree.

―

Two days after the death of her daughter, Pam Ross was in Joanna's bedroom, looking out of the window at a world she could no longer understand or bear to be a part of. The glass was slightly smudged. As she looked closer, the smudge became visible as a faint fan of small fingerprints, Joanna's last touch.

Pam raised her finger towards the glass. Then she held still.

NOTE ON SOURCES

The narrative of *One Morning in March* was constructed using a number of different sources. A principal source of information was the single-volume report written by Lord Cullen and published in October 1996 under the title *The Public Inquiry into the Shootings at Dunblane Primary School on 13 March 1996*. The full transcript of the oral evidence given to the public inquiry over its 26 days is available online and was a key resource while conducting my research. However, the single most valuable resource was the archive of 3,510 individual files, consisting of tens of thousands of pages of witness statements, police records, council minutes, bank records and meeting transcripts now available at the National Records of Scotland (NRS) in Edinburgh under the specific reference heading COM21/4. As far as I can ascertain all the documents relevant to the public inquiry have now been released to the archives except – understandably – the medical records of the children who were shot dead or seriously wounded.

The narrative for the events on 13 March 1996 was written with the assistance of witness statements given to Central Scotland Police in the immediate aftermath of the shooting and now available at the NRS, combined, where possible, with their personal testimony at the Cullen Inquiry and selected interviews specifically for this book. An additional resource was the publication *Dunblane: Our Year of Tears* by Peter Samson and Alan Crow (Mainstream Publishing, 1997), which contained first-person accounts by Eileen Harrild, George Robertson, Rod Mayor, Mick North, Pam Ross, and Joe and Rona Austin and their son Coll. Additional information was drawn from contemporary newspaper reports by *The Scotsman, The Herald, The Times, The Sunday Times, The Guardian, The Independent,* the *Daily Mail* and *Mail on Sunday,* the *Daily Telegraph* and the *Evening Standard,* which were also an assistance in documenting the political campaign to secure a ban on firearms, as were archive news reports by the BBC, ITV, Channel 4 and CNN.

The government's paperwork relating to the shooting and their response, including reports and correspondence between government departments, is available at the National Archives at Kew and online, while the minutes of the Cabinet meeting the day after the shooting are available in the files CAB/128/117. Other publications of assistance were the Home Affairs Committee report *Possession of Handguns* (London: HMSO, 1996), *Maxim* magazine and *Guns Review.*

My research was also assisted by the personal archives of Mick North, who allowed me access to the police reports and legal paperwork provided to the families during the Cullen Inquiry and to his letter from Diana, Princess of Wales; Gill Marshall-Andrews, co-founder of Gun Control Network; and Ann Pearston, who had a voluminous archive of material related to the Snowdrop Petition and campaign.

I am also indebted to Mick North's book *Dunblane: Never Forget* (Mainstream Publishing, 2000) and other publications including *The Alastair Campbell Diaries, Volume One: Prelude to*

NOTE ON SOURCES

Power, 1994–1997 (Hutchinson, 2010), *A Walk-on Part: Diaries 1994–1999* by Chris Mullin (Profile Books, 2011), *Strictly Ann* by Ann Widdecombe (Weidenfeld & Nicolson, 2013), *The Scottish Secretaries* by David Torrance (Birlinn, 2006), *Coming of Age* by Andy Murray (Random House, 2009), *Between You and Me* by Lorraine Kelly (Headline, 2008), *The Insider* by Piers Morgan (Ebury Press, 2005), *Knowing the Score: My Family and Our Tennis Story* by Judy Murray (Chatto & Windus, 2017), *Dunblane Unburied* by Sandra Uttley (BookPublishingWorld, 2006), *The Dunblane Centre: The Gift that Keeps Growing* (Jamieson and Munro, 2014) and the pamphlet *A Dunblane Celebration* (2023).

ACKNOWLEDGEMENTS

The decision to write an account of 13 March 1996 was not lightly taken. Yet I was encouraged by a number of those directly affected who believed the thirtieth anniversary should be marked with an accessible account of the worst crime in Britain in the twentieth century, and the largely forgotten campaign to ban handguns. This book could not have been written without the generosity and support of Mick North, Pam Ross, Kenny Ross, Isabel MacBeath and Deborah Buchanan. I owe each of them a deep debt of gratitude and thanks. Ann Pearston, Jacqueline Walsh and Rosemary Hunter, who formed the Snowdrop Petition, were equally supportive, and my thanks to them also extends to Doug Pearston, who helped clarify key points and, with Ann, source documents. George Robertson and Michael Forsyth, now both Lords, gave me a joint interview in London and I'm deeply grateful for their support. I'd also like to thank Malcolm Robertson; and Ewan Wilson, a retired police officer and son of William Wilson, the chief constable of Central Scotland Police, for his personal insights into his father and the force. My thanks also extend to Peter Watson, Jack Irvine, Lorraine Kelly, Mark Downie, Steve Condie, Liz Mermin, Lydia Murtezaoglu, Dawn Tolland, Yvonne Samson; the staff at the National Records of Scotland in Edinburgh, the National Archives at Kew and all the staff at the Mitchell Library in Glasgow, where so much of this book was written. Creative Scotland supported the research and writing of this book with a grant, and I'd like in particular to thank Alan Bett, head of Literature and Publishing.

I'd like to thank my agents James Spackman and Jason Bartholomew at BKS and my editor at Swift Press, Mark Richards, and all the team who helped put the manuscript into print and onto shelves, including Diana Broccardo, Sam Reynolds, the team at Tetragon, Alex Winckler and Ruth Killick.

Thanks also go to my friends David Wylie and Eben Harrell. Eben's profile of Andy Murray in *Time* magazine was a helpful resource, though any errors in describing his style of play are all my own. Dani Garavelli read early drafts and provided invaluable notes.

Last in the acknowledgements but first in my life, my most sincere thanks and love must go to my wife, Lori.

STEPHEN MCGINTY,
December, 2025

INDEX

.22 calibre weapons
  Cullen Report 250–1, 255–7, 260, 263–4, 267–9
  gun controls 205, 227, 240, 243
  post-Cullen 279, 282–3, 286, 288
  the Scouts 36–7, 39, 50, 56

Albert Halls, Stirling 183, 206, 212, 217
Alexandria 8, 10–11, 15–16, 18
Allston, Roger 93, 103–4
Amateur Photographer 75, 93, 103
ambulances 127, 129–34, 134–6, 143, 160
ammunition
  firearms laws 35–6
  gun amnesties 56
  gun controls debate 205, 207, 233, 251–2
  investigation into Thomas Hamilton 69, 74
  and Thomas Hamilton 26, 52, 89–91, 98, 111–12, 113–14
amnesties 55–6
Anderson, Detective Constable Anne 89–90
Anderson, Ewan 41–3, 55
Anderson, Inspector John 90
Anne, Princess 179–80, 224
Association of Chief Police Officers 202
Austin, Coll 121, 124, 135, 160
Awlson, Agnes 125–6, 129, 210

Baden-Powell, Robert 30, 32
Ball, Councillor Robert 92, 94
Balmaha 5, 12, 15, 31, 40, 65
Bannockburn Boys' Club 37, 90, 94
Bannockburn Family Unit 62, 64–5, 73, 139
BBC
  Dunblane massacre 136, 244
  gun control debate 193, 233, 237, 257, 274, 278
  Murray family 87, 297
Bell, Ian 257, 278
Bell, Nigel 104–6
Beretta handguns 26, 50, 52–3, 55, 104
Bernstein, Tobias Elias (William Bernson) 228–9
Birnie family 171, 293
Bishopbriggs 92, 100–1
Blair, Tony, MP (later Prime Minister)
  control debate 199, 226
  and handgun ban 189
  handgun ban 243, 266–7, 288
  massacre aftermath 167–74, 285
Blake, Mary
  Dunblane school massacre 118–22, 125, 128, 132–4, 145
  massacre aftermath 171, 179, 207
Boal, Ian 92–3
Bonomy, Iain, QC 207, 216
Boys' Brigade 30, 57

INDEX

boys' clubs
 closure 91–2, 94–5
 complaints 22, 25, 49
 Hamilton's complaints 9–10, 107, 109, 164
 photographs 59, 62–3, 78
 and Thomas Hamilton 7, 12, 17, 37–8, 40–3, 88
British Association for Shooting and Conservation 232
British Shooting Sports Council (BSSC) 53–4, 191, 229–31, 262
Browning guns
 boys' clubs 26, 37, 56
 gun clubs 97, 102, 104, 258
 massacre 111, 114, 124, 252
 and Thomas Hamilton 50, 91, 99
Bryant, Martin 201
BSSC (British Shooting Sports Council) 53–4, 191, 229–31, 262
Buchanan, Debbie (Gwen Mayor's daughter) 86, 148–9, 158–9, 296
bullying 8, 14, 272
Butterwick, Karen 22–4

Cabinet meetings 163–80, 186
Callander Rifle and Pistol Club 96, 104
camera business (Hamilton's) 96, 107
Campbell, Alastair 168, 170, 172, 174, 189
Campbell, Colin, QC 209, 215, 218–20, 228, 249
Campbell, William 101
Cardle, James 17–18
Central Regional Council 44, 46, 70, 92, 195
Central Scotland Police
 criticism 174, 196, 219, 231, 254, 260
 firearms certification 91
 gun amnesties 56, 62
 Hamilton complaints 5–6, 20, 21, 23, 213

Hamilton investigation 16–18, 202–3, 212–15
Hamilton's boat destroyed 40
HMIC review 272–3
massacre aftermath 154, 170
Snowdrop death threats 233
Charles, Prince of Wales 222, 244, 245
child abuse 22–3, 41, 67, 95, 164, 217–18
 see also sexual abuse
child protection units 106, 150, 214
Children and Young Persons (Scotland) Act 1937 17
Children's Panel 17, 72
Chisholm, Malcolm 207
Christopher, Ted 276
class register, not yet taken 145
Clydesdale, Victoria 147, 178, 292
compensation
 businesses 232, 261–2, 282–3
 gun clubs 282–3
 gun owners 55, 240, 255
complaints
 about police 21, 68–70, 210, 216
 boys' camps 6, 8, 11, 21, 22–3
 Hagger family 211 14
 Hamilton's 24–5, 33–4, 46–50, 69–70, 90, 94–5, 106–8
 parental 62, 65, 74, 79, 100
 Scouts' 33–4, 44, 46
contempt of court 186–8, 209
Cooke, Professor David 217–18
Coull, Charles 218, 221, 287
criminal intelligence files 70, 89–90
Cringles, Reverend George 117
Crown Office 130, 202, 207, 209, 213–14, 217, 257
Crozier, Alison 223–4, 247
Crozier, Emma
 Dunblane school massacre 120, 127, 147, 184
 massacre aftermath 224, 229, 231, 276, 292, 296

305

Crozier, Jack 223–4, 226
Crozier, John 196, 199, 219, 223–4, 226, 228–9, 245
Cullen, Francis Baird 34–5
Cullen Inquiry 204–20, 223, 228–31, 238
Cullen Report 225, 246–77
Cullen, William Douglas, Lord Cullen
  authority for inquiry 164–5, 186–7
  Cullen Inquiry 204–20
  Cullen Report 246–77
  gun control debate 194, 198, 200, 223, 225, 243
  press conjecture 230–1, 233–4, 238–41
  Snowdrop Petition 218
Currie, John (janitor) 127–9, 210
Currie, Melissa 146, 292

Daily Record 136, 158, 166, 223, 240, 267, 284
Daily Telegraph 190, 230, 236, 239
Davie, Sam 12–13
DCT (Dunblane Charitable Trust) 293
Delaney Fletcher Bozell 281–2
Democratic Unionist Party (DUP) 265
Denny 57, 59–60
Derek (plain-clothes police constable) 150–1
Deuchars, Robert 31–3, 52, 113
Diana, Princess 222–5, 245, 278, 285
Dickson, Ann 274–5
Dickson brothers 193
discipline
  excessive 8, 13–14, 45, 51, 66–7, 78
  gymnastics 38
  shooting 35, 42, 193, 262
disturbing behaviour 21, 78–9, 89, 94, 104–6, 110, 215
division in Dunblane 274–5
Djokovic, Novak 291, 297–8
Duggan, Wilma 171

Dunblane Boys' Club 42, 49
Dunblane Cathedral 82, 178, 181, 244, 246
Dunblane Centre 292–4, 297, 298
Dunblane Charitable Trust (DCT) 293
Dunblane families 80–9
Dunblane Fund 293
Dunblane High School
  boys' clubs 42, 44, 46, 49–50, 62, 71
  George Robertson 153
  Murray family 88
Dunblane Primary School
  aftermath 163, 167, 184, 186, 285
  families 80–8
  Hamilton's complaints 95
  massacre 113, 117–60, 252
Dunblane Rifle and Pistol Club 37, 42, 96
Dunblane Rovers Club 37, 42, 44–7
Duncan, Constable Donna 6–8
Dundee Crematorium 185, 292
Dunlop, Laura 209–10, 218, 219, 228
Dunn, Charlotte 146, 292
Dunn, Martyn 265
DUP (Democratic Unionist Party) 265
Dylan, Bob 276

Elizabeth Emblem 296
Elizabeth II, Queen 106–7, 110, 177, 179–80, 283
Elspeth (social worker) 150–2, 208
erratic behaviour (Hamilton's) 98–9, 99–100

Fairgrieve, Brian 31–3, 73–4
Falkirk and District Royal Infirmary 131, 135, 137, 143
Falkirk Herald 20
family liaison teams 149, 151, 153
Fatal Accidents and Sudden Deaths Inquiry (Scotland) Act (1976) 163

INDEX

Fawcett, Alexis 101, 103
Ferguson, Chief Inspector 70
Firearms Act 1920 35
Firearms Act 1968 192
Firearms (Amendment) Act 1988 54
Firearms (Amendment) Act 1997 288
Firearms (Amendment) Bill 264–5, 269, 278
firearms certificates *see* firearms licences
Firearms Consultative Committee 261, 277
firearms legislation
  Cullen Report 255, 267
  Dunblane families 200, 205, 275
  government debate 165–6, 199, 235, 239, 243, 246
  gun control debate 192
  inadequate 91, 275
  reform 36, 53, 168, 189, 233, 240
firearms licences
  systems 220, 253, 283
  Thomas Hamilton 36–7, 69, 89–91, 105, 150, 203, 214
  UK statistics 191
first aid kits 7–8, 14
five-a-side football 58–62, 107
Fleming, Brenda 170–1
food 7, 10, 20, 38, 59
Forsyth, Michael, MP
  bereaved parents' group 200
  Cabinet meetings 163–9
  Cullen Report 246–53, 256, 259, 265, 270
  firearms legislation 55, 296–7
  government debate 227, 234, 239–41, 243–4
  Hamilton's complaints 20, 49, 69, 95
  inquiries 186–8, 217
  massacre aftermath 153–6, 172–3
  Snowdrop Petition 196–8, 222
Forth Valley Ambulance Service, 131, 133–4
Fox, Albie 258–9

Gallagher, William (Procurator Fiscal depute) 64–5, 69, 71–3
GCN (Gun Control Network) *see* Gun Control Network (GCN)
gifts and tributes 173, 197
see also messages of sympathy
Gillespie, John 98–9
GMTV 175
Gordon, Catherine 124
Guardian, The 235, 278
gun amnesties 55–6
Gun Control Network (GCN)
  establishment 211, 227–8
  gun control debate 230, 243, 260, 265
  Snowdrop wound up 281, 286–7
gun controls *see* firearms legislation
gun laws *see* firearms legislation
gun lobby 190–4, 202, 235–7, 268, 278, 286
Gun Trade Association 260
Gunn, Constable George 6–8, 16, 19–21, 71–2, 134
guns *see* .22 calibre weapons; ammunition; Beretta handguns; Browning guns; gun lobby; handgun ban; hunting rifles; legally held guns; Magnum revolvers; private ownership (of handguns); same calibre gun ownership; self-loading guns; semi-automatic guns; shotguns
Guy (later husband of Isabel MacBeath) 295–6
gymnastics 7, 38, 40, 58–9, 61–3

Hagger, Andrew 9–15, 21, 26, 212
Hagger, Doreen 9–15, 18–19, 21–6, 211–14, 249
Hagger, Victoria 9, 12–13, 15, 18, 212–14
Hamilton, Agnes Graham (Agnes Watt) 28–9, 34, 52, 92, 158, 185, 210
Hamilton, Catherine 28

Hamilton, Constable Ian 175
Hamilton, Thomas
  and boys' clubs 37–50, 69
  Dunblane school massacre 117–60
  early life 28–9
  and firearms 25–6, 29–34, 35–7, 89–114
  and photography 57–79
  and Scouts 19–20, 31–5, 73–4, 94–5, 106, 164
  summer camps 5–27
handgun ban
  bereaved families 205, 219, 237
  Firearms (Amendment) Bill 264
  government debate 188–9, 227, 239
  gun lobby 230
  press conjecture 233
  Snowdrop 183, 242, 247, 257, 287
Handgunner 190
Harrild, Eileen
  Cullen inquiry 206
  Dunblane school massacre 118–22, 125, 128
  firearms legislation 268, 271, 288
  hospitals 132–3, 135, 171, 179
  Princess Diana 223
  Wimbledon win 298
Hasell, Kevin 147, 292
Hastings, Max 239–40
Her Majesty's Inspectorate of Constabulary (HMIC) 249, 272
Herald, The 166, 177
Hill, Tony 55, 211
HMIC (Her Majesty's Inspectorate of Constabulary) 249, 272
Holden, Detective Superintendent Joseph 74, 137–9, 142–3, 148–50, 209–10
Home Affairs Select Committee 194, 201, 229, 235–7, 267–8
homosexuality 41, 44
House of Commons
  firearms debate 187, 227, 257–8, 270

  and Lord Cullen 165–7, 249, 252
  politicians' Dunblane visit 153–4, 167–74
House of Lords 258, 276–7, 282
Howard, John 201
Howard, Michael, MP
  Dunblane families 223, 225–7
  Firearms (Amendment) Bill 264
  firearms debate 165, 240, 243, 247, 250, 269
  firearms review 187
  government compromise 252, 254–7, 262
  press conjecture 234–6
Hughes, Detective Sergeant Paul (later Chief Inspector) 65, 67–71, 90, 214–16
Hughes, Robert 263–4
Hungerford shootings
  Dunblane school massacre 156
  Gun Control Network (GCN) 211
  gun lobby 190–2, 283
  legally held guns 242, 256, 277
  legislative change 52–6, 105, 187
  Thomas Hamilton 108
Hunter, Rosemary
  Cullen inquiry 208
  legislative change 224, 241–2, 257
  Snowdrop 183, 198, 232, 265, 287
hunting rifles 205, 219
Hutchison, Amy Louise 112, 120–1, 179, 247

identification of victims
  Cullen inquiry 204, 210
  parental identification 149–50, 159, 176
  triage 137, 145–7, 169
Inchmoan island 5–8, 10–17, 21, 27, 65, 134
insensitivity 174, 208
insurance payouts 39–40, 96

INDEX

intimidation 89, 174–5
IRA (Irish Republican Army) 200, 202, 236, 263
Irish Republican Army (IRA) 200, 202, 236, 263
Irvine, Ross 147, 292

John (uniformed police constable) 150–1
Johnson, Boris 190

Keenan, Inspector James 21–2, 24
Kelly, Lorraine 175–7, 244–5
Kensington Palace 222–3, 278
Kerr, David 147, 292
Kindness, Detective James 41
kitchen assistant, the 132–3

Labour Party conference 241–3, 280
Law, Richard 191–2, 231, 259
Lawrence, Sir Ivan, QC 194, 201, 235–6, 267–8
legally held guns 52–4, 200, 226, 235–6, 251–2, 254, 277
life jackets 4, 11, 16, 25, 31
Linlithgow 9, 19, 22–3, 25–6, 212–13
Lister, Constable James 206
Loch Lomond
    cabin cruiser 31, 39, 51
    Hamilton's camps 5, 10, 23–4, 57, 64–5, 71
Lord Advocate 165, 188, 204, 206–7, 213, 216–17, 234
Lothian and Border Police 25
Lothian Courier 22–3
Lugton, Michael 154

McBain, Detective Superintendent Ian 15–16
MacBeath, Catherine 144, 159
MacBeath, Isabel
    Dunblane families 80–1, 112
    Dunblane massacre 138, 144, 153
    massacre aftermath 159, 171–2, 174–5, 208–9
MacBeath, Mhairi
    Dunblane families 81, 112, 153
    massacre and aftermath 134, 159, 208–9
    remembrance 292, 295
MacBeath, Murray 80–1, 112
Macdonald, David 111
Macdonald, William 110
McEwan, John 133
McGrane, Sergeant 25
McInally, Sandra 77–9
McIntosh, Reverend Colin 177–8
McKinnon, Brett 147, 185, 292
McLennan, Abigail 147, 196, 292
McLennan, Duncan 196
Macleod, Angus 75–6
McLeod, Claire 118, 148
McMurdo, Douglas, Deputy Chief Constable
    Cullen inquiry 215–16, 220, 249
    resignation 253, 272
    and Thomas Hamilton 21, 70, 90
Magnum revolvers
    Cullen Inquiry 219
    Dunblane school massacre 124, 127
    firearms debate 55, 219, 236, 252–3, 258, 271–2
    gun lobby 37, 114, 193, 258
    and Thomas Hamilton 37, 42, 50–1, 55, 102–3, 114, 124
Major, John, Prime Minister
    Cullen Report 239–41
    Dunblane 167–74, 200
    firearms legislation 163, 243, 250, 265–6
    international response 184
    remembrance 285
Major, Norma 171–2, 200
Marshall-Andrews, Gill 211, 227–8, 243, 260, 287
Mayfair Gun Club 192–3
Mayor, Esther 85–6, 149, 199

Mayor family 151, 158, 160, 199, 265, 268, 271, 296
  see also Buchanan, Debbie (Gwen Mayor's daughter)
Mayor, Gwen
  Cullen Report 253
  Dunblane school massacre 85–7, 118–20, 127, 129
  massacre aftermath 170, 172
  remembrance 178, 292, 296
  victim identification 137, 139–41, 145, 147–9, 151, 160
media village, Dunblane 166, 173
Mellor, David, MP 55, 188–90, 209, 238, 269
messages of sympathy 180, 183–4
  see also gifts and tributes
Mill, Inspector Michael 20, 40
Miller, John (Stirling Procurator Fiscal) 202, 212
Miller, Marion 222
minute's silence 177–8
Moffat, Detective Sergeant Alan 137, 147–8
Moffat, Detective Superintendent James 74–5, 106, 147–8
Moffat, John 96–8
Morton family 144, 147, 219, 256–7, 263–6, 292
Mullin, Chris, MP 26, 194, 202, 235–6
Munn, Inspector Louis 158
Murray, Andy 291–2, 297–8
Murray family 87–8, 113, 139, 157

National Firearms Agreement (Australia) 201
National Pistol Association 261, 268, 284
National Rifle Association (NRA) 36, 204, 261
North, Dr Mick
  bereaved parents' group 182, 195–200, 282

Cullen inquiry 205, 207–8
  Dunblane school massacre 81–3, 140–1, 144, 147, 150–2, 159
  firearms debate 247, 252, 256–7, 263–4, 275
  Gun Control Network (GCN) 211, 227, 243
  Princess Diana 223, 225, 245, 285
  remembrance 292–5
North, Sophie 147, 198, 200, 247, 292
Nottingham Shooting Centre 259–60
NRA (National Rifle Association) 36, 204, 261

Observer, The 192–3
O'Donnell, Andrew 225
O'Donnell, John 225
off-duty police officer 128–30
Ogg, Detective Chief Superintendent John 137, 202, 207–10, 272
Ogilvie, Grace 67–8
Olwen 141, 150–1
ombudsman 25, 48–9
O'Neill, Martin, MP 197, 223, 226

paedophilia 69, 74, 215, 217
Paxman, Jeremy 237–8, 257
Pearston, Ann
  Cullen inquiry 208, 211
  firearms debate 241–3, 256–7, 263–4, 271
  remembrance 296
  Snowdrop 181–3, 197, 221–2, 226–8, 232, 237
  Snowdrop wound up 279–82, 286–7
Pearston, Doug 182, 197, 208, 221–2, 224, 241–2, 286
perimeter cordons 137
petitions 47
  see also Snowdrop
Petrie, John 147, 292
Philip, Prince, Duke of Edinburgh 278–80, 282

INDEX

photography 23, 58–79, 90, 92–4, 215
precognition statements 17, 203
private ownership (of handguns) 183, 205, 227, 237, 243, 251, 256
Procurators Fiscal
  Cullen inquiry 212
  Dunblane school massacre 136, 155
  Hughes' memo 69
  and Thomas Hamilton 16–17, 20, 41, 64–5, 71–3, 75, 216
  Vannet report 202–3
protest song 275–6
public inquiries
  bereaved parents' group 196, 275
  Cullen inquiry 163–6, 168, 186, 204–20
  press conjecture 234
Purves, Robert 179

Reid, Melanie 199, 200
Reilly, Janet 9, 13, 15, 18–19, 22–3, 212–13
resignations 32–3, 47, 92, 247, 249–50, 253, 272
Robb, Alexander 76–7
Robertson, George, MP
  Dunblane school massacre 153–6
  Dunblane visits 164, 166–70, 172
  firearms debate 187, 189
  firearms legislation 253–4, 266, 269–70, 283
  and Lord Cullen 217, 240–1
  remembrance 244, 296–7
  Snowdrop 198–9, 226–7, 243
  and Thomas Hamilton 44–6, 49, 75
Robertson, Malcolm 44–6
Ross, Jimmy and Betty 83, 199
Ross, Joanna 118, 147, 184, 224, 292
Ross, Kenny 83–4, 92, 142–3, 199, 210, 284, 288
Ross, Kenny and Pam 151–2, 160, 175–7, 180, 223–7, 244–5, 294–5
Ross, Pam 83–4, 138–9, 195–6, 237–8, 269, 298

Royal Hospital for Sick Children (Yorkhill, Glasgow) 135, 143, 160
Ryan, Michael 52–6, 108, 211, 260, 277

SAGE (Society Against Guns in Europe) 228–9, 231
Salmond, Alex 187, 198
same calibre gun ownership 50, 91, 97
Savage, Guy 192, 231, 260, 271, 283–4
Scotland on Sunday 263, 275
Scotsman, The 48, 106, 278
Scott, David (student teacher) 126–7
Scott family 147, 195, 257, 292
Scott, Marion 75–6
Scottish Office 136, 225, 248, 253
Scouts
  district commissioner 31, 33, 34, 44
  Hamilton's complaints 19–20, 71, 92, 94–5, 106
  and Thomas Hamilton 28–56, 73–4, 164
search warrants 64–5, 72–3
Secretary of State for Scotland *see* Forsyth, Michael, MP
self-loading guns 54, 97, 105, 192, 248, 251–2
semi-automatic guns 25–6, 37, 52, 54–5, 201, 271
sexual abuse 22–3, 41, 44, 63, 95, 164, 217–18
Shooters' Rights Association (SRA) 191–2, 231–2, 259–61, 271, 283
shotguns
  firearms debate 205, 219, 225, 265
  firearms legislation 35, 54, 166, 201
  gun lobby 191–2, 236, 284
  and Thomas Hamilton 89, 108–9
slapping 3–4, 6, 8, 15–16, 26, 66
Snowdrop 181–9, 182, 197–8, 221, 247, 279–82, 285–7

snowdrops 112, 180, 183, 270–1, 292
social workers 65, 101, 141, 149–52, 208
Society Against Guns in Europe (SAGE) 228–9, 231
solicitor's letters 48
Sportsman's Association 258, 261, 267, 282, 284
SRA (Shooters' Rights Association) 191–2, 231–2, 259–61, 271, 283
Stevenson, Jan 192
Stewart, Linda 132
Stirling High School. 41, 58, 60, 78
Stirling Observer 77, 275, 293
Stirling Rifle and Pistol Club 94, 101
Stirling Royal Infirmary
   Dunblane school massacre 131, 134–5, 137, 142–3, 149, 159, 208
   Dunblane visits 170, 177
   Wimbledon win 298
Strathclyde Police 5–6, 23, 158, 203
Straw, Jack, MP 187, 199, 242–3, 255, 280, 283
Sun, The 212, 233–4, 236, 257, 267, 284
Sunday Mail 75, 188, 196, 198, 257
Sunday Times, The 181, 223, 247
suntan lotion 21, 23
swimming trunks
   boys' camps 6, 11, 13–14
   boys' clubs 40, 50, 58–9
   photography 61, 62–5
   unhealthy interest (in boys) 66–7, 72, 75, 78

Taylor, Gordon 62–4, 72–4
Taylor, Ron
   Dunblane school massacre 109, 117, 125–9, 145–6
   and Lord Cullen 210, 253
   massacre aftermath 155–6, 169–70, 172–3, 186
   telephone wires cut 114, 118

Thursday Night Group (bereaved parents) 195–203
Times, The 181, 230
Togneri, Robert 109
Trading Standards 93, 103
Tribunals of Inquiry (Evidence) Act 1921 186
truants 30, 41
Turner family 143, 147, 199, 200, 245, 292
Tweddle, Grace 124, 126

unhealthy interest (in boys) 40, 69, 74

Valentine, Keith (Procurator Fiscal) 69, 71
Vannet, Alfred (regional Procurator Fiscal) 203

Wallace, Ben, MP 179
Walsh, Dave 232, 280, 286, 287
Walsh, Jacqueline
   political meetings 222, 224, 226
   Snowdrop 181–4, 197–8, 232–3, 279–82, 285–7
Wardlaw, William, 76–7
Watson, Peter 196, 205, 218, 273
Watt, Agnes (née Hamilton) 28–9, 34, 52, 92, 158, 185, 210
Watt, Thomas 28, 158
Westminster Rifle Club 191
Wiggin, Sir Jerry, MP 191, 202, 262, 265
Williams, Steven 13, 15
Wilson, Chief Constable William 137, 142, 155–6, 170, 172, 174, 272–3
Wilson, John 107–9
Woodcraft 30–1, 34–5, 40–1, 46, 76, 107, 111
Woods, Alex 101–3

Yardley, Mike 193–4, 230, 261